Investing in
Indonesia

Investing in
Indonesia

Rosye Buray Salz

Copyright © 2016 by Rosye Buray Salz.

Library of Congress Control Number:		2016904061
ISBN:	Hardcover	978-1-5144-7442-6
	Softcover	978-1-5144-7441-9
	eBook	978-1-5144-7440-2

All rights reserved. No part of this book may be reproduced or transmitted in any form or by any means, electronic or mechanical, including photocopying, recording, or by any information storage and retrieval system, without permission in writing from the copyright owner.

Any people depicted in stock imagery provided by Thinkstock are models, and such images are being used for illustrative purposes only. Certain stock imagery © Thinkstock.

Print information available on the last page.

Rev. date: 05/31/2016

To order additional copies of this book, contact:
Xlibris
1-888-795-4274
www.Xlibris.com
Orders@Xlibris.com

731761

Table of Contents

Acknowledgement ix
Dedication xi
Preface xiii

1. Key Points 1
2. Indonesia Overview 3
3. Political System 7
   A. Central Government of Indonesia 7
   B. Government of Indonesia 9
   C. Types of Legal System 10
   D. National Political Parties 11
4. Cultural Diversity 12
   A. History and Background 12
   B. Indonesian Philosophy 13
   C. Indonesians' Views on Radical Islam 15
5. Time Zones 22
6. Climate 23
7. Demographics 24
8. Economy 27
9. Enterprises In Indonesia 35
   A. Types of Corporate Enterprises 35
   B. Corporate Governance 37
   C. Structure of Capital 39
   D. Type of Shares 39
10. Foreign Investment Regulations and Procedures 41
    A. Investment Overview 41
    B. Direct Foreign Investment 42
       1. Form of Investment 42
       2. Authorities Responsible for Managing Foreign Investment 43
       3. Laws and Government Regulations 44
       4. General Plans of Investment 46
       5. General Licensing Documents 47
       6. General Procedures of Establishing a PT. PMA .. 48
       7. Investing in Existing PMDN or PMA Companies ... 50
       8. Representative Office 50

      9. Approximate Time and Procedure 51
   C. Limitations on Foreign Investment 70
      1. Foreign Ownership Caps and Other Conditions 70
      2. Banned Sectors 74
   D. Indirect Foreign Investment 76
   E. Arbitrating Commercial Disputes 76
11. Indonesian Investment Law 78
   A. General Provisions 78
   B. Principles and Objectives 80
   C. Basic Policies of the Investment 81
   D. The Form and Location of Corporation 81
   E. Treatments to the Investment 82
   F. Employment 84
   G. Business Fields 85
   H. Investment Development for Micro, Small,
      Medium, and Cooperation 86
   I. Rights, Duties And Responsibilities of Investors 86
   J. Investment Facilities 87
   K. Ratification and Licensing of A Corporation 92
   L. Coordination and Implementation of Investment
      Policies 93
   M. Operation of Investment Affairs 94
   N. Special Economic Zones 95
   O. Settlement of Disputes 96
   P. Sanctions 96
   Q. Transitional Provisions 97
   R. Closing Conditions 99
12. Foreign Investment Implementation and Realization 100
   A. Indonesia Progress of Investment
      Realization 100
   B. ASEAN Investment Growth 109
   C. ASEAN Investment Outlook for 2015-2016 122
   D. Sample of Foreign Investment Companies in
      Indonesia 130
13. Government Supports on Foreign Investment 132
   A. Political and Policies Reformations 133
   B. Licensing Process Reformations 134
   C. Fiscal Incentives: Tax Holiday, Tax Allowance and
      Import Duty Facility 139
14. Exchange Control and Landing 154
   A. Medium of Exchange 154
   B. Book Keeping / Records 155

- C. Foreign Exchange Control 156
- D. Offshore Borrowing 157
- E. Onshore Borrowing 158

15. Tax Basics 159
    - A. Taxation Object 160
    - B. Calculation on Taxable Income 161
    - C. Repayment of Income Tax by Taxpayer 163
    - D. Repayment of Income Tax through Other Party 164
    - E. Application of Treaty on Double Tax Agreement & Exchange of Information 166
    - F. Separate Accounting and Changes in Fiscal Year 166
    - G. Exemption or Reduction Corporate Income Tax in Connection with Investment 167

16. Land 168
    - A. Main Laws 168
    - B. Agrarian, Spatial and Land Regulations in Investment Activities 170
    - C. PTSP Procedures 171
    - D. PTSP Implementation Results Reporting 171
    - E. Land Acquisition Procedures in Investment Framework 172

17. Infrastructure 176

18. Industrial Zones 180

19. Trading 181
    - A. Import 182
    - B. Export 183
    - C. General Customs Procedures 187

20. Employment 189
    - A. Company Regulations 189
    - B. Work Agreement 190
    - C. Termination of Contract 191
    - D. Working Hours 192
    - E. Wages and Leave Entitlements 193
    - F. Trade/Labor Union 195
    - G. Industrial Relations 195
    - H. Entrepreneur's Organization 196
    - I. Bipartite Cooperation Institution 196
    - J. Tripartite Cooperation Institution 197
    - K. Employing Foreigners 197

21. Occupational Health and Safety 201

22. Intellectual Property 207
    A. Patent 208
    B. Trademark 209
    C. Copyright 212
    D. Industrial Designs 214
23. Environmental Regulations 219
24. Other Costs Of Doing Business 224
    A. Man Power Costs 224
    B. Comparative Wages in Selected Countries 228
    C. Some Samples of Rental Charge and Service
       Charge per m2/Month in South Jakarta for June
       2015 230
    D. Fuel Costs IDR/Liter Oct – Nov 2015 231
    E. Water Tariff 233
    F. Electricity Costs 233
25. Travel and Visa 237
    A. Visa On Arrival 237
    B. Visit Visa 238
    C. Multiple Visit Visa 238
    D. Indonesian Domestic Luggage Policies 239
    E. Major Infectious Diseases 240
    F. Customs Regulations 241
26. Potential Investment Opportunities 243
27. Challenges 271
    A. Indonesia "Doing Business" Reports 271
    B. Challenges 279
       1. The Governance Development to Create an
          Effective and Efficient Bureaucracy 282
       2. Economic Growth 283
       3. Accelerating Equitable Developments Among
          Regions 284
       4. Global Economic Pressures 284
    C. Efforts and Plans to Tackle Challenges 289
       1. National Medium Term Development Plan 289
       2. Corruption 290
       3. Bureaucracy 293
       4. Licensing Reformation 294
       5. Infrastructure Reformations 297
28. Abbreviation/Acronyms 300
29. About the Cover 309

Acknowledgement

I give thanks to the Lord, God for helping me to complete this book; the Indonesian Investment Coordinating Board (Badan Koordinasi Penanaman Modal, BKPM) in allowing me to use Government data and materials; and the endless support from my husband, Donald L. Salz, Ed.D., for his love and editing the book.

Rosye Buray Salz

The Author received permission from the Indonesian Investment Coordinating Board to use all materials through email from Humas BKPM dated January 19, 2016 at 8:23pm humas@bkpm.go.id ppid@bkpm.go.id

Dedication

*To my son Edwin, my grandson, Ezra,
and to the memory of My Parents and my Brother.*

ROSYE BURAY SALZ

Preface

Within this book, you'll find valuable, even hard-to-find information for those wanting to invest in Indonesia. Even experienced investors should find new and useful facts and points of view. Students and those with a curious mind may be surprised at the complexity of doing business in an up-and-coming economic power. Information in this book is supported by the latest Laws and Regulations available.

In my daily work with investors, manufacturing companies, and other businessmen, I found it difficult to gather necessary information about Indonesian investment. Information came from several sources, some may never before have been translated to English, the language of international business. New foreign investors and even experienced Indonesian business men may not know where to start to find some of the information needed for their endeavors.

In the last few years, I spent hundreds of hours researching and translating documents for various purposes. To make the most of my efforts, I was inspired to put into one package, information on most topics useful for international business in Indonesia: Laws and Regulations, the Government and political system, investment and enterprise in Indonesia, employment, intellectual property, trading, land, tax, travel, and culture.

I have worked in international business for many years, and my insights come from a unique perspective of being an expatriate entrepreneur who has worked in Indonesia, Australia and the USA. Through this book, I would like to attract investors to Indonesia, demystify the investment process, and accelerate your profitability.

Rosye Buray Salz, February 2016

1 Key Points

A. Rapidly Growing Economy

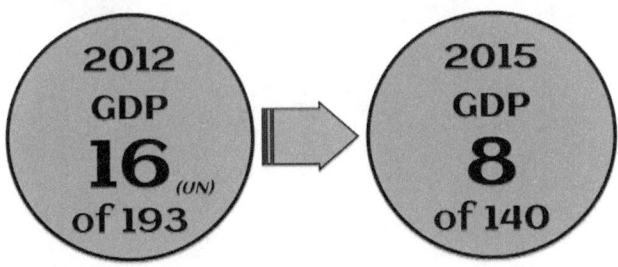

B. Natural Resources
- Indonesia is a renowned market for resource extraction.

C. Demographic
- Indonesia is the 4th most populous nation in the world.
- About 50% of the population is under 29 years old.

D. Domestic Market
- Over 53.7% of Indonesia population lives in urban areas that adopt a modern lifestyle.

E. Strategic Location
- Located at the intersection of the Pacific Ocean, along the Malacca Straits and the Indian Ocean, between Asia and Australia

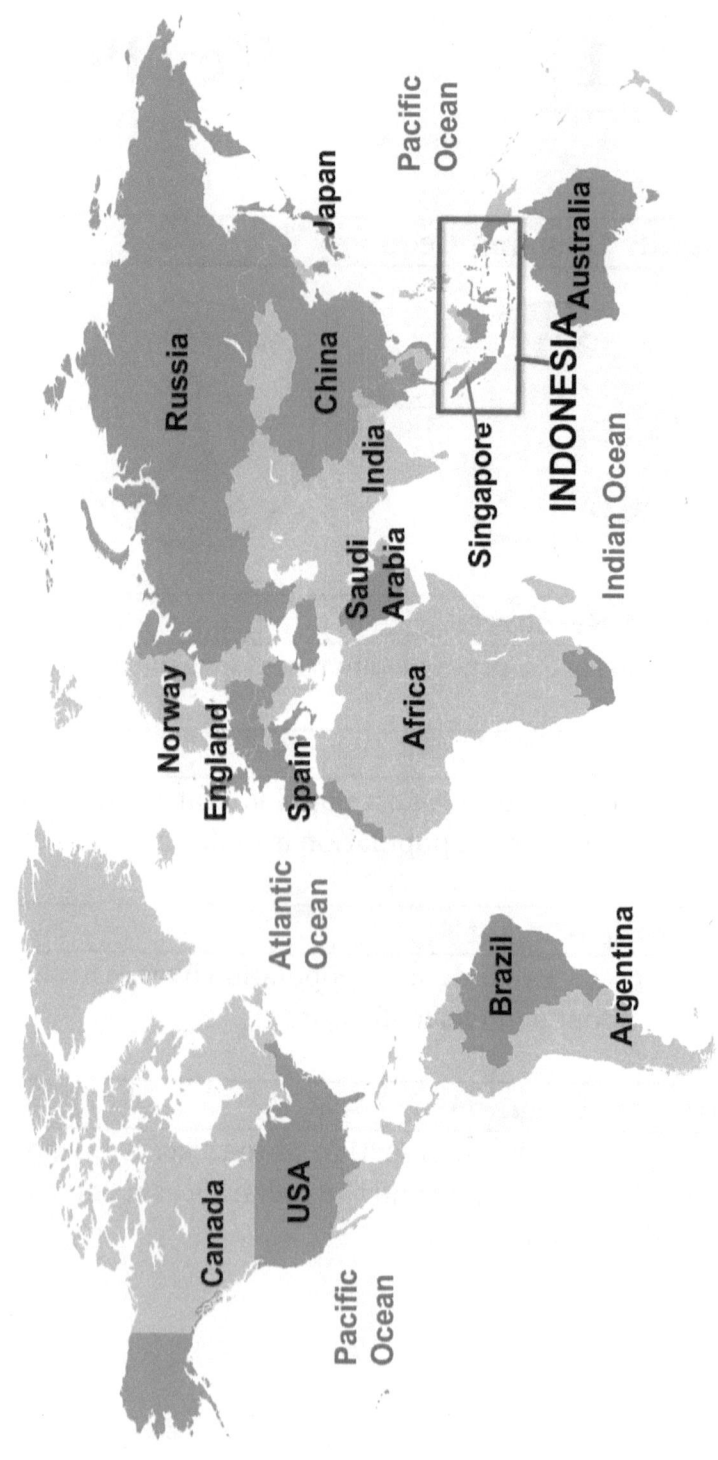

2 Indonesia Overview[1]

---

[1] Data Source: CIA Library https://www.cia.gov/library

ROSYE BURAY SALZ

Name of Country	**Republic of Indonesia**
Capital City	Jakarta
ISO Code	IDN
Currency	Indonesian Rupiah / Rp / IDR
President	Mr. Joko Widodo Since 20 October 2014

Location
Southeast Asia, archipelagic island country
Between Indian Ocean and Pacific Ocean

Coordinates
Latitude 5° 00' N Longitude 120° 00' E

Area
- Total   1,904,569 Km² or 735,358 Miles²
- Land   1,811,569 Km² or 699,451 Miles²
- Water   93,000 Km² (35,908 Miles²) of inland seas
  (Straits, bays, and other bodies of water)
- Distance   East to West   5,200 Kilometers
                North to South   1,870 Kilometers

Islands
17,508 islands; 8,844 islands have been named according to estimates made by the Government of Indonesia, with 922 of those permanently inhibited.

Language
National language is Bahasa Indonesia.
In addition, there are 737 living languages.

Land Boundaries
- Total   2,958 Kilometers
- Coastline   54,716 Kilometers
- Border Countries
  - 228 Kilometers with Timor-Leste
  - 1,782 Kilometers with Malaysia
  - 820 Kilometers with Papua New Guinea

People

Nationality	Indonesia
Ethnicity	300 distinct native ethnics
(2010 est.)	Javanese 40.1%, Sundanese 15.5%, Malay 3.7%, Batak 3.6%, Madurese 3%, Betawi 2.9%, Minangkabau 2.7%, Buginese 2.7%, Bantenese 2%, Banjarese 1.7%, Balinese 1.7%, Acehnese 1.4%, Dayak 1.4%, Sasak 1.3%, Chinese 1.2%, other 15%
Religions (2010 est.)	Muslim 87.2%, Christian 7%, Roman Catholic 2.9%, Hindu 1.7%, other 0.9% (includes Buddhist and Confucian), unspecified 0.4%
Population	253,609,643 (July 2014 est.) – World's 4th largest
Density	±124/Km² or ±322/Mile² – World's 84th place

Natural Resources
Petroleum, tin, natural gas, nickel, bauxite, copper, fertile soils, coal, gold, silver, geothermal

Agricultural Resources
Rice, rubber and similar products, coffee, copra, cassava (tapioca), cocoa, palm oil, peanuts, forest products, spices, medicinal herbs, essential oil, fish and its similar products, shrimp, beef, poultry, eggs.

Industries

Petroleum and natural gas, textiles, automotive, electrical appliances, apparel, footwear, mining, cement, medical instruments and appliances, handicrafts, chemical fertilizers, plywood, rubber, processed food, jewelry, and tourism

Climate

Tropical, hot, humid, more moderate in highlands

Land Use

- Arable land: 13%
- Permanent crops: 12.14%
- Other: 74.88% (2013)

International Organization Participation

ADB, APEC, ARF, ASEAN, BIS, CD, CICA (observer), CP, D-8, EAS, EITI (candidate country), FAO, G-11, G-15, G-20, G-77, IAEA, IBRD, ICAO, ICC (national committees), ICRM, IDA, IDB, IFAD, IFC, IFRCS, IHO, ILO, IMF, IMO, IMSO, Interpol, IOC, IOM (observer), IPU, ISO, ITSO, ITU, ITUC (NGOs), MIGA, MONUSCO, NAM, OECD (Enhanced Engagement, OIC, OPCW, PIF (partner), UN, UNAMID, UNCTAD, UNESCO, UNIDO, UNIFIL, UNISFA, UNMIL, UNMISS, UNWTO, UPU, WCO, WFTU (NGOs), WHO, WIPO, WMO, WTO

3   Political System

A. Central Government of Indonesia

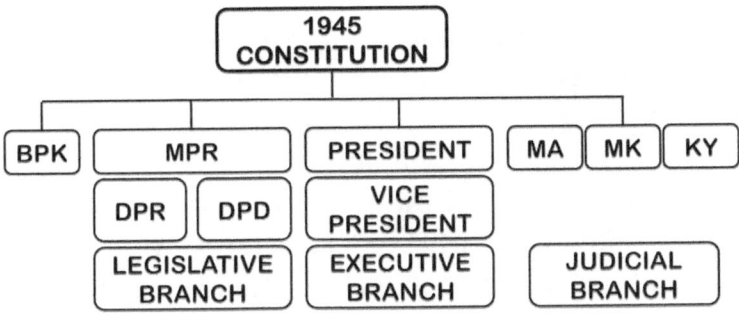

```
MPR    People's Consultative Assembly
MA     Supreme Court
DRP    People's Representative Council
MK     Constituional Court
BPK    Supreme Audit Agency
KY     Judicial Commission
DPD    Regional Representatives Council
DPA    Supreme Advisory Council
```

The President leads the Executive Branch of the Indonesian Government and is the Commander-in-Chief of the Indonesian National Armed Forces.

The President and Vice-President are selected by vote of the citizens for five-year terms, limited up to two terms.

The 695-member of People's Consultative Assembly (Majelis Permusyawaratan Rakyat, MPR) includes 550 members of the People's Representative Council (Dewan Perwakilan Rakyat, DPR) (the House of Representatives), and 130 members of Regional Representatives (Dewan Perwakilan Daerah, DPD), elected by the twenty-six Provincial Parliaments and sixty-five appointed members from Societal Groups.

The MPR is a bicameral parliament, with the creation of the DPD as its second chamber in an effort to increase regional representation. The Regional Representatives Council (Dewan Perwakilan Daerah, DPD) is the upper house of The People's Consultative Assembly. The lower house is The People's Representative Council (Dewan Perwakilan Rakyat, DPR) or the House of Representatives, elected for a five-year term by proportional representation in multi-member constituencies.

The Indonesian Supreme Court (Mahkamah Agung) is the highest level of the Judicial Branch. The Indonesian Supreme Court Judges (Hakim Agung) appointed by the President. The Constitutional Court rules on constitutional and political matters (Mahkamah Konstitusi), while a Judicial Commission (Komisi Yudisial) oversees the Judges.

B. Government of Indonesia

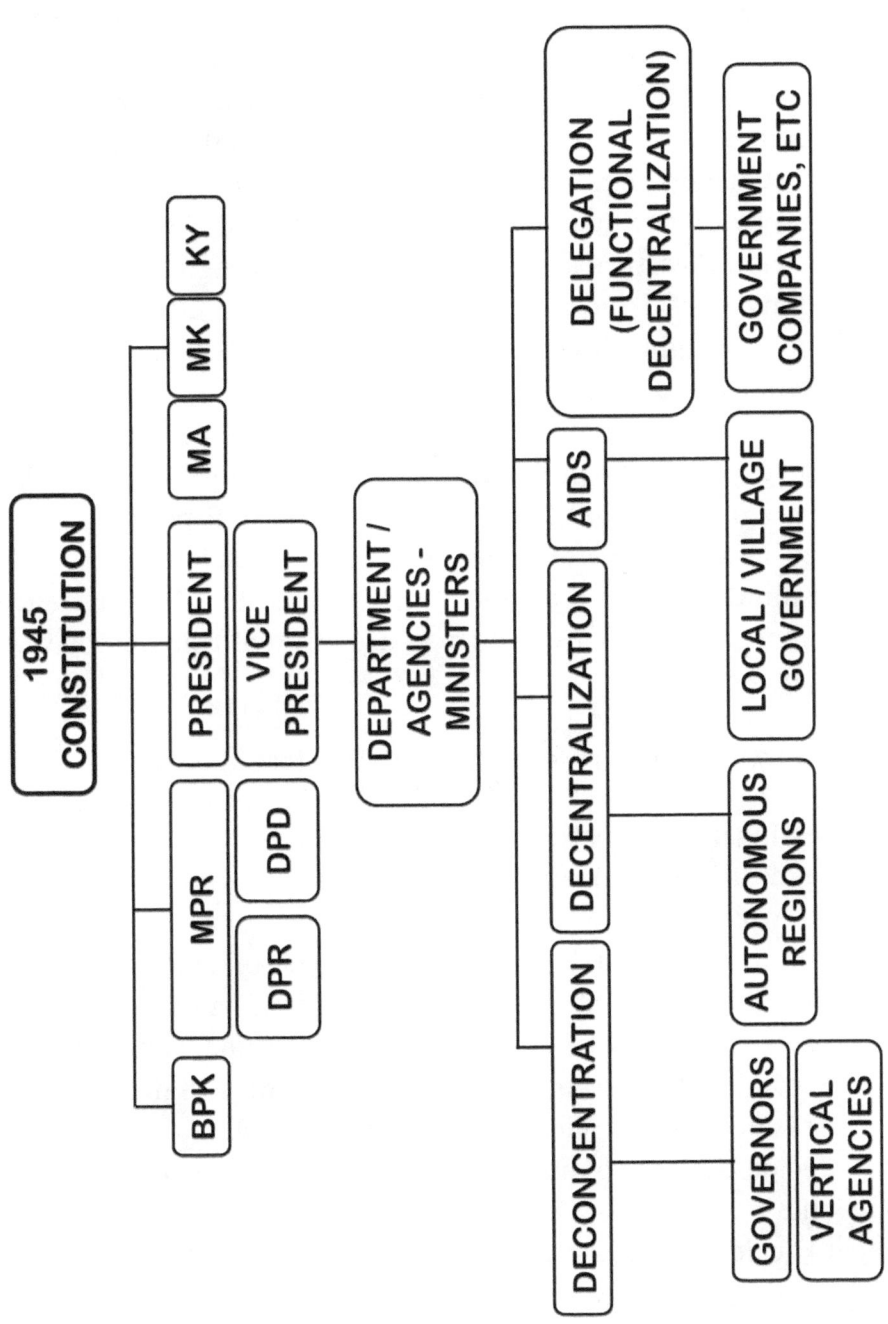

C. Types of Legal System

The judiciary is based on the Supreme Court and separate courts for public administration and military, religious and civil matters. In addition of comprehensive system of Civil Laws that has replaced most of the statutes established by the Dutch, there is an extensive range of decrees and Regulations developed and applied by Government departments. The most relevant areas for foreign investors are Laws regarding: Foreign Investment, Company Law, Land and Buildings, Business Licensing and Trade, Copyrights, Taxation and Customs, Labor and Foreign Workers / Managers, Regional Regulations.

The Judicial Commission (KY) selects Supreme Court Judge nominees, which are presented to the Parliament for approval.

The Constitutional Court (MK) consists of 9 people: three chosen by the House of Representatives, 3 determined by the Supreme Court, and 3 members determined by the President. The Chairman and Vice-Chairman are elected from and by the MK members.

There are five authorities of the Constitutional Court:

a) testing of the constitutionality of the Laws;
b) take a decision on authority dispute between state institutions;
c) take a decision on the opinion of the House of Representatives that the President and/or Vice President has violated the Laws, that do not legally qualify as the President and/or Vice President, therefore to excuse the Assembly to dismiss the President and/or Vice President from office;
d) decide the case of disputes over the results of the election, and
e) to decide a case relating to the dissolution of political parties

D. National Political Parties

Key Indonesian political parties include:

- Partai Golongan Karya (Golkar, a leading party of the Suharto era);
- Partai Demokrasi Indonesia Perjuangan (Indonesian Democratic Party of Struggle, PDI-P, founded and led by Megawati Sukarnoputri, the daughter of Soekarno, a leading party of Joko Widodo);
- Gerakan Indonesia Raya (Greater Indonesia Movement Party, Gerindra);
- Partai Kebangkitan Bangsa (National Awakening Party, PKB);
- Partai Persatuan Pembangunan (United Development Party, PPP);
- Partai Amanat Nasional (National Mandate Party, PAN);
- Partai Keadilan Sejahtera (Prosperous Justice Party, PKS);and
- Partai Demokrat (Democrat Party, PD, a leading party of Yudhoyono era).

4 | Cultural Diversity

A. History and Background

Indonesia is centrally located along trading routes between the Far East, South Asia and the Middle East, resulting in many cultural practices strongly influenced by a multitude of religions, including Hinduism, Buddhism, Confucianism, Islam and Christianity.

> Indian scholars have written about Dwipantara or Hindu kingdom in Java and Sumatra or Swarna Dwipa around 200 BC. There were Hindu – Buddha Kingdoms in Indonesia up to 14 AD, such as Tarumanegara, Kutai, Srivijaya, Majapahit, and many other small kingdoms.

Muslim traders first entered Indonesia in the 7th Century. They migrated through the Strait of Malacca linking the Tang Dynasty in China, the Srivijaya in Southeast Asia and the Umayyads in West Asia. The Hindu / Buddhist kingdoms transferred to Sultanates when the kings converted to Muslims. Islam as government, in the form of sultanate kingdoms, were established in Indonesia beginning in the 13th century.

A Portuguese expedition led by Antonio de Abreu arrived in Maluku around 1511. They traveled to every main island in Indonesia. During this time, Fransiskus Xaverius, a Catholic missionary, spread Christianity. However, the Portuguese left Maluku in 1570 because of 5 years wars with the Sultan of Ternate, Sultan Baabullah. Dutch took this opportunity to come to Indonesia and strengthen their position by establishing the Dutch East India Company (VOC, Vereenigde Oost-Indische Compagnie) in 1602.

List of Indonesian colonists:

Spain	1521 – 1692
Netherlands	1602 – 1945
England	1811 – 1816
Japan	1942 – 1945
Portugal	1511 – 1945 °

1945 Indonesia wins its independence.

° Portugal continued to hold East Timor until 1975 when Indonesia made it one of their own provinces. In 2002, East Timor became an independent country, Timor Leste.

Colonialism, trade, and expeditions, contributed to a complex cultural mixture that is very different from the original indigenous cultures.

Indonesia has a large population, but its many densely populated regions allow for vast areas of wilderness that support the world's second highest level of biodiversity.

B. Indonesian Philosophy

People may identify themselves according to one of 300+ ethnic groups, birthplace or family, and hundreds of languages (737 languages) spoken throughout the country. However most Indonesians are united through the national language, Bahasa Indonesia, as well as through the national philosophical foundation of "Pancasila".

> Indonesia promotes Theocentricity, having God as the central interest and ultimate concern; Theonomy is the state of an individual or society that regards its own nature and norms as being in accord with the divine nature.

Pluralism organizes intercultural affairs. Theocentric and Theonomy are the principles governing the substance of culture, which is the basis for Pancasila Democracy in Indonesia.

"Bhinneka Tunggal Ika" is the official national motto of Indonesia. The phrase is old Javanese translated as *"Unity in Diversity"*. It is declared specifically in article 36A of the Constitution of Indonesia. Also, it is inscribed in the Indonesian national symbol, Garuda Pancasila, stated on the banner gripped by a Garuda's claws. The Garuda is a mythical bird and the disciple, carrier or vehicle (vahana) of Lord Vishnu, symbolizes the virtue of knowledge, power, bravery, loyalty, and discipline.

In its preamble, Indonesia's 1945 constitution declares the Pancasila as the embodiment of basic principles of an independent Indonesian state. Pancasila, is adopted from the Sanskrit words: "pañca" meaning five, and "sīla" meaning principles. It contains five principles held to be inseparable and interrelated. These five principles come from age-old traditions and are said to define Indonesia's nationhood, symbolized in "Garuda Pancasila":

- Belief in the one and only God
- Just and civilized humanity
- The unity of Indonesia
- Democracy guided by the wisdom of deliberations among representatives
- Social justice for all the people of Indonesia

Theonomy (the first principle), is a belief in one God that is absolute. The other four principles are cultures that are related to human needs that are fully recognized, as long as they do not conflict with the first principle.

The constitution gives freedom of worship according to one's religious beliefs, although the first principle of Pancasila, the Indonesian state philosophy, is of the belief in one supreme God. There is a small Jewish community in Indonesia. Animism and Kebatinan (non-religious philosophies) are also practiced.

C. Indonesians' Views on Radical Islam

> Although the population of Muslims in Indonesia is the largest in the world, the 1945 Constitution states it is not a Muslim country.

The Nine Committee formed a Jakarta Charter on June 22, 1945. The Jakarta Charter is a historical document and was made possible by a compromise by the Islamic Party and Nationalist Parties. The compromised was facilitated by the Investigation Committee for the Preparatory Works for Indonesian Independence (BPUPKI) in order to bridge differences in religion and state.

The Jakarta Charter was the basis of establishing the Republic of Indonesia, also five items of Pancasila. It contains lines of revolt against imperialism, capitalism and fascism.

There remain efforts to include Shariah Islam in the constitution. These efforts repeatedly fail, likely because Shariah Islam has never been a part of Indonesian culture.

The Pancasila's promotion of monotheism is a religiously neutral and tolerant statement that equates Islam with the other religious systems: Christianity, Buddhism, and Hindu-Balinese beliefs, and others.

> The Jakarta Charter became the Preamble to the 1945 Constitution after the Nine Committee removed the "Divinity, with the duty of carrying out Shariah Islam for his followers" and changed it to "Belief in the one and only God".

Bellows are clips from various newspapers expressing Indonesians' thoughts regarding the radicals:

- [2]August 4, 2014: The Indonesian government declared, rejecting the ideology brought by militant group Islamic State of Iraq and Syria (ISIS), and prohibit its development in Indonesia.

Indonesia's Coordinating Minister for Political, Legal, and Security Affairs, Djoko Suyanto, announced that the Government banned the Islamic State of Iraq and Syria (ISIS), forbidding the propagation of its teachings in the country.

---

[2] BBC Indonesia. August 4, 2014 Indonesia larang penyebaran ideologi ISIS http://www.bbc.com/indonesia/berita_indonesia/2014/08/140804_indonesia_larang_faham_isis

The Indonesian Government claimed, ISIS is not a religious issue but an ideology or beliefs that are considered contrary to the ideology of Pancasila.

- [3;4]September 11, 2014: Indonesian declared that anyone who join and/or fund ISIS could be prosecuted under Code of Criminal Law (KUHP) 2 Chapter 3 (139a).
- [5]September 15, 2014: Authorities arrested three Indonesian citizens and 4 foreigners (Chinese Moslems) in the area of Central Sulawesi on terrorism-related activities.
- [6]December 15, 2014: Indonesian Police (Markas Besar Kepolisian RI) work together with Malaysian Police (Polisi Diraja Malaysia, PDRM) to prevent their citizens from departing to Syria or other Moslem countries in Middle East to join ISIS
- [7]March 13, 2015: Parliament members demand that Indonesian Representatives or Embassies abroad shall strictly supervise all citizens who visit or live abroad.

---

[3] Fri, 20 Mar 2015, Ini jeratan pasal KUHP bagi WNI pendukung ISIS http://www.hukumonline.com/berita/baca/lt550bd24b29fd7/ini-jeratan-pasal-kuhp-bagi-wni-pendukung-isis

[4] Hukumonline.com, Thur, 11 Sep 2014, Aktivis ISIS bisa dibawa ke pengadilan HAM http://www.hukumonline.com/berita/baca/ lt541119459af84/aktivis-isis-bisa-dibawa-ke-pengadilan-ham

[5] BBC Indonesia, September 15, 2014. WNA yang ditangkap di Poso diduga dari Xinjiang http://www.bbc.com/indonesia/berita_indonesia/2014/09/140915_poso_uighur

[6] Kompas, Mon 15 Dec 2014 Polri benarkan pencegahan terhadap 12 WNI di Kuala Lumpur yang ingin ke Suriah http://nasional.kompas.com/read/2014/12/15/17294471/Polri.Benarkan.Pencegahan.terhadap.12.WNI.di.Kuala.Lumpur.yang.Ingin.ke.Suriah

[7] Republika News, Sat 14 Nov 2015, Jokowi kecaman serangan Paris http://www.republika.co.id/berita/internasional/global/15/11/14/nxsfq5377-jokowi-kecaman-serangan-paris

- [8]November 15, 2015: Indonesia condemns Paris attacks, calls for international action. Jokowi also called on the international community to come together in the fight against terrorism, underlining the importance of strengthening international cooperation. "Terrorism cannot under any circumstances be tolerated," he said. The President said it had become increasingly important for countries to step up global efforts against terrorism.
- [9]November 16, 2015: Haedar Nashir, the Chairman of the second-largest Islamic organization in Indonesia, Muhammadiyah, said that the attacks were "inexcusable" and that all religious groups must join hands to condemn them.

Mr. Nashir, on behalf of Muhammadiyah, offered his condolences to the victims and their families. He also denied that the attacks, for which militant group Islamic State (IS) has claimed responsibility, were representative of Islam and its followers.

"I am not responsible for any groups behind this incident, especially those who claim to act in the name of Islam; they do not represent Islam. Islam does not teach violence or brutality," he said, adding that he hoped no innocent Muslims would be attacked in the wake of the incident.

"These acts of terrorism have tainted Islam's image when Islam, as we know, is based on peace. Peace is a theme found throughout the teachings of Islam," he told The Jakarta Post.

---

[8] *14 Nov 2015, Jokowi mengutuk keras aksi terorisma dan kekerasan di Perancis* http://rri.co.id/post/berita/218693/nasional/jokowi_mengutuk_keras_aksi_terorisme_dan_kekerasan_di_perancis.html

[9] *16 Nov 2015, Religious leaders condemn Paris attacks, demand justice* http://www.thejakartapost.com/news/2015/11/16/religious-leaders-condemn-paris-attacks-demand-justice.html

"This is serious; it has made Islam look bloodthirsty, even though it is not at all."

- [10]November 22, 2015, Minister of Social, Khofifah Indah Parawansa condemned ISIS but also but also regretted if there are those who associate ISIS with Islam. Therefore, this veiled woman encourages all parties, especially the Moslem's schools teach Islam with love and peace. So the acts of terrorism and radical will not recur in the future.
- [11]January 14, 2016: "All elements of this nation should not be provoked into doing harm," Said Aqil Siradj, the chairman of the 40-million-strong Nahdlatul Ulama, said on Thursday in response to the bombing and shooting attack that left five suspected perpetrators and two innocent bystanders dead. Said called on the public "not to be influenced by any parties claiming to act on behalf of religion or jihad but that instead carry out radicalism and terrorism." "We should also remain vigilant, unified and increase our solidarity to create a sense of safety in daily life," Said Aqil Siradj added.

Muhammadiyah, Indonesia's second-biggest Islamic group, with some 30 million members, urged the public "to remain calm and put their trust in the security authorities." "Countering terrorism should be comprehensively conducted through various approaches," said Haedar Nashir, the Muhammadiyah chairman.

---

[10] Liputan6, 22 Nov 2015, Mensos Khofifah: Tidak ada kaitan ISIS dengan Islam http://news.liputan6.com/read/2372190/mensos-khofifah-tidak-ada-kaitan-isis-dengan-islam

[11] NU, Muhammadiyah speak out against terrorist attack, Jakarta, 14 Jan 2016 http://www.jakartaglobe.beritasatu.com/news/nu-muhammadiyah-speak-terrorist-attack/

- [12]January 15, 2016: Chairman of the Board of Nahdlatul Ulama (NU), KH Said Aqil Siradj condemned the bombing and shooting at the intersection of Sarinah Thamrin, Central Jakarta. Mr. Siradj also reminded the Government to take firm action against the perpetrators of terror. "The state should not be defeated by a terrorist act. The omission of the radical groups will grow lush terrorism and radicalism," said Mr. Siradj at the NU office, Jakarta, Thursday January 14, 2016.

Mr. Siradj said that the heinous acts of terror such as bombings and shootings have resulted in decreasing the credibility of Indonesia in the eyes of the world. Terror cannot be called jihad: no religion justifies it. The real Jihad is the struggle to inspire the public to believe, worship, live a moral and dignified life, and be concerned for the welfare of others.

Mr. Siradj claimed, NU is ready to become the frontline in the fight against all forms of terrorism that are disturbing the whole community. For that he invites NU and all elements of the nation, to join hands together against terrorism.

"Nahdliyyin along with all Indonesian people, across faiths, ethnicities, and political parties, ultimately want to join hands to fight terrorism. This is the big enemy, a common enemy, the enemy of all nations and even humanity. All condemn terrorism," said Mr. Siradj, as quoted from NU Online.

NU agrees in an approach against terrorism through discussion, debate, and dialogue to jointly give the sense that no one religion allows violence, especially terrorism.

---

[12] *Satuislam.org, 15 Jan 2016, Ketum PBNU: Teror Bukan Jihad.* http://www.satuislam.org/nasional/ketum-pbnu-teror-bukan-jihad/

Secretary General NU Helmi Faisal Zaini also emphasized that the entire security apparatus must be alert response to this terrorism. NU needs to press the Government to strengthen anticipations.

On January 15, 2016, NU held an interfaith forum to prepare a consolidated diversity rally to respond to acts of terror in Jakarta.

5 Time Zones

Indonesia is divided into three time zones:

a. **Western Indonesia Time/WIT**
   (*Waktu Indonesia Barat*/**WIB**) (UTC+7)
   Islands of Sumatra, Java, Provinces of West Kalimantan and Central Kalimantan

b. **Central Indonesia Time/CIT**
   (*Waktu Indonesia Tengah*/**WITA**) (UTC+8)
   Islands of Sulawesi, Bali, provinces of East Nusa Tenggara, West Nusa Tenggara, East Kalimantan and South Kalimantan

c. **Eastern Indonesia Time/EIT**
   (*Waktu Indonesia Timur*/**WIT**) (UTC+9)
   Provinces of Maluku, North Maluku, Papua, and West Papua.

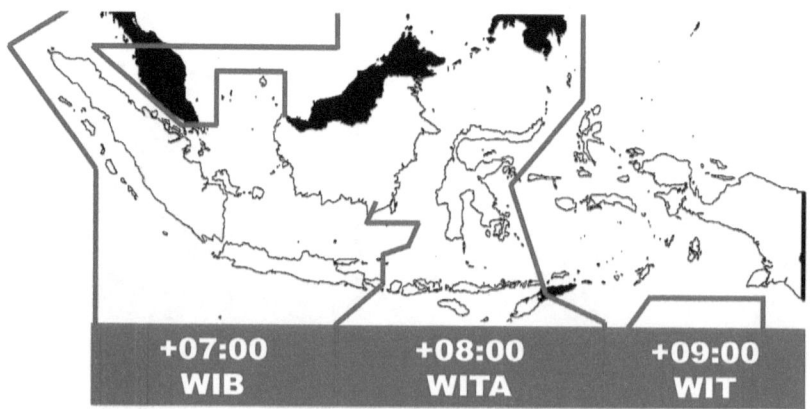

6 Climate

Indonesia is located along the equator, surrounded by 93,000Km² of water that maintains the temperatures on this archipelago fairly constant all year long. The coastal plains average 28 °C (82.4 °F), the inland and mountain areas average 26 °C (78.8 °F), and the higher mountain regions, 23 °C (73.4 °F). The area's relative humidity ranges between 70 and 90%.

Indonesia experiences two seasons, with no summer or winter: a wet season falling mostly between October and April, and a dry season between May and September. Some regions, such as Kalimantan and Sumatra, experience minimal changes in rainfall and temperature between the seasons; whereas others, such as Nusa Tenggara, experience far more pronounced differences with droughts in the dry season, and floods in the wet. Rainfall in Indonesia is plentiful, particularly in West Sumatra, Northwest Kalimantan, West Java, and Western New Guinea.[13]

Sulawesi and islands closer to Australia are dryer, such as Sumba and Timor. Winds are moderate and generally predictable, with monsoons usually blowing in from the south and east in June through October, and from the northwest in November through March. Typhoons and large-scale storms may hit the islands rarely between September and December; however, they pose little hazard to mariners in Indonesia waters. The major danger comes from swift currents in channels, such as the Lombok and Sape Straits.

---

[13] *https://en.wikipedia.org/wiki/Geography_of_Indonesia*

7 Demographics[14]

As of July 1 2014, Indonesian population is estimated 252,812,245. In 2015, population of Indonesia is estimated over 255 million.

- Over 50% of the population is under 29 years old
- 60% of the population is under the age of 39
- Around 52% of the population lives in urban areas
- Indonesia's population covers more than 39% of total population of 10 Southeast Asian countries[15]

Population Growth Rate
0.92% (2015 est.)

Median Age
- Total: 29.6 years
- Male: 29 years
- Female: 30.2 years (2015 est.)

Urban Population
53.7% of total population (2015)

Rate of Urbanization
2.69% annual rate of change (2010-15 est.)

---

[14] CIA Library

[15] Indonesia Investment Coordinating Board, Investing in Indonesia, Opportunities for Growing. Indonesia Investment Seminar, ASEAN-Japan Centre, Tokyo, 22 August 2014. http://www.asean.or.jp/ja/wp-content/uploads/2013/08/3_BKPM_for_Tokyo.pdf

Education Expenditures
3.6% of GDP (2012)
Country comparison to the world: 143rd

Major urban areas – population (2015)
- JAKARTA (capital) 10.323 million
- Surabaya 2.853 million
- Bandung 2.544 million
- Medan 2.204 million
- Semarang 1.63 million
- Makassar 1.489 million

Age Structure (2015 est.)
- 0-14 years
  - 25.82%:
    - Male 33,651,533
    - Female 32,442,996
- 15-24 years
  - 17.07%:
    - Male 22,238,735
    - Female 21,454,563
- 25-54 years
  - 42.31%:
    - Male 55,196,144
    - Female 53,124,591
- 55-64 years
  - 8.18%:
    - Male 9,608,548
    - Female 11,328,421
- >65 years
  - 6.62%:
    - Male 7,368,764
    - Female 9,579,379

Literacy (2015 est.)
- Definition: Age 15 and over can read and write
- Total Population: 93.9%
- Male: 96.3%
- Female: 91.5%

Education is not free; however, it is compulsory for children through to grade 9. Although about 92% of eligible children are enrolled in primary school, a much smaller percentage attends full-time. About 44% of secondary school-age children attend junior high school, and some others of this age group attend vocational schools.

25 March 2015, the Organization for Economic Co-operation and Development (OECD) Secretary-General Mr. Angel Gurría presented a new OECD Education Policy Review of Indonesia with Indonesian Minister of Culture and Elementary and Secondary Education Mr. Anies Baswedan. The Policy Review points out that Indonesia faces a unique window of opportunity: with 43% of its 250 million-strong population under the age of 25, the country is already endowed with the human resources necessary to propel growth, provided its workforce is equipped with the right skills.[16]

This demographic bonus that is higher than any other sector, is Indonesia's commitment to improve productivity and the education level of its youth, with 20% of total Government expenditure on education. Currently, the majority of university graduates are trained in technical fields such as finance and economics (28%) or engineering and sciences (27.5%).

More than 60% of the population is in the working age, which is one of the highest in the region, providing a dynamic workforce, to bring dependency index in the period of 2020-2030 to its lowest point.

---

[16] OECD.org Newsroom, March 25, 2015: Indonesia should accelerate reforms and invest in human capital to ensure sustainable and inclusive growth http://www.oecd.org/ newsroom/indonesia-should-accelerate-reforms-and-invest-in-human-capital-to-ensure-sustainable-and-inclusive-growth.htm

8 Economy

Indonesia is the largest economy in Southeast Asia and an influential global commodity producer. The high domestic consumption and growth in exports of manufactured products and commodities have brought steady growth to the country in the last few years.

Indonesia's share of global exports is 20 percent or more for aluminum, coal, natural rubber, nickel, and palm oil.[17]

In 2014, Indonesia's Gross Domestic Product is USD888.5 Billion; 5% growth.[18] Indonesian has the world's 10th largest economy in terms of purchasing power parity (total USD2,554 Trillion), and is a member of the G-20.

> G-20 (The Group of Twenty) is an international forum for the Governments and Central Bank Governors from 20 major economies. The members include 19 individual countries: Argentina, Australia, Brazil, Canada, China, France, Germany, India, Indonesia, Italy, Japan, South Korea, Mexico, Russia, Saudi Arabia, South Africa, Turkey, the United Kingdom, the United States, and the European Union (EU).

World Bank said that Indonesia has made significant gains in poverty reduction. Its poverty rate went down from 24 percent at the time of the Asian financial crisis to 11 percent by 2014.

---

[17] World Bank Group. 2016. Global Economic Prospects, January 2016: Spillovers amid Weak Growth. Washington, DC: World Bank. Washington, DC: World Bank. doi:10.1596/978-1-4648-0675-9. License: Creative Commons Attribution CC BY 3.0 IGO

[18] http://www.worldbank.org/en/country/indonesia

For a decade up until 2015, Indonesia has had a growth rate of about 6 percent annually, with an active private sector and a burgeoning middle class.[19]

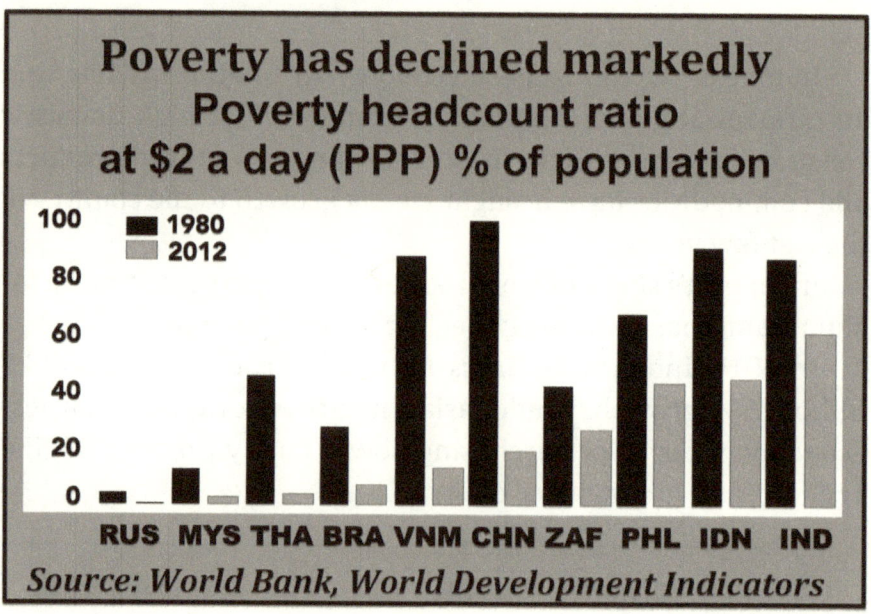

World Bank reported more than half of all FDI inflows to developing regions came from all developing EAP accounts, typically into a wide variety of sectors, including:

- manufacturing (Cambodia, Indonesia, Vietnam),
- construction (Cambodia and Lao PDR),
- tourism (Cambodia, Indonesia, Thailand), and
- resource extraction (Lao PDR, Mongolia, Myanmar).

Although half of the 20 largest developing country stock markets witnessed declines of 20 percent or more from their 2015 peaks, World Bank expects growth in Indonesia in

---

[19] World Bank. 2015. *Indonesia - Country partnership framework for the period FY16 - 20.* Washington, D.C.: World Bank Group.

2016 – 18[20], as reforms are implemented to spur investment growth in Indonesia.

Although revenue losses from lower commodity prices, Indonesia reformed fuel subsidies to cut down fiscal deficits in 2015.[21]

In 2015, Indonesian Gross Domestic Product is in the world's 16th largest GDP by nominal (total of $888,648 Billion). Derived from Purchasing Power Parity (PPP), Indonesia is in the world's 8th largest GDP (total of $2.686 Trillion).[22]

PPPs are the rates of currency conversion that equalize the purchasing power of different currencies by eliminating the differences in price levels between countries. PPPs are used to eliminate the outcomes of the different levels of prices within a group of countries at a point in time. Exchange rates are used to convert GDP in different currencies to a common currency.

Although global foreign direct investment (FDI) inflows fell by 16 percent to $1.23 Trillion in 2014, inward FDI flows to developing economies reached their highest level ever, at $681 Billion with a 2 percent rise.

Some of the reasons behind decline in global inflows in 2014 are:

- the fragility of the global economy,
- policy uncertainty for investors, and
- elevated geopolitical risks.

---

[20] World Bank Group. 2016. *Global Economic Prospects, January 2016: Spillovers amid Weak Growth*. Washington, DC: World Bank. Washington, DC: World Bank. doi:10.1596/978-1-4648-0675-9. License: Creative Commons Attribution CC BY 3.0 IGO

[21] World Bank Group. 2016. *Global Economic Prospects, January 2016: Spillovers amid Weak Growth*. Washington, DC: World Bank. Washington, DC: World Bank. doi:10.1596/978-1-4648-0675-9. License: Creative Commons Attribution CC BY 3.0 IGO

[22] http://data.worldbank.org/country/indonesia

New investments were also offset by some large divestments. Having significantly affected by a single large-scale divestment from the United States, overall FDI flows to developed countries declined by 28 percent to $499 Billion despite a revival in cross-border mergers and acquisitions (M&As).[23]

The FDI's performance to regional groupings and initiatives has influenced by the fall of FDI inflows globally and regionally in 2014. The groups of countries saw their combined share in global FDI flows decline, and discussing in the Transatlantic Trade and Investment Partnership (TTIP) and the Trans-Pacific Partnership (TPP). Two Asian groups bucked the trend:

- The Association of Southeast Asian Nations (ASEAN), with a 5 percent increase inflows to $133 Billion, and
- The Regional Comprehensive Economic Partnership (RCEP), with a 4 per cent increase to $363 Billion

5 developing economies are among the top 10 FDI recipients in the world. Inflows to East Asia rose by 12 percent to $248 Billion. In 2014, the top FDI recipient in the world is China, accounted for more than half of this figure. The United States became the third largest host country, due to large Verizon divestment by Vodafone (United Kingdom). Hong Kong (China) received a 39 percent rise in inflows to $103 Billion. FDI inflows in South-East Asia rose by 5 percent to $133 Billion. Singapore is now the world's fifth largest recipient economy, where inflows reached $68 Billion. Indonesia FDI growth went up by 20 percent to $23 Billion.

---

[23] *World Investment Report 2015, UNCTAD. Reforming International Investment Governance. United Nations Conference on Trade and Development. 25th World Investment Report. Geneva. 2015. ISBN 978-92-1-112891-8.*

Factors that influence FDI trends in regional group, among others are:

- Broader global trends
- Economic performance
- Geopolitical factors

Factors that can increase FDI trends in regional group, among others:

- Longer-term cooperation efforts – by opening sectors to investment and aligning policies for the treatment of investors
- Fewer investment restrictions
- Reduced transaction costs
- Converging policy regimes
- Enlarge market size
- Coordinated efforts to promote regional investment

Investments by developing country multinational enterprises (MNEs), for the first time, became the world's largest investing group, almost one third of the total: Nine of the 20 largest investor countries were from developing or transition economies. MNEs from Asia increased their investment abroad while outflows from Latin America and the Caribbean, and Africa fell. These MNEs continued to acquire developed countries affiliated in developing countries.

In the first half of the year of 2015, Indonesian economy performed below potential due mainly to the commodity price slump and grindingly slow Government spending, due in large part to heightened regulatory uncertainty and infrastructure bottlenecks. Recent data suggest sluggishness carried into Q3.

However, despite the slowdown, Indonesia's economic growth still has outperformed its ASEAN peers:

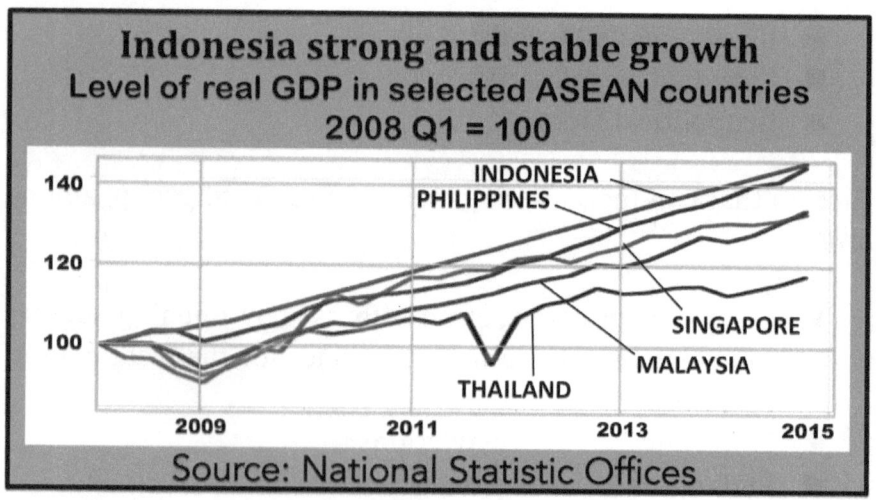

The Survey, presented in Jakarta by OECD Secretary-General Mr. Angel Gurría and Indonesian Minister of Finance Mr. Bambang Brodjonegoro, notes that economic growth has decelerated in recent years and suggests that expediting the pace of reform is needed to provide continuous and comprehensive growth for all Indonesians. Despite a slowdown in 2014 and challenging international environment, Indonesian GDP growth is projected to reach 5.3% in 2015 and 5.9% in 2016, and is forecasted to increase to 6% a year between 2015 – 2019.[24]

---

[24] *OECD. Active with Indonesia. March 2015. Economic Outlook for Southeast Asia, China and India, 2015*

http://www.oecd.org/globalrelations/keypartners/active-with-indonesia.pdf

The Economic Survey identifies that the central Government's strong fiscal position – marked by low deficits and low public debt – offers the opportunity to raise greater revenues to fund higher spending targeted at improving education, boosting infrastructure and expanding the social security system.

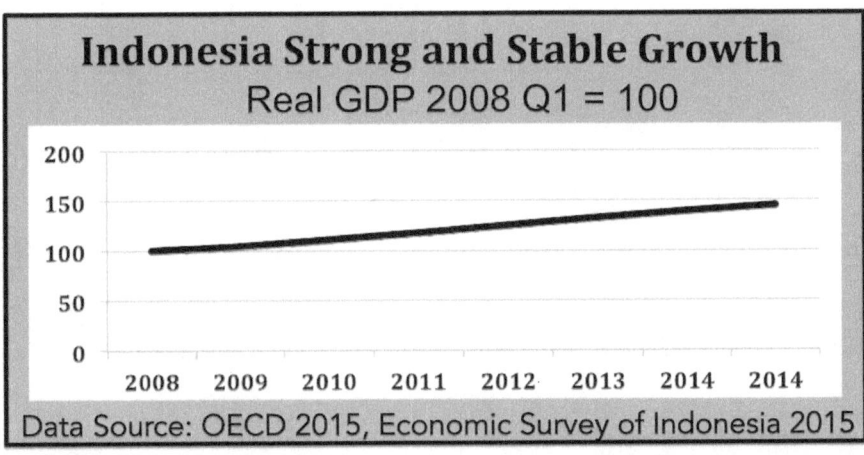

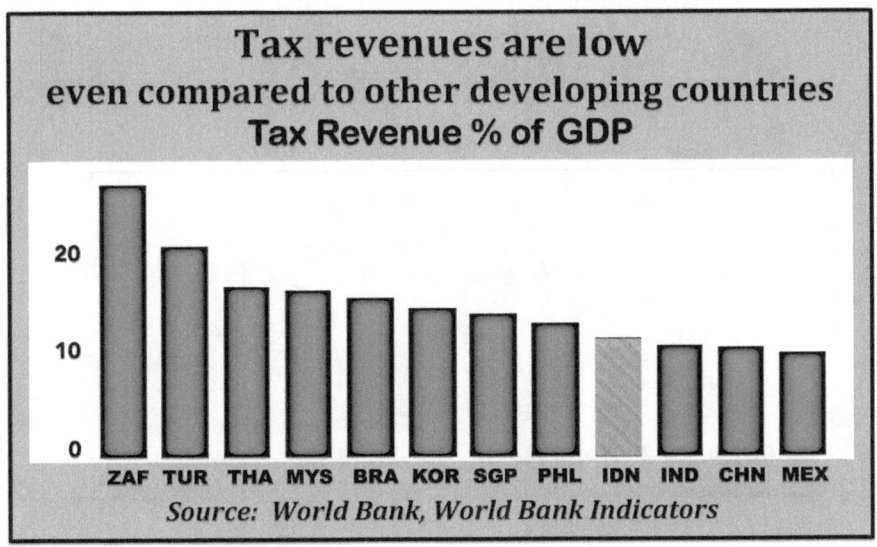

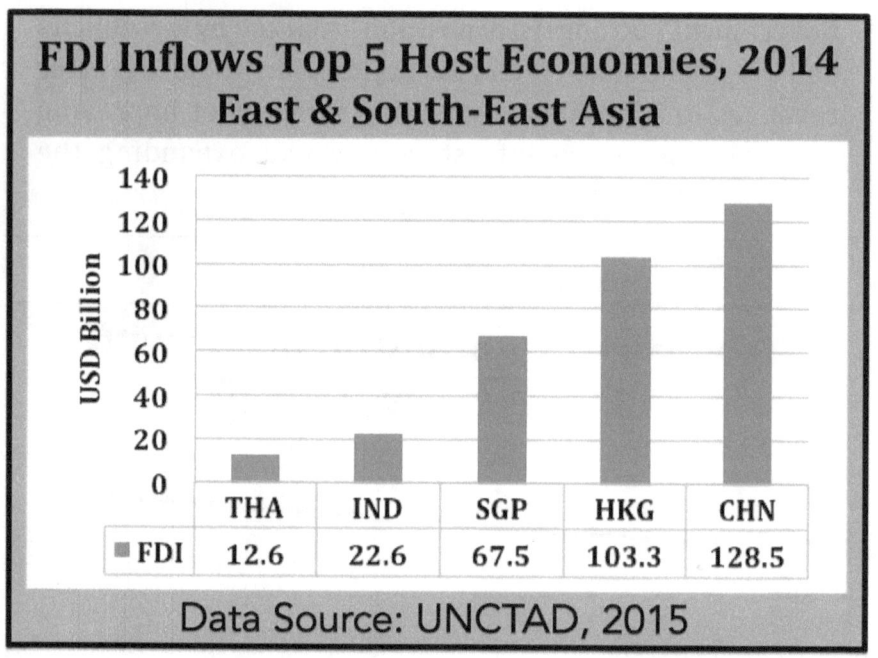

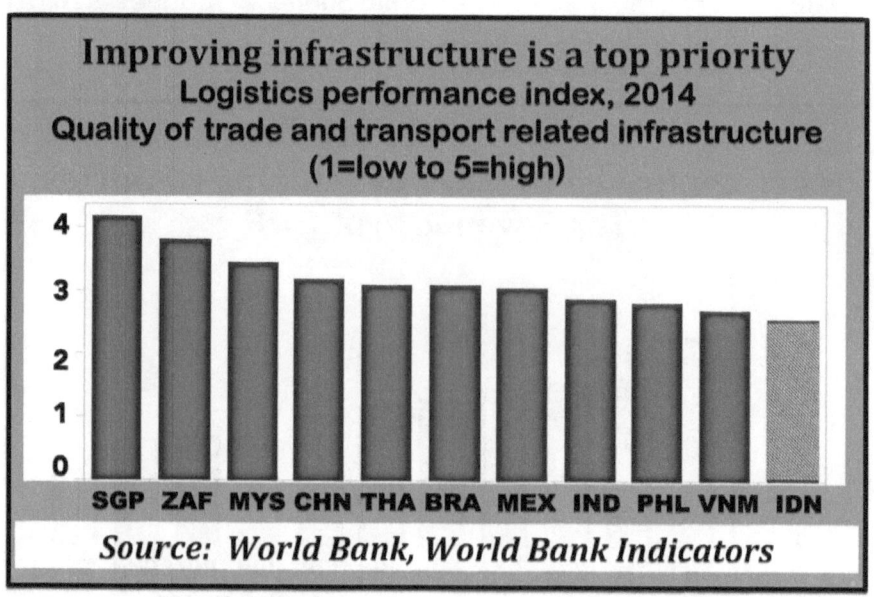

9 Enterprises In Indonesia

A. Types of Corporate Enterprises

There are three main private Limited Liability Company models recognized in Indonesia:[25]

- General Indonesian Companies (Perseroan Terbatas Biasa, PT Biasa)
- Domestic Capital Investment Companies (Perseroan Terbatas Penanaman Modal Dalam Negeri, PT PMDN)
- Foreign Investment Companies (Perseroan Terbatas Penanaman Modal Asing, PT PMA)

PT is a Limited Liability Company, a legal entity to run a business where shareholder liability is limited to the extent of the capital agreed to be contributed by shareholders.

The source of capital of a PT can come from stocks or bonds. Because capital consists of stocks that can be bought and sold, changes in corporate ownership can be done without the need to dissolve the Company. Gains derived by owners of the bonds is a fixed rate regardless of the profit or loss of the PT.

---

[25] *Indonesian Law No. 40/2007: Undang Undang Republik Indonesia Nomor 40 Tahun 2007 Tentang Perseroan Terbatas. Jakarta. 16 Agustus 2007. President Republik Indonesia. Susilo Bambang Yudhoyono. Diundangkan tanggal 16 Agustus 2007. Menteri Hukum dan HAM, Andi Mattalatta. Lembaran Negara Tahun 2007 No. 106.*

Indonesian Law divides PT into two classes:

1. PT. Biasa and PT. PDMN

- Limited to Indonesian citizens and/or Indonesian legal entities;
- A PMDN Company may enjoy certain regulatory or tax advantages;
- The minimum capital requirement for incorporation in Indonesia is IDR50 Million for PT Biasa, but higher amounts are required for PT PMDN.

2. PT. PMA

- Used for Foreign Investment activities;
- Foreign investors may, however, acquire shares in PT PMDN or PT Biasa companies, provided that they comply with the Investment Law and Negative Investment List. The acquired PT Biasa/PT PMDN would also have to be converted into a PT PMA;
- It is possible to have 100 percent foreign shareholding in a PT PMA where the industry sector so permits, provided it has a minimum of two shareholders either as foreign individuals or Company entities;
- The Regulation No. 5 of 2013[26] requires that a minimum of IDR10 Billion be invested in a new PT PMA, excluding the cost from the land and buildings;
- The minimum investment requirement, the Regulation 5/2013 also requires that each shareholder of a PT PMA

---

[26] *Peraturan Kepala BKPM RI No. 5/2013 tentang Pedoman dan Tata Cara Perijinan dan Non Perijinan Penanaman Modal. Jakarta, 8 April 2013, Muhamad Chatib Basri. Promulgated in Jakarta on April 12, 2013 by the Indonesian Minister of Law and Human Rights, Mr. Amir Syamsudin. Berita Negara Republik Indonesia Tahun 2013 Nomor 584.*

holds shares with a nominal value of at least IDR 10 Million;
- The Regulation 5/2013 states that the minimum equity to debt ratio permitted is 25 percent. Although, in practice, there are cases of BKPM approving a 10 percent equity to debt ratio, specifically in the property and plantation sectors.

Based on the source of the capital, there are two kinds of Perusahaan Terbatas (PT):

- **Open PT, or PT Terbuka (Tbk.)**, is a Limited Liability Company that sells its shares to the public through the capital market. For example, PT Telekomunikasi Indonesia (Persero) Tbk, PT. Semen Indonesia (Persero) Tbk, PT Krakatau Steel (Persero) Tbk., etc.
- **Closed PT, or PT Tertutup**, a Limited Liability Company that receives capital from certain shareholders such as relatives, family, friends or business relations, and is not sold to the public.

B. Corporate Governance

Indonesia's Law Number 40 of 2007 on Limited Liability Companies (the Company Law) implementing Regulations establish a 'two-board' system of governance. It adopts the common Law concept of fiduciary duties for each board in carrying out their respective role. While the two boards are separate, the Board of Commissioners may work together in conjunction with the directors to implement strategies of the Company:

a. The Board of Commissioners (Dewan Komisaris):

- Supervises the performance of the Board of Directors and policies made by the board;
- Provides advice to the board;
- May work together in conjunction with the directors to implement strategies of the Company;
- Whether a 100 percent Foreign Owned Company or a Joint Venture Company, may be Foreigners.

b. The Board of Directors (Direksi)

- Manages the Company's operations in good faith and prudently for the benefit of the Company and is personally liable for any loss suffered by the Company for breach of this duty;
- Serves as the authorized organ and representative of the Company in all matters, subject to compliance with the Law, the Company's rules and resolutions of the general meeting of shareholders;
- Have similar responsibilities to directors of companies in Common Law countries and, among other things, must prepare an annual report to shareholders for approval and a business plan for the next financial year, manage the Company's operations and represent the Company in relation to external parties;
- Whether a 100 percent Foreign Owned Company or a Joint Venture Company, may be Foreigners. However, a foreigner is not allowed to take a position as a 'Personnel Director', who is also a member of the boards, and/or a position of authority in a "human resources" capacity;
- BKPM may recommend that there be at least one Indonesian among the Board of Directors if there is an Indonesian shareholder in the PMA Company.

C. Structure of Capital

The Company has its own assets, apart from the assets of each Company's shareholders. Included in the assets of the Limited Liability Company is the capital, consisting of:

- The Company's capital or primary capital, which is the maximum amount of capital referred to in the deed of establishment. The primary capital requirement stipulated in Article 31-32 of Law No. 40 of 2007. The primary capital of the Company is comprised of all the nominal value of shares. *(Article 31, Paragraph 1)*
- Disclosed or placed capital, stipulated in article 33 of Law No. 40 of 2007. At least 25% of the primary capital as referred to in Article 32 must be issued and fully paid *(Article 33, Paragraph 1).*
- Deposited capital, is the capital that has been paid or transferred by the shareholders into the Company's account. Regulated in Article 34 of Law No. 40 of 2007. The payment of this capital can be done in the form of cash and / or in any other forms *(Article 34, Paragraph 2 and 3).*

D. Type of Shares

There are two kinds of share certificates:

- Sero Atas Nama / Stocks, the name of the Company is written above the share certificate after the holdings registered in the book of Limited Liability limited as a corporation.
- Sero Pembawa / Stock Bearer, a share certificate that has no corporation name.

Types of shares in connection with the rights of business entity:

- Sero Biasa / Regular Stocks, usually earn same profits (dividends) as determined by the general meeting of shareholders.
- Sero Preferen / Preference Stocks, receive more rights than Regular Stocks.
- Sero Kumulatif Preferen / Cumulative Preference Stocks, receive more rights than Preference Stocks

10 Foreign Investment Regulations and Procedures

Note from Author: There are translations of Laws and Regulations in this Chapter. I emphasized readability rather than word-for-word. When there are contradictions and discrepancies as to interpretation of any provision of the Law, the original version of the Law written in Bahasa Indonesia shall prevail.

A. Investment Overview

Two common forms of investment in Indonesia:

1. Direct Investment

The investor invests capital in a new or existing Company, in order to establish a business or business presence in Indonesia and to participate in the management of the investee Company. Includes, mergers and acquisitions, building new facilities, reinvesting profits earned from overseas operations and intra Company loans.

2. Indirect Investment

The investor invests through the purchase of securities in the capital markets, such as equity, debt or a combination of both, and is less interested in participating directly in the management or control of the investee Company. This investment is not defined in the Investment Law, however, it is generally understood to be portfolio investment.

B. Direct Foreign Investment

1. Form of Investment

Indonesian direct Foreign Investment is regulated by "Law No. 25 of 2007 regarding Investment" and its implementing regulations (the Investment Law).[27]

Under the Investment Law, any form of direct Foreign Investment in Indonesia must be in the form of a Limited Liability Company (Perusahaan Terbatas, PT).

A Company established with Foreign Investment capital is known as a 'PMA Company' (Penanaman Modal Asing); while an Investment Company established with no foreign investors is known as a 'PMDN Company' (Penanaman Modal Dalam Negeri). A PMA Company itself is also regarded as a Foreign Investment from the Investment Law perspective.

In general, all Indonesian incorporated companies are subject to the Indonesian Company Law (Law No. 40 of 2007 regarding Limited Liability Companies); while PMA and PMDN Companies are also governed by the Investment Law.[28]

---

[27] *Undang Undang Republik Indonesia No. 25 Tahun 2007 tentang Penanaman Modal. Jakarta 26 April 2007. Presiden Republik Indonesia, Dr. H. Susilo Bambang Yudhoyono. Promulgated in Jakarta on 26 April 2007 by the Indonesian Minister of Laws and Human Rights, Hamid Awaludin. Lembaran Negara Republik Indonesia Tahun 2007 No. 67.*

[28] *Undang Undang Republik Indonesia No. 40 Tahun 2007 tentang Perseroan Terbatas. Jakarta, 16 August 2007. Susilo Bambang Yudhoyono. Promulgated in Jakarta on 16 August 2007 by Indonesian Minister of Laws and Human Rights, Mr. Andi Mattalatta. Lembaran Negara Republik Indonesia Tahun 2007 No. 106.*

> **Important**: *Investors are protected by the Investment Law, which states that the Indonesian Government is not allowed to take away ownership rights of any investor, including foreign investors, without paying such an investor a market-based compensation.*

2. Authorities Responsible for Managing Foreign Investment

According to Chapter V Article 7 – 10, the Regulation of the Head of BKPM No. 17 / 2015 on the guidelines and procedures on controlling the implementation of the investment, as well as, development, supervision, control and management of the investment activities, is performed by:[29]

- BKPM (Investment Coordinating Board)
- Board of Investment and One Stop Integrated Services (BPMPTSP) Province
- BPMPTSP Regency / City
- Free Trade Zone and Free Port (KPBPB) Undertaking Agency, or
- The Special Economic Zones (KEK) Administrator in accordance with their field authority.

If the Central Government requires the data of Investment Realization from a Local Government, BKPM can directly monitor the investment under the authority of the Government

---

[29] *Peraturan Kepala Badan Koordinasi Penanaman Modal RI No. 17 tahun 2015 tentang Pedoman dan Tata Cara Pengendalian Pelaksanaan Penanaman Modal. Franky Sibarani. Jakarta 29 September 2015. Promulgated in Jakarta on 8 October 2015 by Director General Legislation, Indonesian Ministry of Laws and Human Rights, Widodo Ekatjahjana. Berita Negara Republik Indonesia Tahun 2015 No. 1481*

of Province, Regency / City, KPBPB Undertaking Agency or KEK Administrator.

Domestic investment is generally organized by the Regional Investment Coordinating Board (Badan Koordinasi Penanaman Modal Daerah, BKPMD) at the local regencies or cities.

Foreign Investment must be approved by the Indonesian Government through the Indonesian Investment Coordinating Board (Badan Koordinasi Penanaman Modal, BKPM), except in the area of:

- Banking and Financial Services Sectors (granted by Indonesia's Financial Service Authority)
- The upstream oil and gas sector (regulated through production sharing contracts with the oil and gas contracting agency Satuan Kerja Khusus Kegiatan Usaha Hulu Minyak dan Gas Bumi (SKK Migas)
- A portfolio investment through the purchase of securities in the capital markets.

Foreign investors must submit to BKPM periodic investor activity reports summarizing investment progress and any obstacles to their investment activities, such as Investment Activities Reports (LKPM), Import Realization Reports, and Foreign Worker's Utilization Reports.

3. Laws and Government Regulations

General Laws and Government Regulations in connection with the establishment of a Foreign Investment Company (PMA) are as below. There are additional Laws and Regulations for specific matters in connection with the field of business. For example, there are Laws and Regulations governing forestry, manufacturing, machinery, finance, trading, food, health, processing, service, mining, transportation, etc.

- ☐ The Law of Indonesia No. 25/2007 on the Investment
- ☐ The Law of Indonesia No. 40/2007 on Perseroan Terbatas
- ☐ The Law of Indonesia No. 13/2003 on Manpower
- ☐ The Indonesian Minister of Manpower Regulation No. 16/2015 on the Procedures of the Employment of Foreigners, and No. 35/2015 on amendment of the Regulation No. 16/2015
- ☐ The Minister of Agrarian and Spatial Planning Regulation No. 5/2015 on Location Permit
- ☐ Indonesian Government Regulation No. 18/2015 on Income Tax facilities
- ☐ The Head of BKPM Regulation No. 8/2015 on how to request Income Tax facilities
- ☐ The Indonesian Minister of Finance Regulation No. 144/PMK.011/2012 on Income Tax facilities
- ☐ The Regulation of President of Republic of Indonesia No. 16/2012 on General Plans of Investment
- ☐ The Acts No. 1/1970 on Work Safety
- ☐ The Indonesian Minister of Trade Regulation No. 70/M-DAG/PER/9/2015 on Angka Pengenal Importir.
- ☐ The Indonesian Government Regulation No. 1/2007 and 52/2011 on Income Tax facilities
- ☐ The Minister of Finance Regulation No. 130/PMK.011/2011 on the provision of exemption or reduction of corporate Income Tax
- ☐ The Law of Indonesia No. 32/2009 on the protection and management of the environment
- ☐ The Decree of the Minister of Finance No.: 609/KMK.04/1994 on holding books in foreign languages and currencies other than Rupiah
- ☐ Indonesian President Regulation No. 39/2014 on Daftar Negatif Investasi (Negative Investment List)
- ☐ The Regulation issued by the Head of Central Bureau of Statistics No. 57/2009 on Klasifikasi Baku Lapangan Usaha Indonesia (KBLI, Indonesia Standard Industrial Classification).

☐ The Head of BKPM Regulation No. 5/2013, amended by No. 12/2013 on guidelines and licensing procedures and non permits of Foreign Investment

4. General Plans of Investment

Regulation of President of Republic of Indonesia No. 16 of 2012 on General Plan of Investment (RUPM)[30]:

- Is planning documents of long-term investment, valid until 2025.
- Listed in the Appendix, and an integral part of the Presidential Regulation No. 16 of 2012.
- Become a reference for the Ministry or Non-Government Institutions and Local Government in formulating policies related to investment activities or potentials development priorities.
- Direction of Investment Policies, which consists of:
    ☐ Improvement of Investment Climates;
    ☐ Distribution of Investment;
    ☐ Focus on Food Development, Infrastructure, and Energy;
    ☐ Environmental Investment (Green Investment);
    ☐ Empowerment of Micro, Small, Medium, and Cooperatives (UMKMK);
    ☐ Provision of Facilities, Facilities, and / or Incentives on Capital investment; and
    ☐ Investment Promotions.

---

[30] *Indonesian President Regulation No. 16/2012: Peraturan Presiden Indonesia No. 16 tahun 2012 tentang Rencana Umum Penanaman Modal. Jakarta 7 February 2012. Dr. H. Susilo Bambang Yudhoyono. Ratified by Dr. H. Susilo Bambang Yudhoyono, the President of the Republic of Indonesia dated 7 February 2012. Promulgated in Jakarta by the Minister of Law and Human Rights of the Republic of Indonesia, Mr. Amir Syamsudin dated 7 February 2012.*

- Roadmap on Implementation of the General Plan of Investment, which consists of:
  - ☐ Phase of investment developments that are easier and fast produce;
  - ☐ Phase of acceleration on infrastructure and energy development;
  - ☐ Phase of large scale industrial development;
  - ☐ Phase of knowledge-based Economy development.

5. General Licensing Documents[31]

The Regulation of the Head of BKPM No. 17/2015 Chapter III Article 3: Investment Licensing scope that became the basis of the implementation of the control implementation the Investment, include:

- Principle Permit, Investment Permit, Expansion Principle Permit and Permit Investment Principles Amendment Permit, Company Merger Principle Permit;
- Business License, Business Expansion License, Expansion License, Business Merger License, and Business Amendment License;
- KPPA and KP3A Permit, and
- Other licensing related to the implementation of the Investment in accordance with the legislation.

---

[31] *Peraturan Kepala Badan Koordinasi Penanaman Modal RI No. 17 Tahun 2015 tentang Pedoman dan Tata Cara Pengendalian Pelaksanaan Penanaman Modal. 29 September 2015. Franky Sibarani. Promulgated in Jakarta on October 8, 2015 by Director General Legislation, Indonesian Ministry of Laws and Human Rights, Mr. Widodo Ekatjahjana. Berita Negara Republik Indonesia Tahun 2015 No. 1481*

General licenses, administratively may be in the form of:

- Certificate / Deed of incorporation and ratification;
- Tax Identification Number (TIN/NPWP);
- Location Permit;
- The lease agreement of land/building;
- Letter of approval on import duty facilities on capital goods;
- Producer Importer Identification Number (API-P);
- Foreign Manpower Utilization Plan (RPTKA);
- Building Permit (IMB);
- Nuisance Act Permit (UUG Permit) / HO or Business Place Permit (SITU), and / or
- Other appropriate licensing in accordance with legislation.

The scope of the non-licensing of Investment which became the basis of control the implementation of Investment includes:

- The decision of facility provision of import duty exemption on machinery and / or goods and materials;
- Import realization reports on Importer Identity Number (API);
- Permits Employing Foreign Workers (IMTA), and
- Other non-licensing related to the implementation of the investment in accordance with Laws and Regulations.

6. General Procedures of Establishing a PT. PMA

There are two options to establish a Foreign Investment Company in Indonesia:

OPTION 1:

- Submission of Principle License to BKPM
- Request a name for the Company (LLC/PT) from the Indonesian Ministry of Law & Human Rights
- Deed of Establishment and Articles of Association

- Certificate of Domicile of Company
- Tax Identification Number
- Legalization of Article of Association by Indonesia Ministry of Law & Human Rights

OPTION 2:

- Request a name of for Company (LLC/PT) from Indonesian Ministry of Law & Human Rights
- Deed of Establishment of PT and Articles of Association
- Certificate of Domicile of Company
- Tax Identification Number
- Submission of Principle License to BKPM
- Legalization of Article of Association by Indonesia Ministry of Law & Human Rights

Type and flow of licensing and non-licensing process in the field of investment[32]:

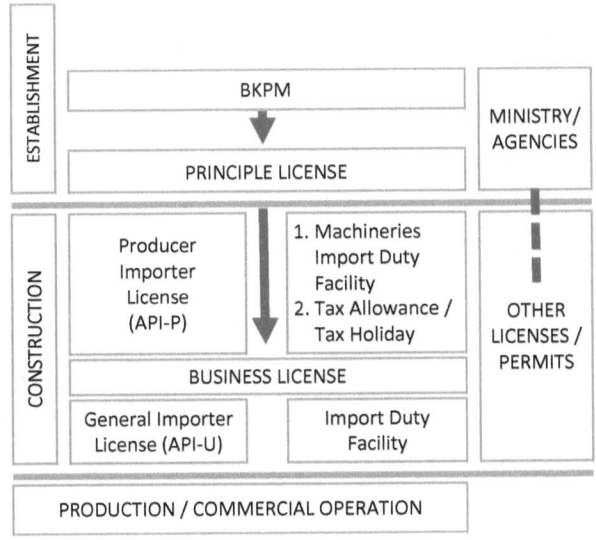

---

[32] *BKPM Strategic Plan 2015 – 2019: Rencana Strategis Badan Penanaman Modal Tahun 2015 – 2019*

7. Investing in Existing PMDN or PMA Companies

A PMDN Company must obtain prior approval from BKPM to transfer all or some of its shares in a Company to a foreign individual or entity. Such shares may only be acquired if the business field is open to investment (see the Limitations on Foreign Investment in section C below). BKPM's prior approval is also required for changes to the shareholding composition of an existing PMA Company.

8. Representative Office

Foreign investors are permitted to open a "representative office" in Indonesia as an alternative to establishing a PMA Company or investing in an existing PMDN or PMA Company.

Three main types of a representative office:

A. A Representative Office Under the Control of the Department of Trade:

- The most common form of representative office
- The range of activities that may be conducted by such a representative office is quite narrow
- May not undertake trading activities, own production facilities or undertake operational business activities
- Cannot accept orders, participate in tenders, sign contracts or engage in the import, export or distribution of goods
- Include marketing and promotional activities and information gathering for the Foreign Company

B. A Representative Office Under the Control of the Department of Public Works:

- Established for the specific purpose
- Joint operation agreement with an Indonesian entity
- To engage in construction and construction consulting services.

C. A Regional Representative Office:

- May be established by a multinational Company
- In one of Indonesia's main cities
- To manage the operations of such Company in the ASEAN region
- The activity is limited to supervising and coordinating the business of its Company within the region
- This office is not allowed to engage in transactions with companies or persons in Indonesia, either for export or import or domestic trading

9. Approximate Time and Procedure

The summary bellow is a sample of approximate times for each step in starting business in Indonesia, as identified by Doing Business (a research project within World Bank Group), through collaboration with relevant local professionals and the study of Laws, Regulations and publicly available information on business entry in that economy.

Summary of Approximate Time, Cost and Procedures for Starting A Business [33]

Legal form: Perseroan Terbatas (PT)
Paid-in minimum capital requirement: IDR12,500,000.00
City: Jakarta
Start-up Capital: 10 times GNI per capita

No.	Procedure	Time to Complete	Cost to Complete
1.	**Company name clearance** ■ The process must be done through a computerized processing system ■ The reservation and clearance is most commonly done in practice by a notary public. ■ The notary must first pay the fee of IDR 200,000 at a bank before obtaining clearance for the proposed Company name. ■ Once the notary pays at a bank, they obtain a payment receipt with a code. *Agency: Notary*	1 day	IDR200,000
2.	**The standard form of the Company deed and clearance for the Indonesian Company's name at the Ministry of Law and Human Rights** ■ The notary reserves the Company name by inserting the code online as proof of payment. ■ The reserved name will be blocked for 60 days. If the founding shareholders are confident that the same name has not been used by another Indonesian Company, this procedure is not necessary.	4 days	Included in procedure 3

---

[33] World Bank. 2016. *Doing Business 2016: Measuring Regulatory Quality and Efficiency*. Washington, DC: World Bank Group. DOI: 10.1596/978-1-4648-0667-4. License: Creative Commons Attribution CC BY 3.0 IGO

http://www.doingbusiness.org/~/media/GIAWB/Doing%20Business/Documents/Profiles/Country/IDN.pdf

Company must not use a name which:
- Has been lawfully used by another Company or is similar to the name of another Company;
- Contravenes public order and/or decency;
- Is identical or similar to the name of a state agency, Government agency, or international agency, except with their approval;
- Does not conform to the purposes and objectives and business activities of the Company, or only designates the purposes and objectives of the Company without having its own name;
- Consists of numbers or a set of figures, a letter or a set of letters that do not form any words; or
- Means a Company, a legal entity, or a civil enterprise (Persekutuan Perdata).

The Ministry of Law and Human Rights may reject a name application reservation if the requested name is, among others, the same or resembles similarities to name of other companies.

Article 4 of MoLHR Reg. No. 4/2014:
An electronic application must be submitted for the use of the Company's name to the Ministry of Law and Human Rights (Minister of MOLHR) through Legal Entity Administration System (SABH). Such application shall be performed by filing the Company's Name Application Form which at least contains of the following information:
- Payment number of the approval of the use of the Company's name from bank; and
- Booked name of the Company.

The approval of the Company's name by the Minister of MOLHR shall be given electronically, as regulated under Article 7 of MoLHR Reg. No.4/2014, which at least contains of the following information:
- Booking number of the name of the Company;
- Name of the Company which may be used;

	■ Date of booking; ■ Expiry date; and ■ Payment code. *Agency: Notary*		
3.	***Notarize Company documents** ■ Government Regulation No. 43 of 2011 on Use of Names of Limited Liability Companies also provides that an application to use a name that is the same or similar to a well-known trademark shall be rejected unless approval is obtained from the holder of the trademark. ■ Law No. 30 of 2004 on Notaries (Article 36 Paragraph 3) stipulates that the maximum notary fee for objects of deed with an economical value of above IDR 100,000,000 up to IDR 1,000, 000,000 is 1.5% of the total value of the object of the deed. *Agency: Notary*	1 day, (simultaneous with previous procedure)	See procedure details
4.	**Approval of the deed of establishment** Article 9, 10, 29 and 30 Indonesian Company Law No. 40 / 2007: The application for approval of Ministry of Law and Human Right on establishment of Company should be able to file electronically by attaching with the certificate of bank account, copy of the relevant bank transmittal advice. The process as follows: ■ The application should be filled at the latest 60 days since the date of establishment deed; ■ Since the application has already fulfilled, the Ministry of Law directly electronically stated no objection on said application. However, if the application is not fulfilled, the Ministry of Law will directly electronically state his objection on said application;	Less than one day (online procedure)	Included in procedure 1

	■ In 30 days since the date of no objection by Ministry of Law, the applicant should submit the original application and supporting documents; ■ 14 days after fulfillment of above requirements, Minis-try of Law will issue the legalization on the establishment of the Company; ■ Data of Company that its establishment has been approved by Ministry of Law i.e. name, domicile, object and purpose, period, Capital Company will be inserted into Company Registry. ■ The Ministry of Law will announce the establishment of Company in Supplement State Gazette (TBNRI) within 14 days of the Ministry's Approval Letter. As of March 2014, the Ministry of Law and Human Rights issues the approval of the deed of establishment electronically. The cost of this procedure is based on the Schedule to the Government Regulation No. 38 / 2009 concerning Types and Tariffs on Non-Tax State Revenues Applied for in the Department of Law and Human Rights which comes into effect on 28 May 2009. *Agency: Ministry of Law and Human Rights*		
5.	**Building Management Domicile Certificate** Business founders of Companies that are located in an office building need to apply the Building Management Domicile Certificate from the Building Management Office before applying for the Certificate of Company Domicile. *Agency: Building Management Office*	1 day	No charge
6.	**Certificate of Company Domicile** ■ All Indonesian Limited Liability Companies must have a Certificate of Company Domicile. ■ Issued by the head of the village (the Lurah) where the Company is located or by the building management if office space is leased.	2 days	No charge

	- There is no official fee for this certificate. - This certificate is required for several documents (SIUP, TDP, etc.) *Agency: Municipal*		
7.	**Non-tax state revenue (PNBP) fees for legal services** - The requirement to pay the non-tax state revenue (PNBP) fee for legal services in relation to the establishment of a PT is obtained in the website of the Legal Entity Administration System known as SABH (www.sisminbakum.go.id). - The obligation for the Company to pay the PNBP is also stated in Article 5 of the MOLHR Reg. No.4/2014. - The cost for the PNBP is further regulated under the Indonesian Government Regulation No.45 of 2014 on Types and Rates of Non Tax State Revenues Prevailing in the Ministry of Law and Human Rights that comes into effect on June 3, 2014. Cost breakdown: - IDR1,000,000 for validation of Company as legal entity - IDR30,000 for publication in State Gazette - IDR550,000 for publication in the Supplement State Gazette *Agency: Notary*	1 day	See procedure details
8.	**The Permanent Business Trading License (SIUP)** - The SIUP constitutes the business license for a non-facility Company engaging in trading business. - Contains details about the Company activities and the person in charge of the Company (normally the President Director). - The Ministry of Trade, which issues the SIUP for a non-facility Company, may require a letter of good conduct from the Indonesian police in support of the person in charge of the Company.	15 days	No charge

Normally, the following copy of documents should be attached for the application for a SIUP:
- The articles of association
- An attestation of location and address of the Company's offices (building management domicile certificate and certificate of Company domicile).
- ID card of the Company President Director.
- Letter of approval from the Ministry of Law and Human Rights

After reviewing the application, the Municipality passes it to the technical agency at the regional office for cooperatives for further review• it takes 2 days to get the signature of the head of that office as the authority is not delegated. Once the application is back, the SUIP is provided.

The Trade Minister Regulation No. 36/M-DAG/PER/9/2007 as amended by the Trade Minister Regulation No. 46/M-DAG/ PER/12/2011. There are no changes to Article 3 under this new Regulation. Classified the SIUP based on the enterprises' net assets as follows:
Article 3
- Small Scale SIUP must be held by businesses engaging in trade having a net asset of more than IDR50,000,000 (fifty million Rupiah) up to no more than IDR500,000, 000 (five hundred million Rupiah) not including land and building on which the business operates;
- Medium Scale SIUP must be held by businesses engaging in trade having a net asset of more than IDR 500,000, 000 (five hundred million Rupiah) up to no more than IDR10,000, 000,000 (ten Billion Rupiah) not including land and building on which the business operates;
- Large Scale SIUP must be held by businesses engaging in trade having a net asset of more than IDR 10,000,000,000 (Ten Billion Rupiah) not including land and building on which the business operates.

Agency: Ministry of Trade

9.	**Company registration certificate (TDP)**	14 days	No charge
	▪ The SIUP must be obtained before the TDP can be issued. ▪ The same documents submitted for the SIUP must also be submitted for the TDP, in addition to the SIUP itself. *Agency: Local Government Office (Trade Sub-division)*		
10.	**Register with the Ministry of Manpower**	1 day	No charge
	Pursuant to Article 6 of the Law No.7 of 1981 concerning Mandatory Labor Affairs Report (Law No.7/1981), the Company shall be obliged to submit a manpower report in the Company to the Ministry of Manpower and Transmigration (Minister of Manpower) or the appointed officer within a period of no more than 30 days as of the establishment of the Company. Such report shall contain the following information: ▪ Company identification; ▪ Manpower relation; ▪ Manpower protection; and ▪ Employment opportunity. The provision regarding the manpower report in the Company is further governed under the Regulation of the Ministry of Manpower & Transmigration of Indonesia No.PER.14/2006 concerning the Guidelines for the Manpower Report in the Company (MOMTR No.14/ 2006). ▪ The manpower report must be submitted in the form of electronic data compiled in the Company's Manpower Database in the Information System on Company's Manpower Mandatory Reports (SINLAPNAKER). ▪ The Company that makes a use of the Sinlapnaker shall be given an Identity Card from the Directorate General of Development of Labor Supervision. ▪ In the event that the region of the Company has not yet installed SINLAPNAKER, the report must be submitted in writing and delivered by hand or by registered mail to the		

	government institution having tasks and responsibility in the field of manpower in the Municipality /City where the Company is located. ■ In order to increase the service of the implementation of mandatory labor affairs report, the Minister of Manpower issues the Circular Letter of Indonesia Ministry of Manpower and Transmigration No.SE.3/MEN/III/2014 concerning the implementation of Mandatory Labor Affairs Report in the Company (MOMTCL No.3/2014). **Time:** Ratification of the registration of mandatory labor affairs report in the Company shall be performed within a period of 1 working day as of the receipt of complete application (signed which has been filled in complete and signed with the Company stamp (MOMTCL No. 3/2014). **Cost:** The registration of the mandatory labor affairs report shall not be subject to any fee(s) (MOMTCL No.3/2014). *Agency: Ministry of Manpower*		
11.	*** Workers Social Security Program (BPJS Ketenagakerjaan)** The Presidential Regulation No. 109 of 2013 on Membership Phasing of Social Security Program regulates that BPJS Ketenagakerjaan covers occupational accident security, old age security, pension security, as well as death security. Under this Regulation, every employers have the obligation to register their workers to BPJS Ketenagakerjaan based on their business scale starting from 1 July 2015, which are as follows: ■ Big and medium business scale to participate on programs including occupational accident security, old age security, pension security, and death security program;	7 days (simultaneous with previous procedure)	No charge

	- Small business scale to participate on programs including occupational accident security, old age security, and death security program; - Micro business scale to participate on programs including occupational accident security and death security. The Company shall obtain application forms (form 1 for data and form 1A for employees' data) at the nearest BPJS Ketenagakerjaan office (list of BPJS Ketenagakerjaan in DKI Jakarta: http://www.bpjsketenagakerjaan.go.id/kanwil/903/KANWIL-DKI-JAKARTA.html). The application forms shall be submitted to the BPJS Ketenagakerjaan at the latest 30 days after obtaining application forms with following attachments: receipt of first contribution payment, SIUP, Company's NPWP, Deed of Establishment, and employees' National Identity Card, Photograph, and Family Registration Card. After 7 days of the submission, BPJS Ketenagakerjaan will issue the membership card and certificate of registration. If there is any changes on the Company's address, business activity, and the amount of employees, as well as employee's wages, at the latest 7 days following to such changes, the employer is obliged to convey it to BPJS Ketenagakerjaan. *Agency: Social Security Administrative Bodies (BPJS Ketenagakerjaan)*		
12.	* **Healthcare insurance** Complete manual registration form and provide the data of future participants to BPJS Health or through appointed third parties, and submit the personal data of the participant candidates. During application, the employer must provide at least the following personal data of the candidate participants: - Name and Date of birth; - Name of the health service provider selected by the employee; and	7 days (simultaneous with previous procedure)	No charge

	■ Other personal information, including: ☐ Employee and his/her family member(s), who will be covered by the health insurance program; ☐ Employee's salary info; ☐ Information on participation status *Agency: Social Security Administrative Bodies (BPJS Kesehatan)*		
13.	*** Taxpayer ID number (NPWP) and a VAT collector number (NPPKP)** Regulation of Directorate General of Taxation No. Per-38/PJ /2013 on Procedures of Application of Taxpayer Registration and/or Taxable Entrepreneur Number, Amendment of Data and Transfer of Taxpayer and/or Taxable Entrepreneur aimed to enhance the service to the taxpayer: ■ The relevant Tax Office will conduct field confirmation regarding the correct data/ identity of the taxpayer within 1 year as of the issuance of NPWP. ■ The person /entity can apply for NPWP in the relevant tax office where the Company is located or can apply it online through http:// www.pajak.go.id, choose e-registration to make account as a taxpayer and then follow the procedures, by filling the form and attaching copies of the following: ● Deed of establishment ● ID card/KTP of one of active Director ● Statement letter regarding confirmation on place of business from one of the active Director (form is provided), ● POA and ID card/KTP of the authorized. The NPWP card and Registered Statement Letter is obtained within 1 calendar day upon the completeness of the required document without and fee, charge and/or retribution. *Agency: Tax Office*	1 day (simultaneous with previous procedure)	No charge

* Takes place simultaneously with another procedure.
Source: Doing Business database.
Note: Online procedures account for 0.5 days in the total time calculation.

Summary of Approximate Time, Cost and Procedures for Starting a Business[34]

Legal form: Perseroan Terbatas (PT)
Paid-in minimum capital requirement: IDR 12,500,000.00
City: Surabaya
Start-up Capital: 10 times GNI per capita

No.	Procedure	Time to Complete	Cost to Complete
1.	**Clearance of Company Name** ■ The process must be done through a computerized processing system ■ The reservation and clearance is most commonly done in practice by a notary public. ■ The notary must first pay the fee of IDR 200,000 at a bank before obtaining clearance for the proposed Company name. ■ Once the notary pays at a bank, she/he obtains a payment receipt with a code. *Agency: Notary*	1 day	IDR 200,000
2.	**The standard form of the Company deed and clearance for the Indonesian Company's name** ■ The notary reserves the Company name by inserting the code online as proof of payment. ■ The reserved name will be blocked for 60 days.	4 days	Included in procedure 3

---

[34] World Bank. 2016. *Doing Business 2016: Measuring Regulatory Quality and Efficiency.* Washington, DC: World Bank Group. DOI: 10.1596/978-1-4648-0667-4. License: Creative Commons Attribution CC BY 3.0 IGO

http://www.doingbusiness.org/~/media/GIAWB/Doing%20Business/Documents/Profiles/Country/IDN.pdf

	■ If the founding shareholders are confident that the same name has not been used by another Indonesian Company, this procedure is not necessary. Government Regulation No. 43 of 2011 on Limited Liability Company, Company must not use a name which: ■ Has been lawfully used by another Company or is similar to the name of another Company; ■ Contravenes public order and/or decency; ■ Is identical or similar to the name of a state agency, Government agency, or inter-national agency, except with their approval; ■ Does not conform to the purposes and objectives and business activities of the Company, or only designates the purposes and objectives of the Company without having its own name; ■ Consists of numbers or a set of figures, a letter or a set of letters that do not form any words; or ■ Means a Company, a legal entity, or a civil enterprise (Persekutuan Perdata). The Ministry of Law & Human Rights may reject a name application reservation if the requested name is, among others, the same or resembles similarities to name of other companies. *Agency: Notary*		
3.	*****Notarize Company documents** ■ Once the notary gets the Company name approval from the Ministry of Law & Human Rights, the founders can sign the deed of establishment. ■ Standard articles of association are available at the notary office.	1 day (simulta-neous with previous procedure)	See procedure details

	▪ The notary fees associated with this procedure cover the following services: a. Name check b. Deed drafting & approval Commonly, local notary associations set the scale of notary fees. In practice, the fee depends on the agreement between notary and client. The average notary fee for Surabaya is IDR 7,000,000. *Agency: Notary*		
4.	**The non-tax state revenue (PNBP) fees for legal services** ▪ The requirement to pay the non-tax state revenue (PNBP) fee for legal services in relation to the establishment of a PT is obtained in the website of the Legal Entity Administration System known as SABH (www.sisminbakum.go.id). ▪ The obligation for the Company to pay the PNBP for the legal services in relation to the establishment of the Company is also stated in Article 5 of the MOLHR Reg. No. 4/2014. ▪ The cost for the PNBP is further regulated under the Indonesian Government Regulation No.45/2014 on Types and Rates of Non Tax State Revenues Prevailing in the Ministry of Law and Human Rights that comes into effect on June 3, 2014. Cost breakdown: • IDR1,000,000 for validation of Company as legal entity • IDR30,000 for publication in State Gazette • IDR550,000 for publication in the Supplement State Gazette *Agency: Notary*	1 day	See procedure details

5.	**Building Management Domicile Certificate** Business founders of Companies that are located in an office building need to apply the Building Management Domicile Certificate from the Building Management Office before applying for the Certificate of Company Domicile. *Agency: Building Management Office*	1 day	No charge
6.	**Certificate of Company Domicile** ■ All Indonesian limited liability companies must have a certificate of Company domicile. ■ Issued by the head of the village (the Lurah) where the Company is located or by the building management if office space is leased. ■ There is no official fee for this certificate. ■ This certificate is required for several documents (Ministry of Law and Human Rights approval, SIUP, TDP, etc.) *Agency: Head of the village (Lurah)*	2 days	No charge
7.	**Approval of the deed of establishment** Article 9, 10, 29 and 30 Indonesian Company Law No. 40 year 2007: The application for approval of Ministry of Law & Human Right on establishment of Company should be able to file electronically by attaching with the certificate of bank account, and copy of the relevant bank transmittal advice. The process are as follows: a. The application should be filled at the latest 60 days since the date of establishment deed; b. Since the application has already fulfilled, the Ministry of Law directly electronically stated no objection on said application. However, if the application is not fulfilled, the Ministry of Law will directly electronically state his objection on said application;	Less than one day (online procedure)	Included in procedure 1

	c. In 30 days since the date of no objection by Ministry of Law, the applicant should submit the original application and supporting documents; d. 14 days after fulfillment of above requirements, Minis-try of Law will issue the legalization on the establishment of the Company; e. Data of Company which its establishment has been approved by Ministry of Law i.e. name, domicile, object & purpose, period, Capital Company will be inserted into Company Registry. f. The Ministry of Law will announce the establishment of Company in Supplement State Gazette (TBNRI) within 14 days of the Ministry's Approval Letter. As of March 2014, the Ministry of Law and Human Rights issues the approval of the deed of establishment electronically. The cost of this procedure is based on the Schedule to the Government Regulation No. 45/2014 on Types and Tariffs on Non-Tax State Revenues Applied for in the Department of Law & Human Rights that comes into effect on May 30, 2014. *Agency: Ministry of Law and Human Rights*		
8.	**Taxpayer registration number (NPWP) and a Value Added Tax (VAT) collector number (NPPKP)** ■ The Company must be registered with the Tax Office maximum 1 month from the start of business operations. ■ The Company must obtain a VAT collector number (NPPKP) if it anticipates annual revenue of more than IDR600 million from the sales of goods and services. ■ The Company domicile certificate, articles of association, and identity cards of the directors must be submitted to obtain the tax numbers. NPWP and NPPKP can be arranged simultaneously in one package.	1 day	No charge

	■ The applicant submits the required documents to the Tax Office and gets the receipt of application. ■ The Tax Officer will inform the applicant when the NPWP and NPPKP cards are ready for pick up. ■ The NPWP application can also be arranged on-line but the applicant still needs to provide hard copies of documents and visit the Tax Office to pick up the NPWP Card. Most applicants visit the Tax Office in person. ■ In practice, unofficial fees may apply and range from IDR50,000 to IDR 300,000 specifically for the technical surveyor. *Agency: Tax Office*		

9.	**Permanent business trading license (SIUP) at the One Stop Shop (UPTSA)**
	
	■ The SIUP constitutes the business license for a non-facility Company engaging in trading business.
	■ Contains details about the Company active-ties and the person in charge of the Company.
	■ The following documents should be attached based on local Regulation No. 1/2010, enacted in April 2010:
	  ● Copy of ID Card;
	  ● An attestation from the applicant (stamp duty IDR 6,000) on the business area;
	  ● Copy of the deed of Company establishment;
	  ● 2 passport photos of 3x4cm
	  ● Copy of NPWP.
	■ Only the SIUP can be obtained at the one-stop shop.
	
	Agency: One Stop Shop
		14 days	No charge

10.	**Company Register and Registration Certificate (TDP)** TDP cannot be applied for at the same time as SIUP because SIUP is a pre-requisite for TDP.	14 days	No charge

		The following documents should be attached: a. Copy of deed of establishment; b. Copy of ID Card; c. Copy of technical permit related the business; d. Copy of NPWP; e. Copy of SIUP. Based on Mayor Regulation No. 35/2010 on the business services industry and the trade sector, it is mandatory to register the Company no later than 3 months after the business operations started. *Agency: City Agency of Trade and Industry Affairs*		
11.	**Register with the Ministry of Manpower at the local Manpower Office** Law No. 7/1981: Companies with more than 10 workers or a monthly payroll of IDR 1 million must register with the Ministry of Man power. This procedure can be completed concurrently with other post-registration procedures by filing the manpower compulsory report and Company regulations with the Ministry of Manpower. Although there is no official fee, there may an un-official administrative fee that depends on negotiation and usually starts at IDR100,000. *Agency: Ministry of Manpower*	14 days	No charge
12.	*** Workers Social Security Program (BPJS Ketenagakerjaan)** Law No. 3/1992: it is mandatory for every Company or individual employing 10 workers or more or generating a monthly payroll of at least IDR 1million a month to apply for the Workers Social Security Program (BPJS Ketenagakerjaan), operated by the executing agency. This social security program covers occupational accident security, death security and old age security.	7 days (simultaneous with previous procedure)	No charge

	Government Regulation No. 14/1993, as amended by Government Regulation No. 28/2002): A Company or an individual is not obligated to enroll its employees in the social security program if it offers an independent employee social security program with benefits comparable or better than those offered by the Package of Basic Health Maintenance Security. *Agency: Social Security Administrative Bodies (BPJS Ketenagakerjaan)*		
13.	*** Healthcare insurance with BPJS Kesehatan** Under the enactment President Decree No. 12/2013, as amended by President Decree No. 111/2013 on Health Insurance, PT Jamsostek (Persero) will no longer operate the health maintenance security program. As of January 1, 2014 BPJS-Kesehatan has taken on that role. Jamsostek has changed its name to BPJS Ketenagakerjaan. BPJS health maintenance membership is compulsory starting from 1 July 2015. *Agency: Social Security Adm. Bodies (BPJS Kesehatan)*	7 days (simultaneous with previous procedure)	No charge

* Takes place simultaneously with another procedure.
Note: Online procedures account for 0.5 days in the total time calculation. Source: Doing Business database.

C. Limitations on Foreign Investment

1. Foreign Ownership Caps and Other Conditions[35]

Under Presidential Decree No. 39 of 2014, foreign investors are allowed to hold up to 100 Percent ownership in some industries, while in other sectors the maximum amount of foreign ownership is capped at a figure between 20 and 95 percent. There are several further sectors that are subject to specific Regulations, such as banking and horticulture, where the foreign ownership may be capped as low as 20 percent.

This table is intended to give an overview of some of the sectors that were affected by the changes to the Negative Investment List in April 2014 and does not cover all lines of business subject to Foreign Investment caps.

Business field	Cap
ENERGY AND MINERAL RESOURCES	
Electrical power installation services	Closed to Foreign Investment (before 24 April 2014: open for up to 95% foreign capital).
Large-scale power plants (capacity of >10MW)	Foreign Investment limit for power plant projects carried out in a public-private partnership is 100%. Under the partnership terms, a foreign investor can wholly own the power plant during the concession period, after which some equity must transfer to the Government. (Before 24 April 2014: subject to a 95% limit).
Small-scale power plants (capacity of 1-10MW)	Subject to foreign ownership limit of 49% (before 24 April 2014: small-scale electricity generation could be carried out in partnership with local businesses with no express restriction on foreign capital).

---

[35] *Peraturan Presiden Republik Indonesia No. 39 Tahun 2014 tentang Daftar Bidang Usaha yang Tertutup dan Bidang Usaha yang Terbuka dengan Persyaratan di Bidang Penanaman Modal. 23 April 2014. Dr. H. Susilo Bambang Yudhoyono. Promulgated in Jakarta on April 24, 2014 by Indonesian Minister of Laws and Human Rights, Mr. Amir Syamsudin. Lembaran Negara Republik Indonesia Tahun 2014 No. 93.*

Land drilling services	Closed to Foreign Investment (before 24 April 2014: open for up to 95% foreign capital).
Offshore drilling services	Subject to a foreign ownership limit of 75% (before 24 April 2014: subject to a 95% limit).
Certain oil and gas support services	Closed to Foreign Investment (before 24 April 2014: open for up to 95% of foreign capital).
Certain oil and gas construction services	Either closed to Foreign Investment or subject to limits ranging from 49% to 75% (before 24 April 2014: were not mentioned in the Negative List).
COMMUNICATIONS AND INFORMATICS	
Advertising	Open to investment by ASEAN member countries subject to a foreign ownership limit of 51% (before 24 April 2014; entirely closed to Foreign Investment).
Broadcasting	Open to 20% foreign ownership in existing radio or television broadcasting companies by way of new capital injection by fo-reign investors. This was not, strictly speaking, a new rule, since the 2002 Broadcasting Law already provided that a foreign investor may participate in the capital of an existing broadcasting Company for its business expansion. It is possible that this change to the Negative List was made to harmonize the Regulations.
Fixed telecommunication network provider services (includes the operation, maintenance or provision of network access for facilities used for voice, data, text, sound and video transmission using wired telecommunications infrastructure)	Subject to foreign ownership limit of 65% (before 24 April 2014: subject to a 49% limit).
Provision of content services (e.g. ring tone, premium SMS), call centers, data communication system services and internet services	Subject to foreign ownership limit of 49% (before 24 April 2014: only be conducted in partnership with local partners and there was no express limit on the foreign ownership).

HEALTHCARE	
Sub-specialized hospital services, specialized medical clinics, specialized dental clinics and specialized nursing treatment services	Open to investment by ASEAN member countries subject to a foreign ownership limit of 70% in certain regions of Eastern Indonesia, and 67% in the rest of the country. (Before 24 April 2014, the limits were tighter).
Pharmaceuticals (manufacture of drugs, raw pharmaceutical materials and finished drugs)	Subject to foreign ownership limit of 85% (before 24 April 2014: subject to a 75% limit).

TRANSPORTATION	
Construction of land terminals (e.g. passenger land transport terminals and general cargo terminals)	Subject to foreign ownership limit of 49% (before 24 April 2014: was not covered under the Negative List, so the revised list now clarifies what limit applies).
Periodical motor vehicles testing services	Subject to foreign ownership limit of 49% (before 24 April 2014: was not covered under the Negative List, so the revised list now clarifies what limit applies).
Provisions of port facilities	Subject to foreign ownership limit of 95% for port provision services in a public–private partnership scheme (before 24 April 2014, it was subject to a 49% limit).

FINANCE	
Venture capital	Subject to foreign ownership limit of 85% (before 24 April 2014: subject to an 80% limit).

TRADE	
Small-scale retail business lines	Closed to Foreign Investment (before 24 April 2014, most retail business lines were, in practice, not open to Foreign Investment but the position has now been confirmed by the revised list).

Large-scale retail business lines	Not expressly mentioned in the Negative List, so in theory it would be considered open to Foreign Investment; however, there is no clarity on what would constitute 'large-scale' retail business.
Distribution, ware-house & cold storage (except cold storage in areas listed below)	Subject to foreign ownership limit of 33% (before 24 April 2014: entirely open to Foreign Investment).
Cold storage businesses in Kalimantan, Sulawesi, Nusa Tenggara, Maluku & Papua	Subject to foreign ownership limit of 67% (before 24 April 2014: entirely open to Foreign Investment).

Apart from limitations in terms of percentage of foreign shareholding, there are other conditions that attach to some of the remaining 'open' business fields. Certain subsectors of forestry, maritime and fishery, energy and mineral resources, industrial, defense, public work (e.g. construction for public buildings), trade, culture and tourism, transportation, communication and informatics, finance, banking, manpower and transmigration (e.g. labor service providers), education, health and security, have one or more of the following conditions:

- They are reserved for micro, small and medium enterprises and cooperatives (as defined in Law Number 20 of 2008 on Micro, Small, Medium Enterprises and Cooperatives);
- They require a partnership;
- They are required to be in a certain location; and
- They require a special license from the relevant Minister.

Obtaining professional advice on how the business field of a particular proposed investment is categorized is strongly recommended, as navigating the various Laws can be difficult.

2. Banned Sectors[36]

Not all business fields are 'open' to Foreign Investment. Under Presidential Regulation No. 39 of 2014 the 'Investment Negative List' (the Negative List), which was last revised on 23 April 2014, business sectors are either completely 'closed to' investment or 'conditionally open', they are subject to foreign ownership limits or require special arrangements and permits.

The Negative List prohibits any investment activities from being conducted in those fields, whether by the PMA Company itself or by subsidiaries of the Company. Decisions to close business fields to Foreign Investment are based on health, moral, cultural, environmental, national defense and security concerns, and other national interests.

Article 3 of the Negative List states that business sectors that are not specifically mentioned are unconditionally open for investment.

It would be prudent to re-confirm with BKPM that there is no unwritten policy in place, or condition imposed, that restricts Foreign Investment into business lines that are not listed in the Negative List. Where new business sectors have been introduced, although a new foreign ownership limit may now apply where previously there was no formal restriction, investors at least have some certainty as to what restriction or condition applies.

---

[36] *President Regulation No. 39/2014 on List of Business Fields Closed to Investment and Business Fields Open, with Conditions, to Investment. 23 April 2014. Peraturan Presiden Republik Indonesia No. 39 Tahun 2014 tentang Daftar Bidang Usaha yang Tertutup dan Bidang Usaha yang Terbuka dengan Persyaratan di Bidang Penanaman Modal. 23 April 2014. Dr. H. Susilo Bambang Yudhoyono. Promulgated in Jakarta on April 24, 2014 by Indonesian Minister of Laws and Human Rights, Mr. Amir Syamsudin. Lembaran Negara Republik Indonesia Tahun 2014 No. 93.*

List of Business Fields Closed to Investment

Sector	Business field
Agriculture	Marijuana cultivation
Forestry	1. Capturing of Fish Species as listed in Appendix I Convention on International Trade in Endangered Species of Wild Fauna and Flora. (CITES) 2. The use (removal) of coral/atoll from nature for construction material/lime/calcium and souvenir/jewelry, also live or dead coral (recently dead coral) from nature.

Industry	1. Manufacture of Alcoholic Beverages (Hard Liquor, Wine, and Malt Containing Beverages)
	2. Manufacture of chemicals that can damage the environment:
	  a. Mercury processed Chlorine Alkali
	  b. Manufacture of active ingredients of pesticides
	  c. Industrial chemicals: Polychlorinated Biphenyl (PCB), Hexachlorobenzene
	  d. Manufacture of the ozone depleting substances listed in President Regulation No.39/2014
	3. Chemical Material Industry Schedule 1 Chemical Weapons Convention (Sarin, Soman, Tabun Mustard, Levisite, Ricine, Saxitoxin, VX, etc)

Transportation	■ Providing and Implementation of Land Terminals ■ Implementation and Operation of Weight Stations ■ Implementation of Motor Vehicle Type Tests ■ Implementation of Motor Vehicle Periodic Tests ■ Telecommunication/Supporting Facility of Shipping Navigation ■ Vessel Traffic Information System (VTIS) ■ Air Traffic Guiding Service
Communication and Informatics	Management and Implementation of Radio Frequency and Satellite Orbit Spectrum Monitoring Stations
Culture and Tourism	a. Government Museums b. Historical and Ancient Heritage (temple, castle, epigraphy, remains, ancient buildings, etc.) c. Gambling/Casinos

D. Indirect Foreign Investment

The primary form of indirect Foreign Investment into Indonesia is through the country's stock exchange, which is regulated by the Financial Service Authority, or Otoritas Jasa Keuangan (OJK), whose main function is to regulate capital market activities. Because the Investment Law states that it does not apply to indirect or portfolio investments, it is unclear whether public companies deals fall within the jurisdiction of BKPM and require pre-approval. In 2013, Indonesia introduced Regulation No. 5 / 2013, which had the effect of subjecting public companies to the authority of BKPM, depending on whether the 'controlling' shareholder of the Public Company was a foreign investor. Some of these provisions were subsequently revoked, and so, at the time of writing this guide, it is unclear what Regulation applies to Foreign Investments in public companies. As such, obtaining further advice on this issue is strongly recommended.

E. Arbitrating Commercial Disputes

Main Laws:

- Law No. 30 of 1999 on Arbitration and Alternative Dispute Resolution;
- Law No. 5 of 1968 regarding Ratification of the Convention on the Settlement of Investment Disputes between States and National of Other States;
- Presidential Decree No. 34

According to the Article 5 of the Law No. 30 of 1999[37],

- Only trades disputes that can be settled by arbitration
- The rights under the Laws and Regulations are fully controlled by the parties to the dispute.
- Civil disputes can be resolved through alternative dispute resolutions in the District Court.
- The parties gather for meeting to resolve the dispute within a period of 14 days, with the results of the meeting set forth in a written agreement.
- If a dispute is not solved with a written agreement, a third party advisory expert is required to enter as a mediator.
- If the mediator fails to help to reach an agreement between the parties within 14 days, the parties may contact an arbitration institution or agency to mediate for an alternative dispute resolution.
- Mediation should begin within a period of 7 business days. Both parties should reach a written confidential agreement within a period of 30 days.
- The agreement settlement of disputes is final and shall be registered in the District Court within a period of 30 days of signing.
- The settlement of the disputes should be implemented within 30 days after the registration.
- If the peace effort fails to be achieved, the parties may apply for a business solution through an arbitration institution or ad-hoc arbitration.

---

[37] *Undang Undang Republik Indonesia No. 30 tahun 1999 tentang Arbitrase dan Alternatif Penyelesaian Sengketa. 12 August 1999. Bacharuddin Jusuf Habibie. Promulgated in Jakarta on August 12, 1999 by Indonesian Secretary of the State Minister, Muladi. Lembaran Negara Republik Indonesia Tahun 1999 No. 138.*

11. Indonesian Investment Law

Although it is now amended, Indonesian domestic and Foreign Investment are based on *Indonesian Law No. 25 of 2007 on Investment*.

Note from Author: The following is my own translation of the Investment Law. I emphasized readability rather than word-for-word. When there are contradictions and discrepancies as to interpretation of any provision under the Indonesian Law No. 25 of 2007, the original version of the Law written in Bahasa Indonesia shall prevail.

Indonesian Investment Law No. 25 of 2007 described in Bahasa Indonesia as "Undang Undang Republik Indonesia Nomor 25 Tahun 2007 Tentang Penanaman Modal". Signed in Jakarta, Indonesia, on April 26, 2007 by Dr. H. Susilo Bambang Yudhoyono, the President of the Republic of Indonesia. Promulgated in Jakarta by the Minister of Laws and Human Rights of the Republic of Indonesia, Mr. Hamid Awaludin dated 26 April 2007. Recorded in the State Gazette of the Republic of Indonesia No. 67 of 2007.

A. General Provisions

Chapter I. Article 1 – 2.
The provisions in this Act apply to investments in all sectors in the territory of the Republic of Indonesia.

- Investments are all forms of investing activities by both domestic investors and foreign investors in order to do business in the territory of the Republic of Indonesia

- Domestic investment are all investment activities to conduct business in the territory of the Republic of Indonesia by domestic investors using domestic capital
- Foreign Investment are all investment activities to conduct business in the territory of the Republic of Indonesia, made by foreign investors using fully foreign capital, as well as joint ventures with domestic investors.
- Investors are individuals or entities that perform foreign and domestic investment.
- Domestic investors are Indonesian citizens, Indonesian business entities, the country of Republic of Indonesia, or an Indonesian region that makes an investment in the territory of the Republic of Indonesia.
- Foreign investors are foreign individuals, foreign business entities, and/or foreign Governments that undertake investments in the territory of the Republic of Indonesia.
- Capital is an asset in the form of money, or other asset that is not in the form of money, that has economic value and is held by investors.
- Foreign capital is capital belonging to a foreign country, foreign individual, foreign corporation, foreign entity, and/or Indonesian entity, that is owned partly or entirely by foreigner(s).
- Domestic capital is capital owned by the country of Republic of Indonesia, Indonesian citizen as individual, or corporation or non-corporation of the Republic of Indonesia.
- One Door Integrated Services is a government agency for comprehensive implementation of license and non-license activities, delegated or authorized by other institutions or agencies, to provide all license and non-license required for businesses, started from the application up to the issuance of the document, all in one place.
- Local autonomy is rights, authority, and obligation of local autonomy to regulate and manage its Government and

the interest of local community in accordance with the requirements of the Laws.
- Central Government, here and after referred as Government, is the President of the Republic of Indonesia who governs the country of the Republic of Indonesia as described in the Indonesian Constitution 1945.
- Local Government is the governor, regent, major, and local officials as the organizing element of local Government

B. Principles and Objectives

Chapter II. Article 3.

Indonesian investments are organized by these principles: legal certainty, openness, accountability, equal treatment regardless of country of origin, togetherness, efficiency of justice, sustainability, being environmentally sound, independence, and having a balance of progress and national economic unity.

The objectives of investment, among other things, are to:

- Increase the growth of national economic
- Create jobs
- Increase sustainable economic development
- Improve competitiveness of the national business world
- Improve the capacity and capability of national technology
- Encourage the development of a democratic economy
- Cultivate economic potential into real economic strength by using funds derived from both domestic and from abroad
- Improve public welfare

C. Basic Policies of the Investment

Chapter III. Article 4.
The Government sets basic policies of investment to:

- Encourage the creation of a conducive national business climate for investment in order to strengthen the competitiveness of the national economy
- Accelerate the increase in investment

The Government sets the basic policies by:

- Providing equal treatment for domestic investors and foreign investors with regard to national interests;
- Ensuring legal certainty, business certainty, and business security, for investors, from obtaining permits until the end of investment activities, in accordance with the provisions of the legislation;
- Extending opportunity for growth and provide protections to micro, small, medium enterprises and cooperatives.

The basic policies are embodied in the form of the General Plan Investment.

D. The Form and Location of Corporation

Chapter IV. Article 5
1. Domestic investment can be done in the form of a legal business entity, non-corporation, or individuals, in accordance with the provisions of Laws and Regulations
2. Foreign Investment should be in the form of a Limited Liability Company, under the Laws of Indonesia and domiciled in the territory of the Republic of Indonesia, unless otherwise stipulated by Law.

3. Domestic and foreign investors, investing in the form of Limited Liability Company, can be done by:
   a. Becoming a shareholder of a Limited Liability Company;
   b. Purchasing shares; and
   c. Other means in accordance with the provisions of the legislation.

E. Treatments to the Investment

Chapter V. Article 6.
1. Government gives equal treatment to all investors originating from any country that conducts investment activities in Indonesia in accordance with the provisions of Laws and Regulations.
2. The treatment in Paragraph above shall not apply to investors of a country that gained the privilege pursuant to an agreement with Indonesia.

Chapter V. Article 7.
1. The Government will not undertake nationalization or expropriation of property rights of investors, except by Law.
2. In the event that the Government uses nationalization or expropriation of property rights, the Government will compensate the amount determined based on market prices.
3. If both parties do not reach agreement on compensation, the settlement will go through arbitration.

Chapter V. Article 8.
1. Investors may transfer their assets to others.
2. The assets do not include assets in item (1), to be designated by Law as the assets controlled by the state.
3. The investors shall have the right to transfer and repatriate in foreign currency, among other things:
   a. Capital;

b. Profits, interest, dividends, and other income;
   c. The funds required for:
      - Purchase of raw and auxiliary materials, semi-finished goods, or finished goods; or
      - Replacement of capital goods in order to protect the viability of the investment;
   d. Additional funds required for financing investment;
   e. Funds for loan repayment
   f. Royalties or fees
   g. Income of foreign individuals working in the Investment Company;
   h. Proceeds from the sale or liquidation of the investment;
   i. Compensation for losses;
   j. Compensation for expropriation;
   k. Payments for technical assistance, costs to be paid for technical services and management, payments under project contract, and payment of intellectual Property rights; and
   l. The sale of assets referred to in item (1).
4. The right to transfer and repatriate as referred in item (3) shall be done in accordance with the provisions of the legislation.
5. The provisions as referred in item (1), without reducing:
   - ☐ Government authority to enforce the provisions of the legislation, which requires reporting of the implementation of the transfer of funds;
   - ☐ Government's right on tax and/or royalty and/or other Government income from investments in accordance with the provisions of the legislation;
   - ☐ Implementation of Laws protecting the rights of creditors; and
   - ☐ Implementation of the Law in order to avoid losses to the state.

Chapter V. Article 9.
1. In terms of liability that has not been resolved by the investor:
    a. The investigator or the Minister of Finance may ask the bank or other institution to suspend the right to transfer and/or repatriate; and
    b. The court is authorized to determine postponement of the right to transfer and/or repatriate based on a lawsuit.
2. Bank or other institutions carry out the determination of the postponement based on the determination of the court as referred in the Paragraph (1)b until the completion of the entire responsibility of the investor.

F. Employment

Chapter VI. Article 10
a. The Investment Company should give priority to Indonesian citizens for manpower.
b. The Investment Company is entitled to use foreign national experts for certain expertise and positions in accordance with the provisions of the legislation.
c. The Company's capital investment requires improving the competence of Indonesian citizen's workers through trainings.
d. Investment companies that employ foreign workers are required to conduct training and transferring technology to the Indonesian citizen workforce.

Chapter VI. Article 11
a. Settlement of industrial disputes shall be pursued by amicable discussions between the Investment Company and the workforce.
b. If the settlement referred to in subsection (1) does not achieve results, the settlement is done through the efforts of the tripartite mechanism.

c. If the settlement referred to in Paragraph (2) did not achieve the results, investment companies and workers resolve industrial disputes through the industrial relations court.

G. Business Fields

Chapter VII. Article 12
1. All areas of business or types of businesses are open to investment activity, except the areas of business or type of businesses that are declared closed and opened with requirements.
2. Business fields closed to Foreign Investment are:
   a. Production of weapons, ammunition, explosives and war equipment;
   b. Business fields explicitly declared closed by Law.
3. Pursuant to Presidential Decree, Indonesian Government establishes business fields closed to investment, both foreign and domestic, based on criteria of health, morals, cultural, environment, defense and national security and other national interests.
4. Criteria and requirements of business fields that are closed or open with conditions, and list of business fields that are closed or open with requirements, will be regulated by Presidential Decree individually.
5. Government establishes opened business fields with requirements is based on the criteria of national interest:
   a. The protection of natural resources,
   b. Protection, development of micro, small, medium enterprises and cooperatives,
   c. Supervision of production and distribution
   d. Enhancement of technology capacity
   e. Participation of domestic capital
   f. Cooperation with business entities appointed by the Government.

H. Investment Development for Micro, Small, Medium, and Cooperation

Chapter VIII. Article 13

The Government shall determine the field of business reserved for micro, small, medium enterprises, and cooperatives, and opened business fields for large businesses with the requirements that the large business should work with micro, small, medium enterprises and cooperatives.

Government to provide guidance and development of micro, small, medium enterprises and cooperatives through partnership programs, increased competitiveness, encouragement of innovations and market expansions, as well as the greatest possible extent of dissemination of information.

I. Rights, Duties And Responsibilities of Investors

Chapter IX. Article 14
Each investor is entitled to have:
a. Certainty of rights, Law, and protection;
b. Transparent information regarding their business sector;
c. Service rights; and
d. Any form of convenience facility in accordance with the provisions of the legislation.

Chapter IX. Article 15
Each investor is obliged to:
a. Apply the principles of good corporate governance;
b. Implement corporate social responsibility;
c. Submit the report of the investment activities to the Investment Coordinating Board;

d. Respect the cultural traditions of local communities around the location of business investments; and
e. Comply with all Laws and Regulations.

Chapter IX. Article 16
Each investor is responsible to:
a. Guarantee the availability of capital derived from sources that are not contrary to the provisions of Laws and Regulations;
b. Bear and settle all liabilities and losses if the investment stop or leave or abandon unilaterally its business activities, in accordance with the provisions of the legislation;
c. Create a fair competition business climate, prevent monopoly practices, and other practices that hurt the country;
d. Preserve the environment;
e. Provide for the safety, health, comfort and well-being of workers; and
f. Comply with all Laws and Regulations.

Chapter IX. Article 17
Investors exploiting natural resources that are not renewable must allocate funds gradually for the location recovery that meets the standards of environmental feasibility, the implementation of which is set in accordance with the provisions of Laws and Regulations.

J. Investment Facilities

Chapter X. Article 18
1. The Government shall provide facilities to investors making investment.
2. Investment facilities referred to in Paragraph (1) may be given to investments on:
   a. Business expansion; or
   b. New investment.

3. Investment granted facilities referred to in Paragraph (2) should at least meet one of the following criteria:
   a. Absorb a lot of labor;
   b. Include a high priority scale;
   c. Include infrastructure development;
   d. Transfer technology;
   e. Pioneer new industry;
   f. Locate in remote, underdeveloped regions, border areas, or other areas deemed necessary;
   g. Preserve the environment;
   h. Conduct research, development and innovation;
   i. Partner with micro, small, medium or cooperatives; or
   j. Use domestic capital goods or domestic machinery or equipment for industry
4. Facilities given to the investments referred to in Paragraph (2) and (3) can be in the form of:
   a. Income Tax through a reduction of net income to a certain extent on the amount of investment made in a certain time;
   b. Exemption or reduction of import duty on the import of capital goods, machinery, or equipment for the purpose of production that can not be produced domestically;
   c. Exemption or reduction of import duties on raw materials or auxiliary materials for production purposes for a specific period and specific requirements;
   d. Exemption or suspension of Value Added Tax on the import of capital goods or machinery or equipment for the purpose of production that can not be produced in the country for a certain period;
   e. Depreciation and amortization; and
   f. Land and building tax relief, particularly for certain sectors, in the region or a particular area or region.
5. Exemption or reduction of corporate Income Tax in the certain amount and time can only be granted to new capital investment which is an industry pioneer, the industry has

extensive connections, value-added and high externality, introduces new technology, and has a strategic value for the national economy,
6. For the replacement engine or other capital goods on existing investment, may be granted in the form of relief or exemption of import duty.
7. Further provisions on fiscal facility as referred in Paragraph (4) to Paragraph (6) is regulated by the Regulation of the Minister of Finance.

Chapter X. Article 19
Facilities referred in Article 18 Item (4) (5) are given by the national industrial policies set by the Government.

Chapter X. Article 20
Facilities as referred in Article 18 do not apply to Foreign Investments, which do not form in a Limited Liability Company.

Chapter X. Article 21
In addition to the facilities as referred in Article 18, Government provides facility service and/or licenses to investment companies to acquire:
- Land rights;
- Immigration service facilities; and
- Import licensing facilities.

Chapter X. Article 22
1. The service facility and/or licensing rights to the land as referred in Article 21a can be given and extended in advance as well can be renewed at the request of investors, in a form of:
   - Hak Guna Usaha, may be awarded as a total of 95 years, by granted and extended in advance at once for 60 years and can be renewed for 35 years;

- Hak Guna Bangunan, may be awarded as a total of 80 years, by granted and extended in advance at once for 50 years and can be renewed for 30 years;
- Hak Pakai (Right of Use), may be awarded as a total of 70 years, by granted and extended in advance at once for 45 years and can be renewed for 25 years.

2. The right to land as referred to in Paragraph (1) may be granted and extended in advance as well as to investment activities, with requirements, among others:
   a. Long-term investment, more competitive economy and related to changes in the structure of Indonesian economy;
   b. Level of risks of investment that requires long term capital in accordance with the type of investment activity;
   c. Investments that do not require a large area;
   d. Investments that involving state rights land;
   e. Investments that do not interfere with the public's sense of justice and not harm the public interest.
3. The right to land can be renewed after evaluation that the land is further used properly in accordance with the circumstances, the nature and the purpose of entitlements.
4. Granting an extension of land rights are given in advance and can be renewed as described in Paragraph (1) and (2) may be suspended or canceled by the Government if the Investment Company abandoned the land, harmed the public interest, or land use and exploitation are not in accordance with the intent and purpose of their land rights, as well as in violation of the provisions of the legislation in the land sector.

Chapter X. Article 23

1. Service and/or licensing for immigration facility as referred to in Article 21b may be given to:
   a. Investment that requires the employment of foreigners in the realization of the investment;

b. Investment that requires the employment of temporary foreign workers in order to repair machines or other production equipment and tools, and for after-sales service; and
c. Prospective investors who will do an assessment of investment.
2. The immigration service and/or licensing facilities granted to investments referred to in Item (1) a, b are given after investors receive a recommendation from the Investment Coordinating Board.
3. The facilities to be given to foreign investors are:
   a. Limited Stay Permit for foreign investors for 2 years;
   b. Change of status from a Limited Stay Permit for investors becomes Permanent Residency after living in Indonesia for 2 consecutive years;
   c. Re-entry Permit for several trips to Limited Residential Permit Holders with a validity period of 1 year, for a maximum period of 12 months, valid from the date of Limited Stay Permit granted;
   d. Re-entry Permit for several trips to Limited Residential Permit Holders with a validity period of 2 years, for a maximum period of 24 months, valid from the date of Limited Stay Permit granted; and
   e. Re-entry Permit for several trips to Permanent Resident Permit Holders with a validity period of 24 months, valid from the date Permanent Residency is granted.
4. The provision of Limited Stay Permit for foreign investors as referred to in Paragraph (3)a and b carried out by the Directorate General of Immigration based on the recommendation of the Investment Coordinating Board.

Chapter X. Article 24

Ease of service and/or licensing on import facilities referred to in Article 21c may be granted for import of:

a. Goods that do not conflict with the provisions of the legislation that regulates trade in goods;
b. Goods that do not impact the nation negatively on the basis of safety, security, health, environmental, and morals;
c. Goods for factory relocation from overseas to Indonesia; and
d. Capital goods or raw materials for their own production needs.

K. Ratification and Licensing of A Corporation

Chapter XI. Article 25.

1. Investors making investments in Indonesia must comply with the provisions of Article 5 of this Law.
2. Ratification of the establishment of a Domestic Investment Company, either in the form of a legal entity or a non-corporation, to be done in accordance with the provisions of Laws and Regulations.
3. Ratification of the establishment of a Foreign Investment Company in the form of a Limited Liability Company conducted in accordance with the provisions of Laws and Regulations.
4. Investment Company that will conduct business activities must obtain permits pursuant to the rules and Regulations of the authorized agencies, unless otherwise stipulated in Laws.
5. Permits referred to in Paragraph (4) obtained through One Stop Integrated Services.

Chapter XI. Article 26.
a. One Stop Integrated Service aims to assist investors in obtaining service convenience, fiscal facilities, and information about investments.
b. One Stop Integrated Service conducted by authorized institutions agencies in the field of investments that received delegation of authority from institutions or agencies that have authority in licensing and non-licensing at the national level, or the Province or District / City.
c. Provisions concerning the modalities and implementation of One Stop Integrated Services are regulated by Presidential Decrees.

L. Coordination and Implementation of Investment Policies

Chapter XII. Article 27.
a. Government coordinates investment policies, coordination:
   1. Among Government agencies,
   2. Inter-Governmental agencies with Bank Indonesia,
   3. Among Government agencies with local Governments,
   4. Between local Governments.
b. Coordination of the implementation of the investment policies conducted by the Investment Coordinating Board.
c. The Investment Coordinating Board led by a chief who is responsible to the President.
d. Head of the Investment Coordinating Board shall be appointed and dismissed by the President.

Chapter XII. Article 28.
1. Duties and functions of Investment Coordinating Board are as follows:
   - perform duties and to coordinate the implementation of policies in the field of investment

- Review and propose policies of investment services
- Establish norms, standards, and procedures for the implementation of activities and investment services
- Develop investment opportunities and potential in Indonesian regions by empowering enterprises
- Create a map of Indonesian investment
- Promote Indonesian investment
- Develop business sector investment through fostering investment to, among other things:
  - Improve partnerships & competitiveness
  - Create healthy competition,
  - Disseminate information to the greatest possible extent within the scope of investment activities.
- Help resolve barriers and consultation issues faced by the investors in implementing investment activities.
- Coordinate domestic investments outside the territory of Indonesia
- Coordinate and implement the One Stop Service.

2. In addition, the Investment Coordinating Board is in charge of implementing investment services under the provisions of legislation, involving competent and authorized officials from related sectors and related areas. *Chapter XII. Article 29*

M. Operation of Investment Affairs

Chapter XIII. Article 30.
1. Government and/or Local Government to ensure certainty and security sought for the implementation of investment.
2. The Local Government organized the affairs of investment under its authority, except in matters of investment activities under the Government affairs.
3. Obligatory functions of the implementation of investment activities of Government affairs in local Governments based on externality, accountability efficiency.

4. Cross Province investment implementation to be managed by the Government; Cross regencies / cities investment implementation into the affairs of the Province; Implementation of the investment within the scope of the Districts / cities into the affairs of the District / City.
5. Government affairs in the field of investment, the authority of the Government are:
   - Capital investments related to un-renewable natural resources at the level of the high risk of environmental damage
   - Investments in a high priority national scale industry
   - Investments related to the function of unifying and connecting inter-regional or cross-province
   - Investments associated with the implementation of national defense and security
   - Foreign Investments and foreign investors using foreign capital, comes from foreign Governments, based on agreement made by the Government and Foreign Governments
   - Another fields of investment into Government affairs according to Laws.
6. Government may organize, or delegate Governor or District / City Government to manage the jobs.

N. Special Economic Zones

Chapter XIV. Article 31.
1. Special economic zones can be defined and developed to accelerate economic development in certain areas that are strategic for national economic development, and to maintain balance in the progress of a region.
2. The Government is authorized to determine the investment policies independently in special economic zones.

O. Settlement of Disputes

Chapter XV. Article 32.
1. In the event of a dispute in the field of investment between the Government and investors, the parties must first resolve the dispute through consultation and consensus.
2. In case a dispute settlement is not reached, the dispute resolution can be made through arbitration or alternative dispute resolution or a court
3. In the event of a dispute in the field of investment between the Government and domestic investors, the parties can resolve the dispute through arbitration by agreement of the parties, and if the settlement of disputes through arbitration is not agreed upon, the settlement of the dispute will be conducted in court.
4. In the event of a dispute in the field of investment between the Government and foreign investors, the parties will resolve the dispute through international arbitration that must be agreed upon by the parties.

P. Sanctions

Chapter XVI. Article 33.
1. Domestic investor and foreign investor who invests capital in the form of a Limited Liability Company are prohibited from making agreements and/or statements confirming ownership of shares in a Limited Liability Company for and on behalf of third party.
2. In the case of domestic and foreign investors making an agreement and/or statement referred in Paragraph (1), the agreement and/or the statement is declared null and void.
3. In the case of an investor conducting business pursuant to an agreement or contract with the Government committing corporate crime in the form of a tax crime, inflating costs of

recovery, and other costs to minimize advantages resulting from loss to the state, based on the findings or inspection by the competent authorities, and has received a legally binding court ruling, the Government shall terminate the agreement or contract with the investor.

Chapter XVI. Article 34.
Any companies or individuals referred to in Article 5, which do not fulfill the obligations specified in Article 15, may be subject to administrative sanctions in the form of written warning, restrictions on business activities, suspension of business and/or investment facility, revocation of business activities and/or investment facility issued by the agencies or authorities. In addition to administrative sanctions, entities or individuals may be subject to other sanctions in accordance with Laws and Regulations.

Q. Transitional Provisions

Chapter XVII. Article 35.
Bilateral, regional or multilateral international agreements in investment that were approved by the Indonesian Government before the enactment of this Law shall remain valid until the expiry of the agreement.

Chapter XVII. Article 36.
Draft of bilateral, regional or multilateral international agreements in investment that has not approved the Government of Indonesia at the time this Law applies, shall be adjusted to the provisions of this Law.

Chapter XVII. Article 37.
- At the time of this Act was implemented, all the provisions of legislation implementing Regulations of Law No. 1/1967 on

Foreign Investment, as amended by Law No. 11/1970 on the Amendment and Supplement to Law No. 1/1967 on Foreign Investment, and Law No. 6/1968 on Domestic Investment as amended by Law No. 12/1970 on the Amendment and Supplement to Law No. 6/1968 on Domestic Investment, shall remain valid as long as there is no contradictory to the Law, and has not been regulated by a new Regulations.

- Investment approval and implementation permits granted by the Government based on Law No. 1/1967 on Foreign Investment, as amended by Law No. 11/1970 on the Amendment and Supplement to Law No. 1/1967 on Foreign Investment, and Law No. 6/1968 on Domestic Investment as amended by Law No. 12/1970 on the Amendment and Supplement to Law No. 6/1968 on Domestic Investment, shall remain valid until the expiration of the investment approval and implementation permits.
- Investment request and other requests relating to investment that have been submitted to relevant agencies, and not yet approved by the Government on the date of enactment of this Act, shall be adjusted to the provisions of this Law.
- Investment Company that was given a permit by the Government based on Law No. 1/1967 on Foreign Investment, as amended by Law No. 11/1970 on the Amendment and Supplement to Law No. 1/1967 on Foreign Investment, and Law No. 6/1968 on Domestic Investment as amended by Law No. 12/1970 on the Amendment and Supplement to Law No. 6/1968 on Domestic Investment and, if the permanent business license has expired, it can be extended based on this Law.

R. Closing Conditions

Chapter XVIII. Article 38.
With the enactment of this Law the following are declared revoked and invalid:

1. Law No. 1/1967 on Foreign Investment (State Gazette of the Republic of Indonesia 1967 No. 1, Supplement to State Gazette of the Republic of Indonesia No. 2818) as amended by Act No. 11/1970 on the Amendment and Supplement to Law No. 1/1967 on Foreign Investment (State Gazette of the Republic of Indonesia 1970 No. 46, State Gazette of the Republic of Indonesia No. 2943), and
2. Law No. 6/1968 concerning Domestic Investment (State Gazette of the Republic of Indonesia of 1968 No. 33, Supplement to State Gazette of the Republic of Indonesia No. 2853) as amended by Law No. 12/1970 on the Amendment and Supplement to Law No. 6/1968 on Domestic Investment (State Gazette of the Republic of Indonesia Year 1970 No. 47, State Gazette of the Republic of Indonesia No. 2944),

Chapter XVIII. Article 39.
All legislative provisions related to the investment shall adjust its structures based on this Law.

Chapter XVIII. Article 40.
This Law applies on the date of promulgation.

12 | Foreign Investment Implementation and Realization

A. Indonesia Progress of Investment Realization

Based on data of Principle Licenses published by BKPM, there are investment plans of IDR1,660.5 Trillion for January to November 2015, consisting of IDR1,079.7 Trillion (about USD86.4 Billion) for Foreign Investment (PMA), and IDR580.8 Trillion (about USD46.5 Billion) domestic investment (PMDN), with the plan of employment for 871,640 people.[38]

BKPM targets the realization of the investment of IDR519.5 Trillion (about USD41.5 Billion) in 2015 and IDR594.8 Trillion (about USD47.6 Billion) in 2016.

According to the Investment Coordinating Board of the Republic of Indonesia, the total investment realization in January – September 2015 was IDR400 Trillion (about USD32 Billion), a 16.7% increase compared to the same period of 2014 (IDR342.7 Trillion or about USD27.4 Billion).

The most important targeted industries were mining; food; transportation and telecommunications; metal, machinery and electronics; and chemical and pharmaceutical. Oil and Gas, Banking, Non-Bank Financial Institution, Insurance, Leasing, and Home Industry are excluded. The investment value is in

---

[38] *Siaran Pers. BKPM. Jakarta, 14 Desember 2015. BKPM dan Ditjen Bea Cukai Fasilitasi Percepatan Importasi Mesin/Peralatan Perusahaan yang Sedang Konstruksi*

Indonesian Rupiahs, and the currency rate of USD 1 = IDR12,500, based on Revised State Budget 2015.

> The five contributing countries in Indonesia FDI realization in January – September 2015 are Singapore (USD3.5 Billion, 16.4%), Malaysia (USD2.9 Billion, 13.6%), Japan (USD2.5 Billion, 11.8%), South Korea (USD1 Billion, 4.7%), and Netherlands (USD0.9 Billion, 4.2%). [39]

In Quarter III 2015, the top five contributing countries in Indonesia FDI realizations are Singapore (USD1.2 Billion, 16.2%), Japan (USD0.9 Billion, 12.2%), Netherlands (USD0.5 Billion, 6.8%, Malaysia (USD0.3 Billion, 4%), and China (USD0.2 Billion, 2.7%).

Total "new" investment from Singapore in 2014 is US$5.8 Billion, followed by Japan (US$2.7 Billion) and the Malaysia (US$1.8 Billion). As one of the fastest growing economies in the world, Indonesia offers many business opportunities to foreign investors.

Below are Indonesian Government exchange rates for budgeting and reporting:

Year	USD1 = IDR	State Budget
2010, 2011, 2012	9,000	
2013 (Q1 & Q2)	9,300	2013
2013 (Q3 & Q4)	9,600	2013 Revision
2014 (Q1, Q2, Q3)	10,500	2014
2014 (Q4)	11,600	2014 Revision
2015 (Q1, Q2, Q3)	12,500	2015 Revision

---

[39] *Indonesia Investment Coordinating Board. 22nd October 2015. Domestic and Foreign Direct Investment Realization in Quarter III and January – September 2015*

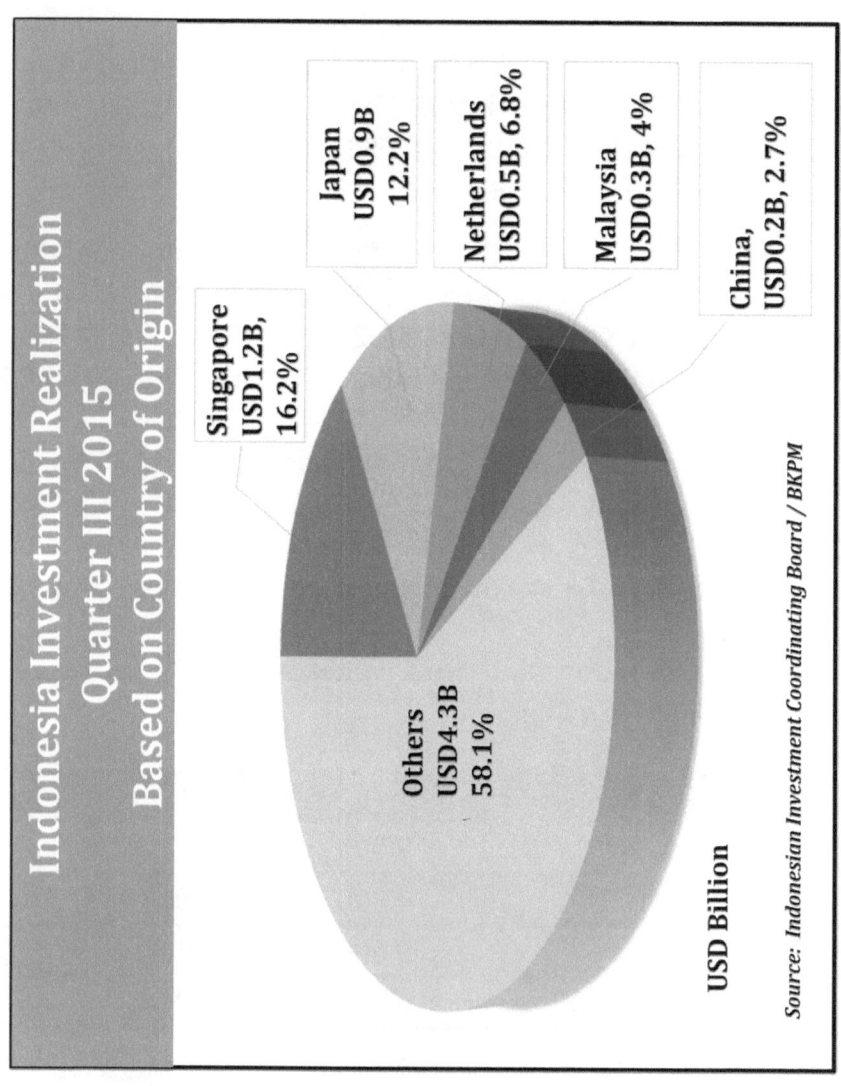

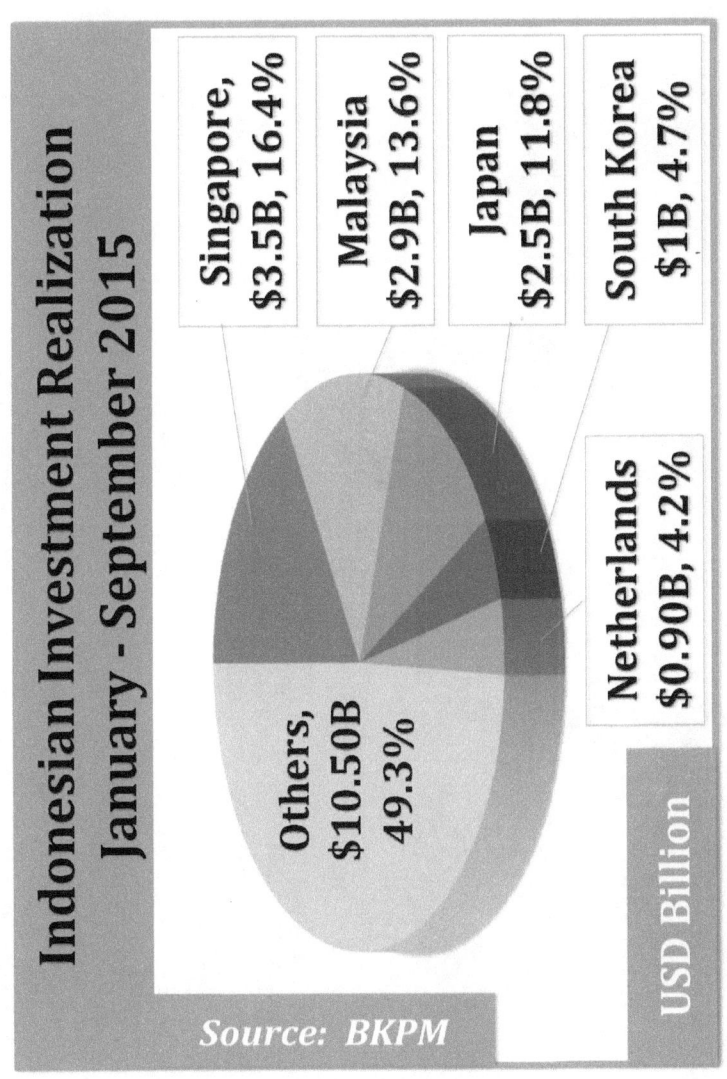

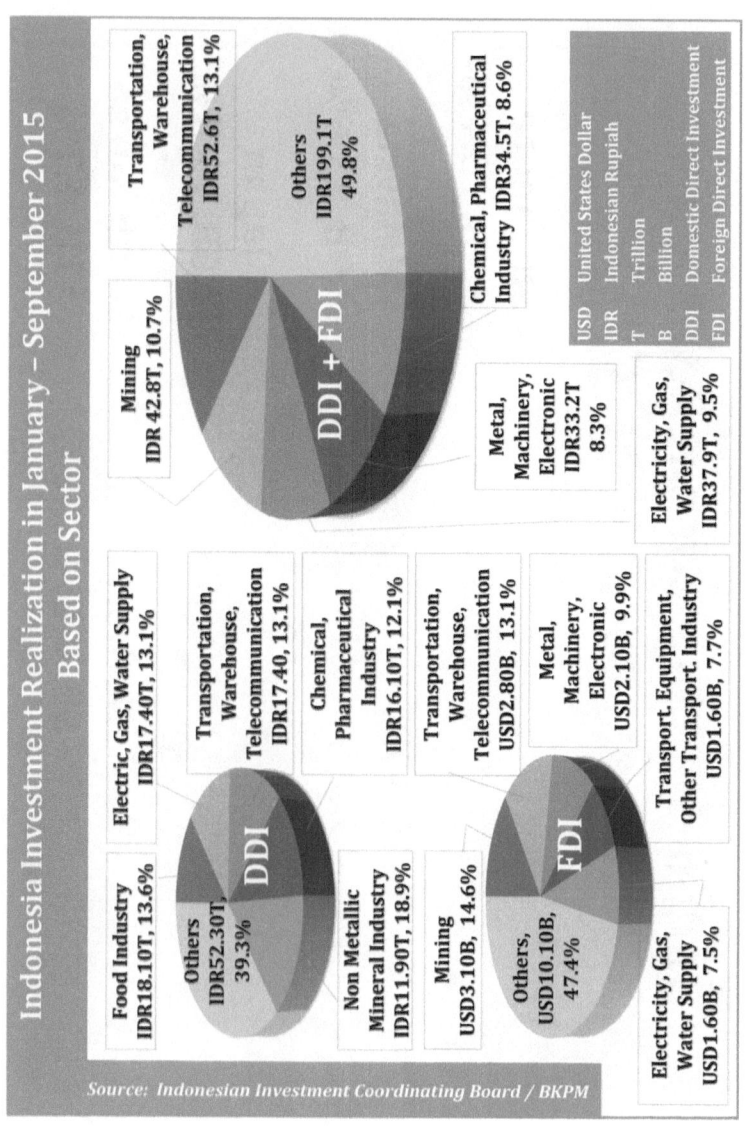

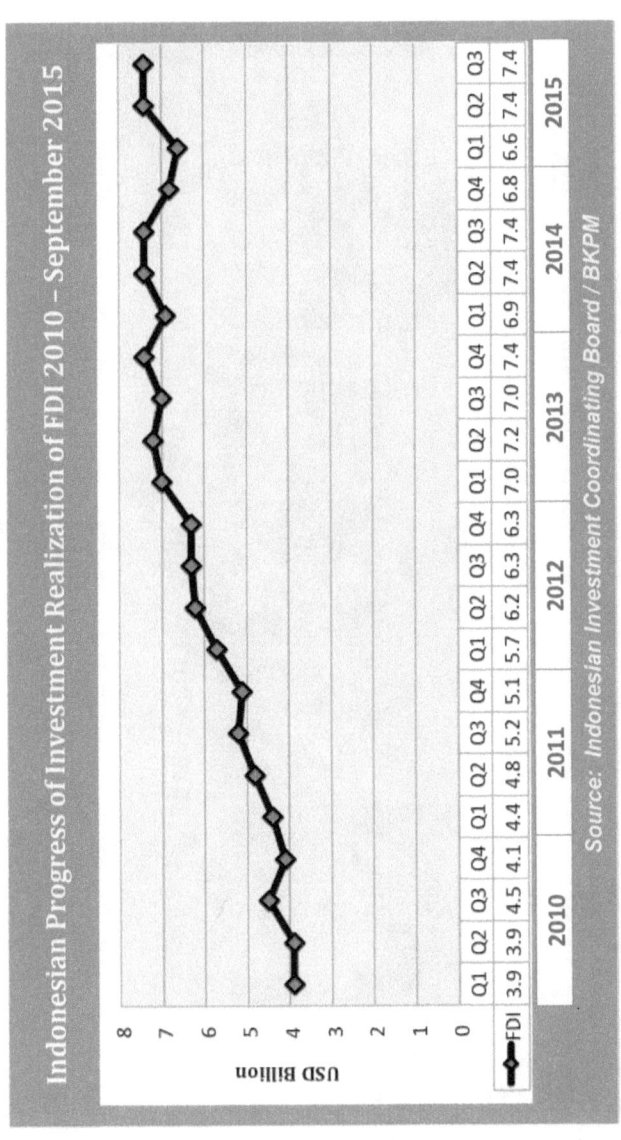

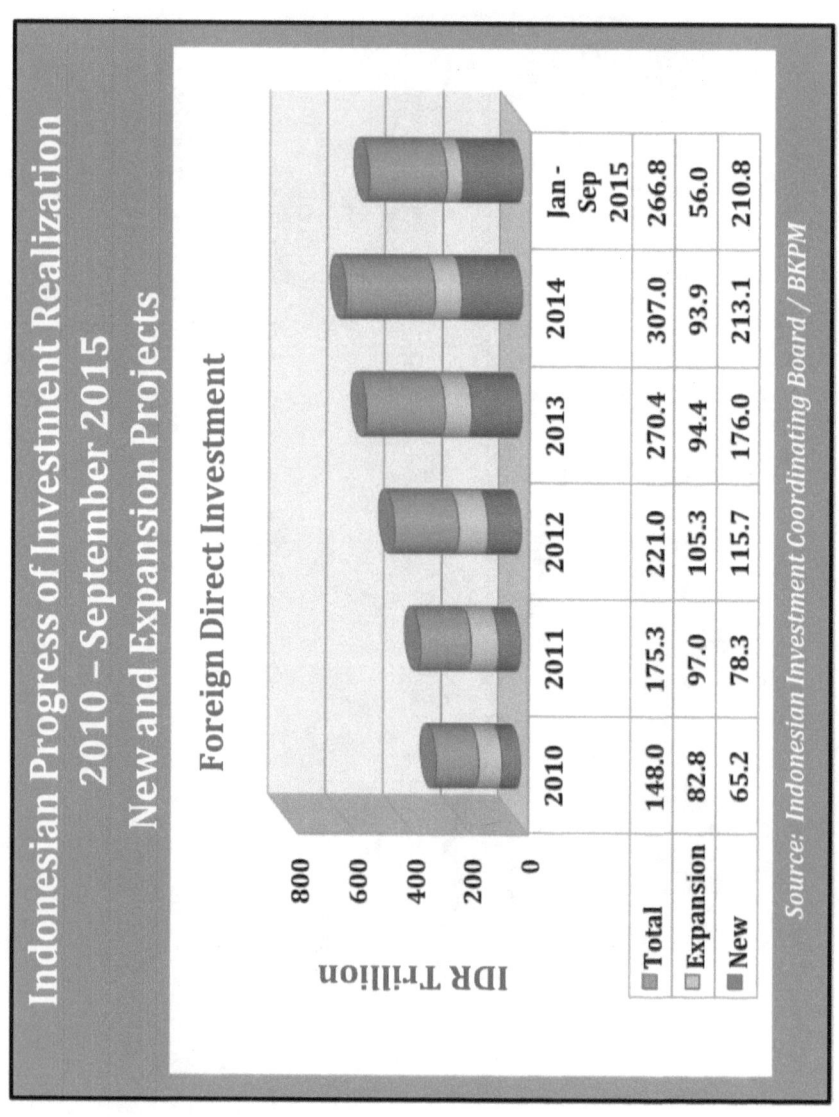

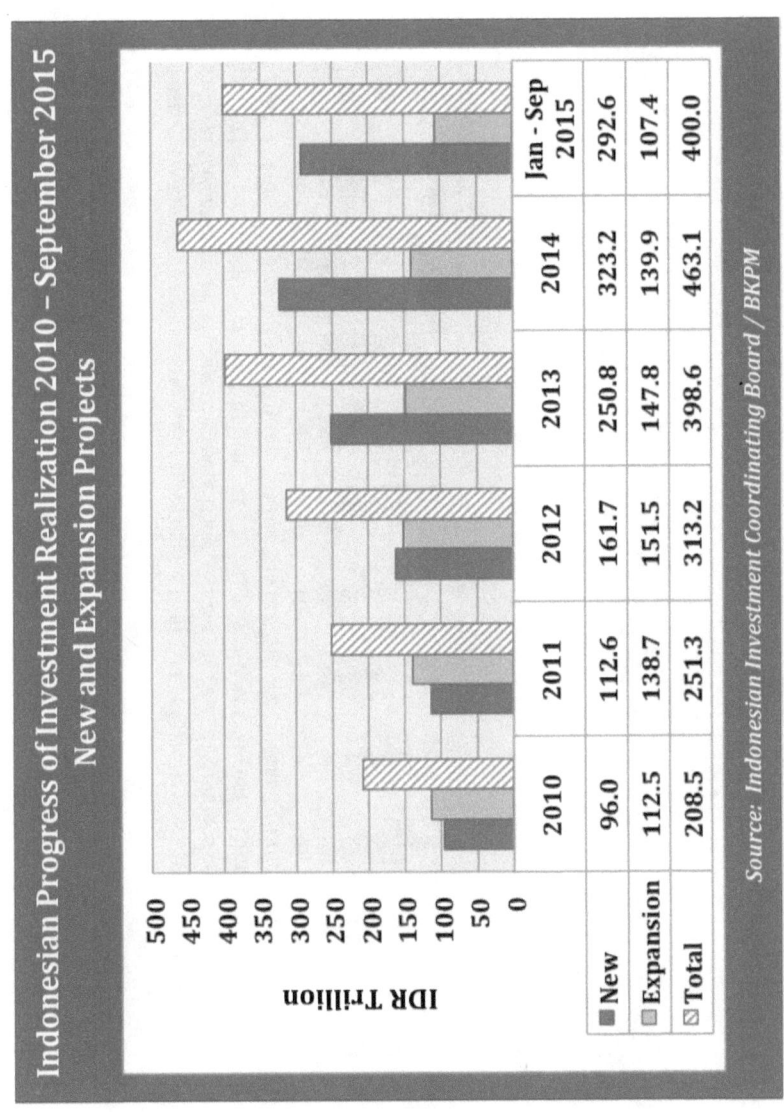

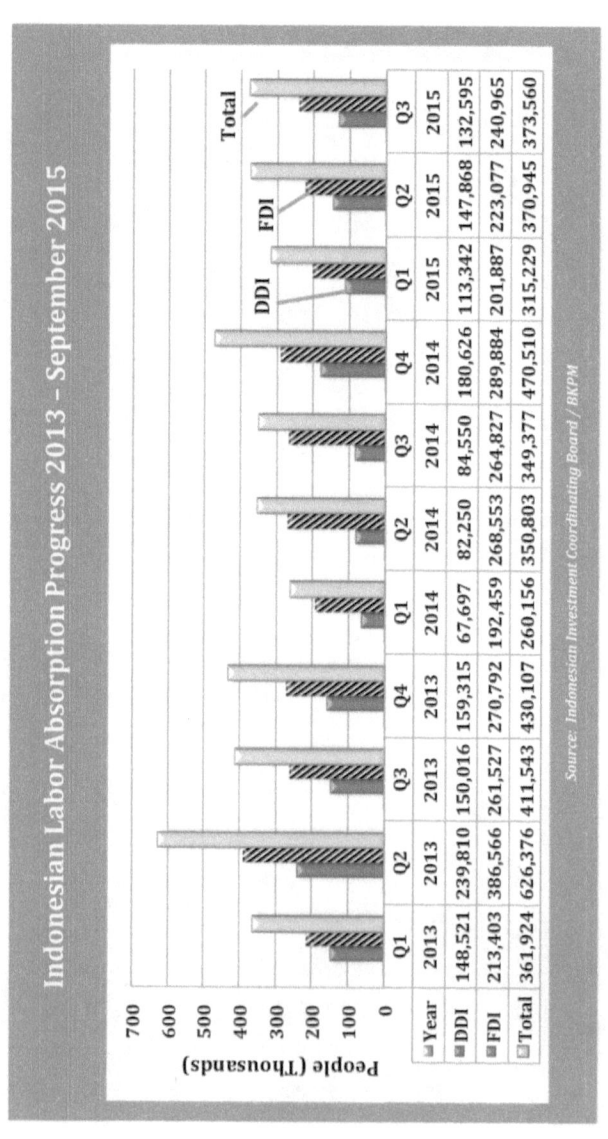

B. ASEAN Investment Growth

Unless marked individually, reports below were taken from:

- ASEAN 2015. A Blueprint for Growth. ASEAN Economic Community 2015: Progress and Key Achievements Jakarta: ASEAN Secretariat, November 2015. ISBN 978-602-0980-55-3

- The ASEAN Secretariat. ASEAN Investment Report 2015: FDI Infrastructure Investment and Connectivity. Jakarta, ASEAN Secretariat, November 2015. ISBN 978-602-0980-51-5.

Investors do not see ASEAN as a collective single investment destination anymore, but 10 stand-alone economies.

ASEAN is both a major recipient and a source of FDI. The region is an important source of, and partner in, South–South Cooperation.

> South-South Cooperation is a development cooperation comprising several developing countries under the United Nation working together towards economic growth, industrial development and poverty reduction.

Outward FDI flow from this region to the world rose by 19% in 2014, to $80 Billion – greater than FDI outward flows from France and Spain combined, and 2.6 times greater than FDI outward flows from the Republic of Korea.

To strengthen South South Partnerships, internationalization will be increased by ASEAN Companies in 2015 and beyond, including using more M&A strategies.

Outward FDI flows from ASEAN have been growing steadily since 2012 with significant outflow going to developing economies. Indonesia, Philippines, Malaysia, and Singapore received investment from abroad actively last year because of emerging investment opportunities, while FDI from Thailand and Viet Nam declined. Outward flows from ASEAN increased financial strength, strong profitability, and cash holdings. However, some countries have land and labor constraints, limited markets and/or saturated growth, which become key drivers on outward FDI flows[40].

In 2014, the top 100 ASEAN companies, by market capitalization, had combined cash holdings of $228 Billion, and combined assets of nearly $3 Trillion. Most of these have operations in other ASEAN Member States. Some are subsidiaries of a group of companies, which have extensive regional presence and overseas investment outside the region.

> These 100 top ASEAN companies have cash reserves greater than the combined global FDI made by companies from France, Germany, Italy and the Netherlands in 2014. These cash reserves are also greater than the combined 2014 GDP of Cambodia, Lao PDR and Viet Nam. These companies and their cash reserves are potential sources of investment for other developing economies. They operate in different sectors, such as agriculture, extractive, manufacturing, and services industries. Many of these companies aspire to be strong regional or international players in their industries.

Examples of ASEAN companies that are active in developing and operating infrastructure assets in developing economies, including those in their own region, are:

- Indonesia: Waskita Karya, Wijaya Karya and Semen Indonesia;
- Philippines: International Container Terminal, San Miguel, and Ayala and Manila Water;
- Singapore: Sembcorp, Keppel Corporation, City Development, CapitaLand, and Changi Airports International;

---

[40] *ASEAN Investment Report 2013 and ASEAN Investment Report 2014*

- Thailand: ITD, EGCO, Ratchaburi, Banpu, Amata, Siam Cement and EGATi; and
- Viet Nam: Viettel, EVN and VLP

ASEAN companies also have been active in using M&As in their internationalization processes, indicating the burgeoning financial capability and abilities to acquire strategic assets abroad. ASEAN companies have been consistently raising global cross-border M&A purchases since 2009. As in 2013, most cross-border M&A purchases by ASEAN companies were made in developing Asian economies. By 2014, ASEAN companies acquired more assets abroad than cross-border M&A sales marked in the region.

Example of private companies from Singapore, Malaysia, Thailand, Indonesia and the Philippines that made significant M&As abroad in various industries:

- OCBC (Singapore) bought 97.8% of Wing Hang Bank (Hong Kong, China) for $4.8 Billion;
- St James Holdings (Singapore) bought Perennial Real Estate Holdings (China) for $2.8 Billion;
- RGE (Indonesia) acquired Sateri Holdings Ltd-Viscose fiber assets (China) for $863 million; and
- JG Summit Holdings (Philippines) purchased NZ Snack Food Holdings (New Zealand) for $608 million.

Further evidence of the growing financial strength of ASEAN Companies that support procuration of assets abroad is that, in 2014, ASEAN companies made 35 deals greater than $250 million, as compared with only 21 in 2013.

As a consequence of the growing of FDI and corporate expansion, Regional network of production (CPNS) and regional value chains (RVCs), are expected to inspire more foreign and ASEAN companies to position themselves to operate in in different Member States. Companies do so partly because of their corporate strategies, that includes:

- gaining access to resources and markets;
- increasing input and operation efficiency; and
- accessing complementary locational benefits provided in the region.

Lower transaction costs contributed by regional integration also play a role:

- 95.9% of all tariff lines in ASEAN will have zero rates for intra-ASEAN imports by the end of 2015, supporting further intraregional trade and production networks.
- Export tariffs on final goods or intermediate products manufactured in one Member State for another Member State are to be eliminated.

Companies are producing as if they were within a single-country model of operation rather than across a number of Member States connected through RVCs. Regional corporate expansion is another important source of ASEAN connectivity contributed by intra and inter Company linkages involving the facilities of MNEs and ASEAN companies located in different parts of the region.

The development and expansion in manufacturing FDI in the CLMV countries and the relocation of labor-intensive operations to these locations, as well as in other Member States is contributing to regional connectivity. Production from these locations is being supplied to affiliates or customers based in the other ASEAN Member States. This connectivity enriches the growth of supporting industries and the regional division of labor. The increase in regional economic activities involving MNEs and ASEAN companies overpasses the improvement through investment and production, especially between the CLMV countries and the other Member States.

> Developing Asia became the world's largest investor region. In 2014, MNEs from developing economies invested $468 Billion abroad, a 23 percent increase from the previous year. They reached 35 percent of total share in global FDI, a 13 percent increase from 2007.[41]

Unless marked individually, reports below were taken from:

- The Association of Southeast Asian Nations (ASEAN) 2015. A Blueprint for Growth. ASEAN Economic Community 2015: Progress and Key Achievements Jakarta: ASEAN Secretariat, November 2015. ISBN 978-602-0980-55-3

Although tariff elimination alone does not create an open market, significant progress has been made. Member States eliminated import duties among themselves by 2010 for the ASEAN-6 (Brunei Darussalam, Indonesia, Malaysia, the Philippines, Singapore and Thailand), and – by 2015 with flexibility to 2018 – for the CLMV (Cambodia, Lao PDR, Myanmar and Viet Nam) pursuant to the commitments made in the AFTA in 1992, and later in the ATIGA in 2010. To date, the ASEAN-6 has eliminated their intra-regional tariffs, resulting in an ASEAN average of 95.99%:

- 99.2% for 0% tariff lines
- 90.86% for the CLMV (Cambodia, Lao PDR, Myanmar and Viet Nam)

---

[41] UNCTAD. World Investment Report 2015: Global Investment Trends. Chapter I. UNCTAD. 2015. Reforming International Investment Governance. United Nations Conference on Trade and Development. Geneva. 2015

The ASEAN wide self-certification scheme is underway, being established by cooperative efforts. Intra-regional trade preferences can be made easier, among other factors, with continuous simplification of:

- Rules of Origin (ROO); and
- The ASEAN Self-Certification Project.

Traders and manufacturers are responsible to meet the origin certification. This motivates regional trade links by allowing certified exporters the freedom to declare that their products have satisfied ASEAN origin criteria, that allows them to benefit from trade preferences under ATIGA. Ten Member States are on board on one of the two Self-Certification Pilot Projects.

Central to ASEAN's trade facilitation agenda is transparency and resulting business certainty. A major highlight in facilitating the free flow of goods is establishing an ASEAN Trade Repository (ATR), documenting Trade and Customs Laws and Procedures accessible in the public domain that was authorized under ATIGA.

Entered into force in 2012, the ASEAN Comprehensive Investment Agreement (ACIA) contains commitments to liberalize, facilitate, promote, and protect cross-border investment, based on international best practices. In line with their commitments in the ACIA, Member States strive to improve their investment regimes to help create a competitive investment environment in the region.

The AEC administers a business-supportive environment through regulatory frameworks promoting fair competition and freer flow of capital. To date, almost all Member States have in place consumer protection Laws as well as competition Laws. Co-operation and capacity building in the area of intellectual property (IP) rights are enhanced to build an innovation-supportive environment.

The main catalyst for the development of the financial sector is

- financial integration;
- improved efficiency; and
- lowered cost of capital.

To facilitate greater trade and investment in the ASEAN region, financial integration aims to achieve a well-functioning regional financial system:

- with more liberalized financial services,
- capital account regimes, and
- inter-linked capital markets.

SMEs form the backbone of ASEAN economies comprising over 90% of enterprises in ASEAN, and responsible for generating employment for the majority of ASEAN's working population.

An important aspect of the changing landscape of FDI in ASEAN is advancing the transfer of labor-intensive manufacturing activities from higher-cost locations in ASEAN, and other Asian economies, to other ASEAN Member States, such as Indonesia and the CLMV (Cambodia, Lao PDR, Myanmar and Viet Nam). This expansion is enhancing further regional production networks and regional value chains - boosting connectivity between CLMV countries and the other ASEAN Member States as production from the former is supplied to affiliates or customers based in the latter.

Several factors contributed to the annual increase in FDI flows in ASEAN in 2014. For example,

- improved regional perception among international investors,
- increased investment opportunities in the region, and
- ASEAN companies investing more last year as they continued to pursue regional investment plans.

Rapid growth in market-seeking FDI in the region, such as in the retail industry, was led by:

- economic growth,
- anticipation of the AEC,
- ASEAN MNEs in the region,
- burgeoning per capita income, and
- accumulation of affluent consumers.

Cost advantages, such as low labor costs, are contributing to a growing regional division of labor and value chains that are connecting the ASEAN Member States more closely. It is attracting greater manufacturing FDI from outside and within the region.

Because demand for various infrastructure services are increased, private investors' increased interest in the region increased. These influenced by rapid urbanization, rising per capita income, and growing populations.

In addition to winning contracts, infrastructure-related companies from Indonesia, Malaysia, the Philippines, Singapore, Thailand and Viet Nam have established subsidiaries in other ASEAN Member States in 2014–2015.

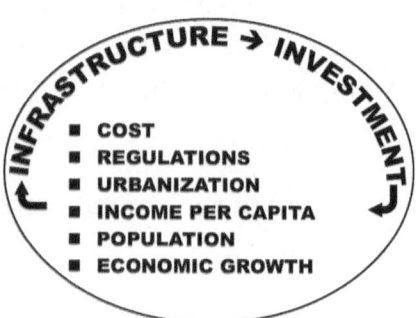

Corporate endeavors to regionalize, or to be major regional players, along with increasing costs and market limitations at home, continue to drive ASEAN companies to invest in neighboring Member States. Strong corporate profitability and the growing cash reserves of the major ASEAN companies have become stimulants for their regionalization and internationalization plans, which are also helping strengthen South-South cooperation.

Other contributory key factors in the 2014 FDI situation are continuing improvement of the region's investment environment through policies introduced in past years, as well as emerging investment opportunities.

Indonesia and Myanmar received significantly exceptional FDI and intra-ASEAN investment in the extractive industry, in part, through production sharing and concession arrangements due to their predominant access to natural resources such as in mining of coal, oil and gas, and other minerals.

ASEAN was the largest investor in Indonesia, accounting for 60% of FDI flows last year, primarily in agriculture, manufacturing and finance.

Real estate activities were about 80% of Indonesian investment in the region in 2014, suggesting the growing interest of Indonesian companies in investing regionally, particularly in industry.

Numbers of ASEAN companies have announced significant investment plans in the region. For example, Lippo Group Indonesia is planning to invest about $600 Million to $1 Billion over the next five years in several industries in Myanmar that include hospitality, health care, and education services.

The expansion of regional investment into new plants and new product categories is encouraged by rapid growth of industries such as the electronics and automotive industry, including parts and components production. For example, many Japanese MNEs expanded in Indonesia and Thailand in 2014.

- Japanese automotive MNEs such as Mazda, Nissan, Mitsubishi, Toyota and Honda, which already had significant presence in these Member States, have been expanding their production capacities into so-called eco-cars in Thailand, and automotive manufacturing in Indonesia.

Agro-climatic factors and access to agricultural land and low-cost labor supply have influenced the agriculture investment in the region. Indonesia continued to capture significant palm oil and agriculture investment.

It is an important motive to keep costs low. FDI into the manufacturing industry continues to be determined by cost and market factors. It hinges on the host country and the stage of development of an industry in the different Member States. For example,

- **Cost motivated investment:** low value added manufacturing of electronics, automotive parts, textiles, garments, shoe manufacturing and components in Indonesia, Cambodia, Myanmar and Viet Nam.
- **Cost and market factors investment:** automotive manufacturing in Indonesia, Thailand and the Philippines.

The transfers of labor-intensive activities are another significant development in MNEs. The transfers are from higher-cost locations in other Asian economies and within ASEAN to the CLMV countries, as well as other ASEAN Member States such as Indonesia. Manufacturing companies such as textiles and garments are responsible in the making MNEs transfers, for example:

- Mitsubishi's trading house was investing $60 million to build seven factories in Central Java, Indonesia in 2014, with a local joint venture partner;
- Aoyama Trading (Japan) and Makalot Industrial (Taiwan Province of China) are shifting production to Central Java, Indonesia because of cost reasons.

Some MNEs are not only expanding in the same host country but, also, concurrently in other ASEAN Member States through their other subsidiaries. For example:

- AEON, a major Japanese retailer, has expanded rapidly in ASEAN in recent years. In May 2015, AEON was opening its first store in Indonesia, and plans to open 20 more new malls in West Java and Jakarta after 2016.
- Mitsubishi Hitachi Power Systems built a new plant in Indonesia in 2015. Its subsidiary Hitachi Automotive Systems Indonesia was established in November 2014.
- Volvo (Sweden) announced to build a $140 million factory in Indonesia in 2015.
- Denso (Japan) is operating a new plant in Indonesia. Suzuki started a new plant in Indonesia in 2015.
- Mitsubishi is expanding in Indonesia, with a new plant to start operation in 2017.
- TOA Paint (Thailand) is planning to expand operations to Indonesia in 2015.
- Thai Oil, a refinery Company of PTT (Thailand), is planning to expand in Indonesia with new refinery capacity.
- Parkson, a subsidiary of the Lion Group (Malaysia), has 14 stores in Indonesia since the opening in 2014, and it plans to open more stores in the region.
- Keppel Land (Singapore) is expanding its real estate operations in ASEAN. In 2015, has completed its Phase 1 of the International Financial Centre Jakarta in Indonesia in 2015, with Phase 2 to be completed by 2020.
- Sembcorp (Singapore) is building an integrated port and industrial estate in Indonesia.
- Ingress has set up two manufacturing facilities in Indonesia. Ingress is a Malaysian automotive components manufacturers and a recent recipient of "ASEAN Economic Community Priority Integration Sector Award in Automotive" at the 6th ASEAN Business Awards Malaysia in 2015.

Cross-border M&A sales in ASEAN were down, but purchases made by ASEAN companies rose. As a strategy for participating in and accessing the ASEAN market, MNEs continued to use cross-border M&A, to establish quick production or service platforms, and acquire strategic assets in the region. The use of cross-border M&As tends to be by MNEs from some key source countries and concentrated in ASEAN Member States with more mature M&As environments.

The M&As declined from 17 in 2013 to just 10 in 2014. It was due to the drop in the size of deals, including mega deals, those exceeding $500 Million, for example:

- Japanese companies cross-border M&A declined by nearly $4 Billion in deals;
- The United States companies cross-border M&A declined by nearly $3.1 Billion.

However, deals by Chinese companies rose by 13 times to $2.4 Billion in 2014. Indonesian and Korean companies also made significant acquisitions in the region.

Although three key economic sectors (i.e. primary, manufacturing and services) of cross-border M&As in the region declined, deals in infrastructure-related industries bucked the trend.

- Cross-border M&A values in ICT raised significantly from $0.4 Billion in 2013 to $3.6 Billion in 2014;
- Transportation and storage deals rose by 25% to $1.5 Billion; and
- Electricity, gas, water and sanitation deals by 4% to $1.1 Billion in 2014.

Trade, manufacturing and finance witnessed significant declines in cross-border M&A sales.

In Indonesia, Japanese companies made significant acquisitions in finance, in particular, in the insurance industry:

- Sumitomo Mitsui Financial Group acquired a 15.7 % stake in Bank Tabungan Pensiunan Nasional for $526 million;
- Nippon Life Insurance acquired a 20% interest in Asuransi Jiwa Sequis Life for $424 million; and
- Sumitomo Life Insurance acquired 40% ownership of BNI Life Insurance for $357 million.

---

[42] Sumitomo has extensive operations in ASEAN in different infrastructure sectors. It has built power plants in Indonesia, Malaysia, the Philippines and Viet Nam and has subsidiaries across the region. It plans to further expand its regional footprint, including in EPC activities.

In Indonesia, Sumitomo also the EPC contractor for the Kamojang geothermal power station (35 MW capacity) owned by Pertamina Geothermal Energy (Indonesia).[a] By 2014, Sumitomo Corporation had been involved with 11 EPC geothermal power construction projects in Indonesia, including some for which it was awarded contracts by Pertamina last year.[b] These projects account for about 50% of current and anticipated geothermal power generation in the country.

---

[42] UNCTAD and ASEAN Secretariat, based on information from Sumitomo Corporation Company website and annual reports. a Sumitomo Corporation, "Sumitomo Corporation Signs Deal with PT. Pertamina Geothermal Energy for Construction of the Fifth Unit of the Kamojang Geothermal Plant", news release, 7 Oct 2013 (http://www.sumitomocorp.co.jp/english/news /detail/id=27206).

b Sumitomo Corporation, "Contract Awarded by PT Pertamina Geothermal Energy for Construction of Units 5 and 6 at Lahendong Geothermal Power Station in Indonesia", news release, 12 Dec 2014. (http://www.sumitomocorp.co.jp/english/news/ detail/id=28151).

Samples of deals were made in infrastructure related industry that demonstrating the growing use of the M&A strategy to establish a presence in the region:

- China Mobile acquired a 23% stake in True Corporation (Thailand) for $882 million;
- Solusi Tunas Pratama (Indonesia) acquired Malaysian-owned Axiata-Telecom Towers in Indonesia for $459 million;
- Electricity Generating (Thailand) acquired a 45% interest in Masin-AES in Singapore for $453 million; and
- Angat Hydroelectric Power Plant, a Korean Company acquired in the Philippines for $441 million.

C. ASEAN Investment Outlook for 2015-2016

Unless marked individually, reports below were taken from:

- *The Association of Southeast Asian Nations (ASEAN) 2015. The ASEAN Secretariat. ASEAN Investment Report 2015: FDI Infrastructure Investment and Connectivity. Jakarta, ASEAN Secretariat, November 2015. ISBN 978-602-0980-51-5.*

Global economic fragilities and slower growth in the region resulting the FDI inflows in 2015 are likely to decline marginally or stay at about the same level as in 2014. In the first half of 2015, cross-border M&A sales and FDI flows to the region were down. Those weak numbers do not augur well for the region to record higher annual FDI flows in 2015 to surpass the level achieved in 2014.

Although it's cautiously optimistic, the health of the global economy, corporate investment plans as well as the delivery of the AEC in terms of depth and scope influence the outlook for 2016.

Factors to support investment into the region in 2016 and beyond are:

- the region's strong macroeconomic fundamentals;
- its economic resilience;
- the influences of regional integration;
- the cost competitiveness of the region;
- the strong cash holdings of ASEAN companies; and
- the continued regional investment expansion plans of investors.

ASEAN highlighted factors:

- **Middle-income consumers**: The number of region's middle-income consumers and its comparatively higher economic growth as compared with the world average will continue to attract market-seeking FDI and influencing corporate investment plans.

- **More integrated region:** Companies are positioning themselves strategically with more expected to expand regionally in post AEC 2015 as the region becomes more integrated. AEC to increase the competitiveness of the region and connectivity between ASEAN Member States that will help to reduce the transaction costs of investment and the cost of doing business in the region across a wide range of industries.

- **The growing competitiveness of the region**: It is a key role in attracting FDI, with MNEs continually searching for lower-cost locations and opportunities for production networks to boost their efficiency. The high in production costs in locations outside the region and within ASEAN will attract efficiency-seeking FDI to and within the region.

- **Effective supply chain strategy and achieving production efficiency**: MNEs, both foreign and ASEAN will continue to exploit these complementary locational advantages within the region. This leads to investment and production operations that are based on differences in locational cost structures, factors of production and skill levels that match MNEs' strategy. They are connecting the Member States through production, investment and inter and intra firm linkages as MNEs engage in regional division of production for reasons of markets, costs, or access to natural resources, making the region a stronger magnet for attracting FDI from new and existing investors.

- **The huge infrastructure plans:** Announced by ASEAN Member States. Their commitment to attract private investment into infrastructure will contribute to the rise in investment in the industry, including in industrial estate development and construction activities. Private participation in infrastructure should not be examined from FDI statistics alone but also from analysis of non-equity approaches to participation by the private sector.

- **Continuous reforms and favorable investment measures to improve investment environment:** The ASEAN Member States continue to announce reforms and favorable investment measures that will improve the investment environment in the region, while stakeholders show interest in addressing international investment governance issues at the international level.

OECD Development Centre 2016 Press Release:[43] Kuala Lumpur, 20/11/2015. Emerging Asia (Southeast Asia, China and India) is set for robust growth. This is according to the latest OECD Development Centre's Economic Outlook for Southeast Asia, China and India. Although there is concern that the outlook for growth for many OECD countries will be more moderate than in recent years, robust growth remains expected over the medium term.

Growth projection in Emerging Asia is average 6.5% for 2015, and 6.2% annually over 2016-20. Growth projection in the Association of Southeast Asian Nations (ASEAN) region is expected to average 4.6% in 2015 and 5.2% over 2016-20.

Removing tariffs and non-economic boundaries can stimulate integration and facilitate trade and demand for renewable energy. Stronger economic integration will provide tangible opportunity as local businesses transform into regional players or ASEAN enterprises, by expanding their operations beyond national borders.

It is very important to reduce the gaps that inhibit sustainable and inclusive growth, primarily the persistence of poverty and the uneven state of the infrastructure in the whole development of the impact area.

According to Outlook's country structural policy notes, it is required to adopt a comprehensive package of reforms for small and medium enterprises, finance, infrastructure, labor market and environmental policy, agriculture, education, social security and tourism sectors, in the formulation of a new development strategy.

---

[43] *OECD (2016), Economic Outlook for Southeast Asia, China and India 2016: Enhancing Regional Ties, OECD Publishing, Paris. Press Release. Kuala Lumpur, 20 November 2015. http://www.oecd.org/dev/asia-pacific/economic-outlook-southeastasia-china-india-2016-press-release.htm*

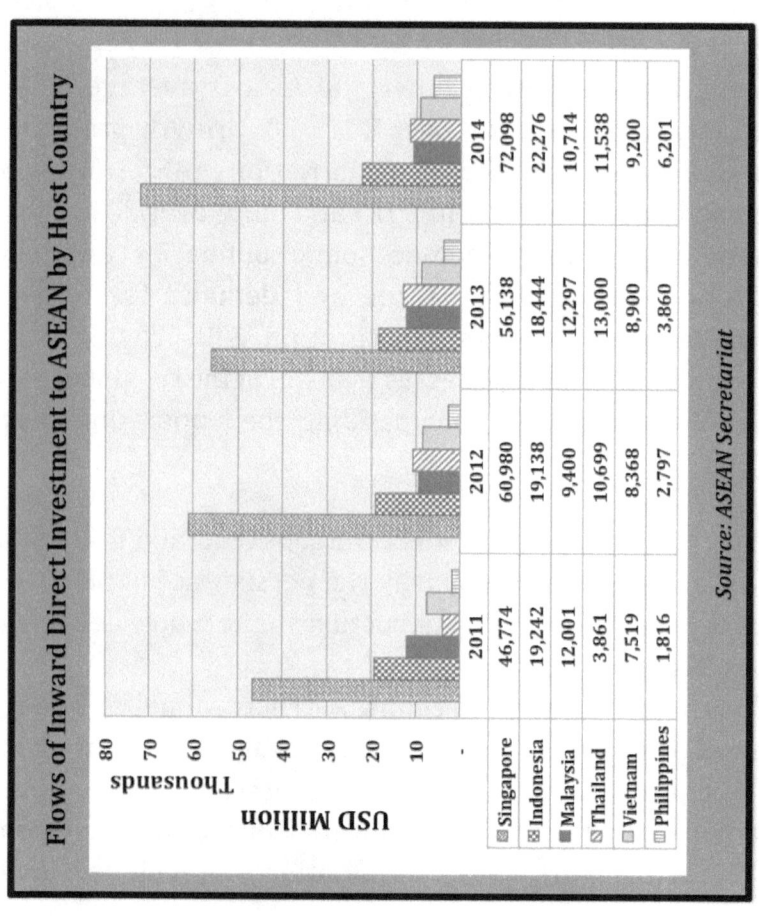

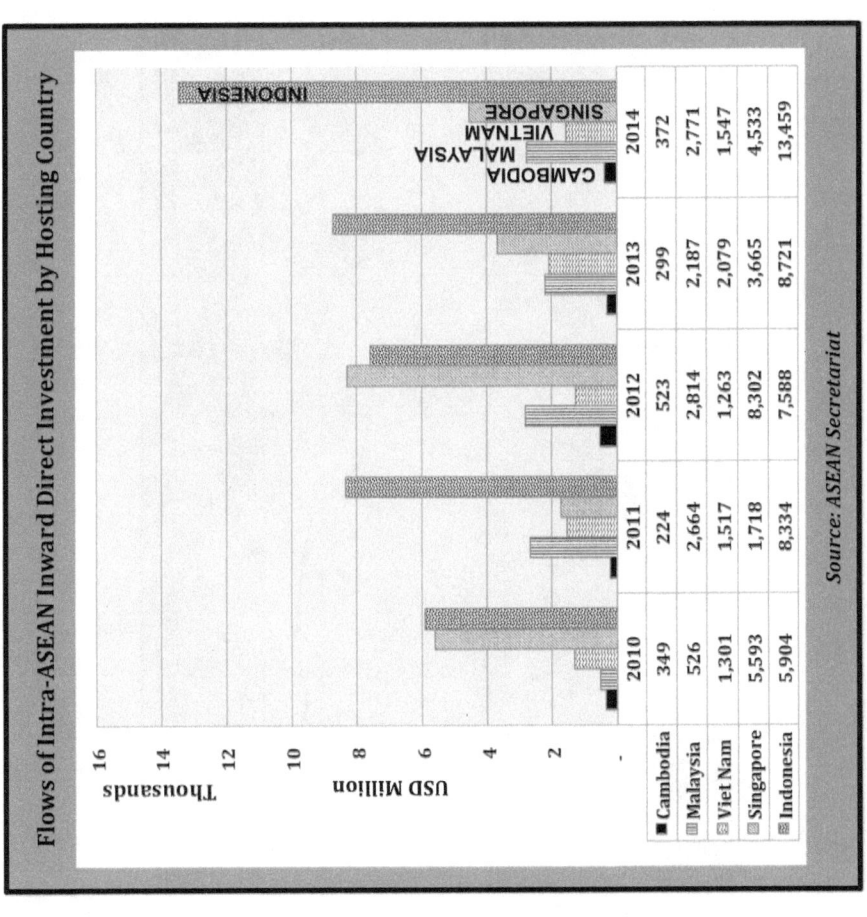

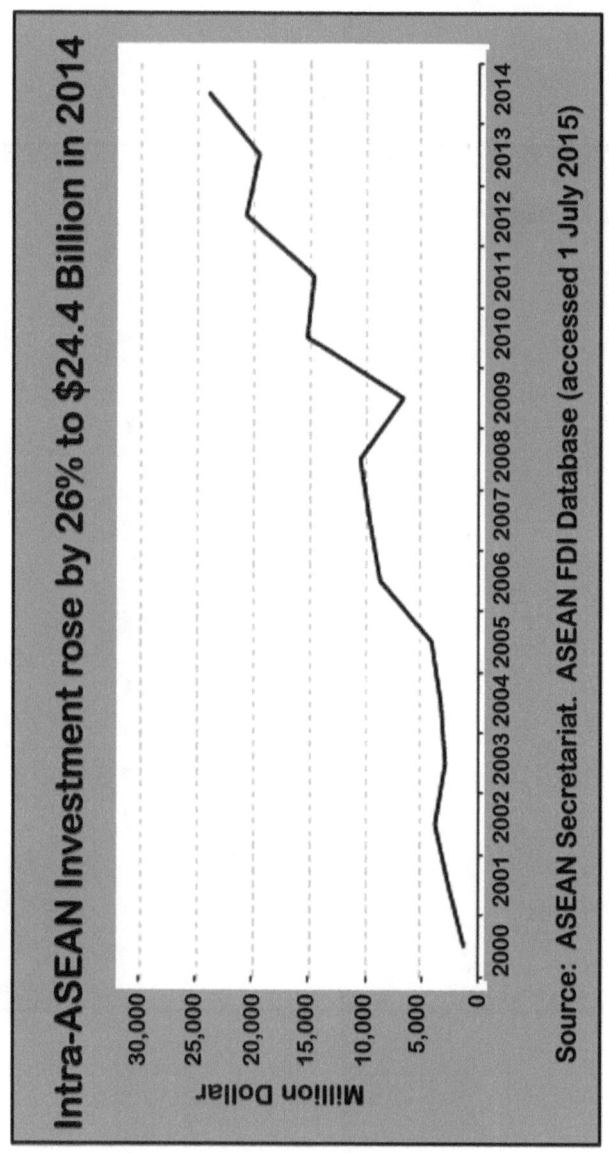

The Importance of ICT

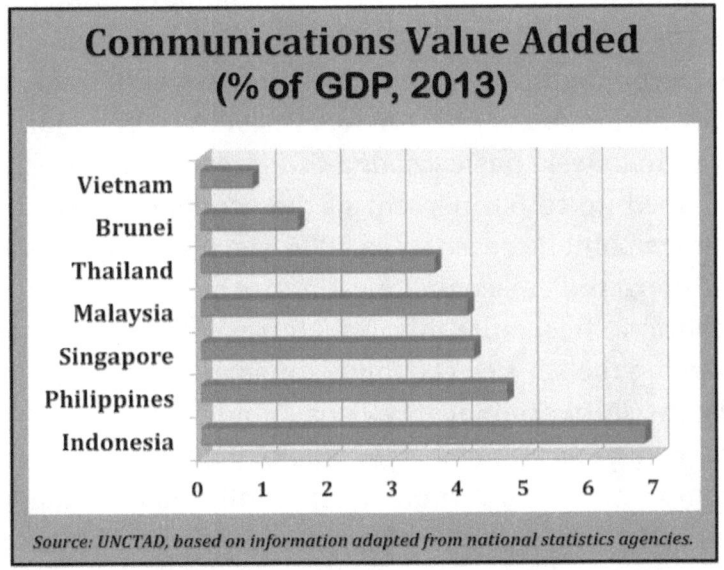

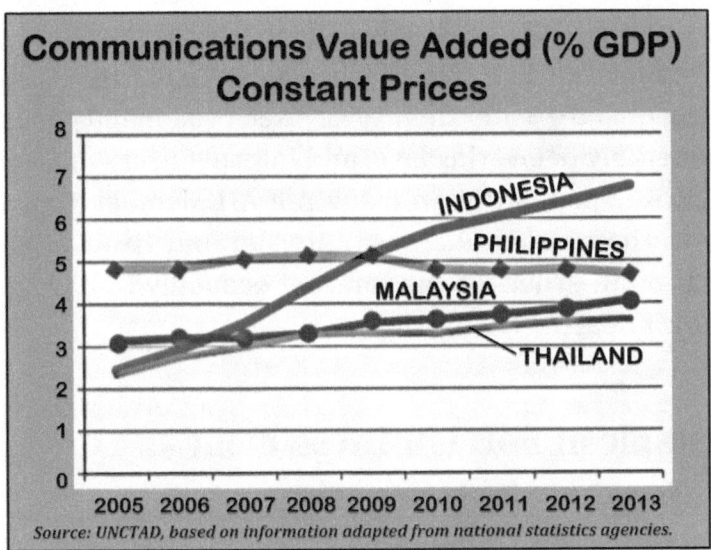

Note: Communications refers to telecommunication and posts. Data for Viet Nam refer to Information and communication, which includes telecommunication, broadcasting, publishing and computer and information services.

In most ASEAN Member States where data are available, has seen an increase in access to telecommunications that fit within the size of the communications sector. The value added of the telecommunication sector has grown over the last decade. Its contribution to overall GDP has varied. The communication sector in Indonesia has exceeded GDP growth. Its contribution has climbed up to 6.8 percent of the economy in 2013, a 4.2 percentage point increase since 2005, the highest in ASEAN.

The impacts of telecommunication are broader than its direct contribution. Telecommunication infrastructure is essential for enabling the service economy, supporting e-commerce and driving the software industry. Broadband access, in particular, is a critical general-purpose technology essential for growth and competitiveness. A number of studies have attempted to measure the link between broadband access and economic growth. Although the methodologies differ, they generally find that increases in fixed broadband access contribute to an increase in GDP. The evidence is mixed, particularly where penetration levels have not reached a particular threshold, e.g., fixed broadband greater than 10%. Fixed broadband penetration is considerably below this level and Internet users make up less than half the population in many ASEAN Member States. This points to the need to increase Internet and fixed broadband penetration in order for the Internet economy to have greater economic impact.

D. Sample of Foreign Investment Companies in Indonesia

1. ABN Amro
2. Pirelli (PT Astra Otoparts Tbk)
3. PT. BlueScope Steel Indonesia
4. PT Bridgestone Tire Indonesia

5. Cargill Asia Pacific
6. PT. Coca Cola
7. CIMB Niaga Bank
8. Olam International
9. PT Freeport Indonesia Tbk
10. PT Goodyear Indonesia
11. Hankook Tire
12. Holcim
13. Compagnie Financiere Michelin (PT Chandra Asri Petrochemical Tbk)
14. PT. Honda Prospect Motor
15. International Finance Corporation
16. PT. Krakatau Posco
17. MEC Holdings
18. PT. Nestle Indonesia
19. PT. Newmont Nusa Tenggara
20. PT. Newmont Minahasa Raya
21. Qatar Telecom
22. Royal Dutch Shell Plc.
23. PT. Samsung Electronics
24. Siemens Indonesia
25. The Tata Power Company Ltd
26. PT. Toyota Motor Manufacturing Indonesia
27. PT. Tirta Investama (Danone Aqua – Danone Group – Aqua Golden Mississippi)
28. PT. Unilever Indonesia Tbk
29. PT World Bank

13 Government Supports on Foreign Investment

Note from Author: There are translations of Laws and/or Regulations in this Chapter. I emphasized readability rather than word-for-word. When there are contradictions and discrepancies as to interpretation of any provision of the Law, the original version of the Law written in Bahasa Indonesia shall prevail.

The Regulation of BKPM No. 17 of 2015 on guidelines and procedures for controlling the implementation of the investment[44], make sure that every Investor is entitled to:

- Certainty of rights, Law, and protection;
- Transparency regarding the information about business fields;
- Service rights; and
- Various forms of convenience facilities in accordance with the provisions of the legislation.

---

[44] *Peraturan Kepala Badan Koordinasi Penanaman Modal Republik Indonesia No. 17 Tahun 2015 Tentang Pedoman dan Tata Cara Pengendalian Pelaksanaan Penanaman Modal. 29 September 2015. Franky Sibarani. Promulgated in Jakarta on October 8, 2015 by Director General Legislation, Indonesian Ministry of Laws and Human Rights, Mr. Widodo Ekatjahjana. State Gazette No. 1481 of 2015.*

A. Political and Policies Reformations

Indonesia continued their treaty terminations, while formulating new IIA (International Investment Agreement) strategies[45].

Indonesia has undertaken some reformation on several fronts of its IIA policy: The country has initiated the termination of its BITs (Bilateral Investment Treaties), and developing a new model BIT for (re)negotiation that will consider the exclusion of portfolio investment from the definition of investment and will add a contribution to economic development requirement in its definition clauses. National treatment will be subject to exceptions related to special treatment in favor of domestic small and medium enterprises and investments and measures affecting natural resources. The new model will also clarify in greater detail the scope of the FET (Fair and Equitable Treatment) standard and will provide a list of State obligations including a prohibition against denial of justice in criminal, civil or administrative proceedings and assurance of police protection from any physical harm. Investor-State arbitration will be subject to host country consent. An investor may submit a case to international arbitration if the host country provides a specific consent letter.

Some industries have begun to open to foreign participation in Indonesia that may lead to more intraregional FDI. For example, service industries such as port management are now allowed as part of Government efforts to enable Indonesia to become a strong maritime country.

---

[45] *United Nations Conference on Trade and Development. UNCTAD. World Investment Report 2015. Reforming International Investment Governance.*

Foreign ownership ceiling in several industries were in several industries, however it was increased in several others. For example, foreign investors ownership on:

	Before	Now
Onshore oil production facilities	95%	0%
Data communications system services	95%	49%
Construction, health services and electricity generation, pharmaceuticals	75%	85%
Venture capital operations	80%	85%
Power plant projects carried out as public-private partnerships	95%	100%

B. Licensing Process Reformations

On 23rd August 2013, the Government of Indonesia announced economic policy packages, among others aimed at increasing investment.[46]

- **Streamlining Investment Licensing**
  - ☐ Cutting barriers, particularly licensing procedures.
- **Revising the "Negative Investment List"**
  - ☐ To make the investment Law more and more investor-friendly.
  - ☐ The new updated list of sectors open for FDI will be announced soon in within this year.
- **More Tax Incentives**
  - ☐ Tax dispensation to labor-intensive industries: textile, apparel, footwear, furniture, and toys industries.

---

[46] *http://www.bkpm.go.id*

☐ Additional tax deduction to firms with at least 30 percent export-oriented products.

The main target of the Policy Package to Improve the Ease of Doing Business is to make any one all who wants to do a business to receive faster and easier service. The Government sets a target of eight areas of improvement to increase the ease of doing business, namely:

- Starting a Business
- Getting Electricity
- Paying Taxes and Insurance Premium
- Enforcing Contract
- Resolving Insolvency
- Registering Property
- Dealing With Construction Permits
- Getting Credits

In these areas, the Government sets a total of 17 actions. Each area covers one or more actions. All actions have been implemented by February 2014.

Progress on licensing simplification:[47]

	BEFORE	NOW
Power Generation	49 permits 923 days	25 permits 256 days
Agrarian	HGU 3000-6000ha 123 days	4 improvements 90 days
Forestry	Land Use – 111 days	13 improve. – 27 days

---

[47] *Indonesian Investment Coordinating Board (BKPM)*

Transportation	Special Terminal – 30 days	4 improve. – 5 days
Agriculture	Plantation Permit – 751 days	9 improve. – 182 days
Industry	Business Permit – 672 days	8 improve. – 152 days
Tourisms	TDK – 661 days	6 improve. – 188 days
Tax Allowance	Unclear	28 days

Progress of Ease of Doing Business in Indonesia (EODB)[48]

EODB Indicators	2015	2016
Starting a business	10 procedures, 52.5 days	7 procedures, 9.2 days
Dealing with construction permit	17 procedures, 202 days	10 procedures, 149 days
Registering property	5 procedures, 5 days	5 procedures, 11 days
Getting electricity	5 procedures, 94 days	4 procedures, 35 days
Paying taxes and assurance	65 payments	43 payments
Enforcing contract	40 procedures, 460 days, costs 118.1% of claim costs	3 procedures, 56 days, no costs
Resolving insolvency	23 months, costs 20-22% of assets	11 months, costs 5.08% of assets

---

[48] *Indonesian Investment Coordinating Board (BKPM)*

In October 26, 2015, Indonesian Investment Coordinating Board (BKPM) announced the reformation on licensing process to facilitate the realization of investment interests in Indonesia, in the form of the launch of the 3-Hour Licensing Investment Services.

It is Principle License with certain criteria processed in a single package with the issuance of the Deed of Establishment and Approval from the Ministry of Justice and Human Rights, Tax Identification Number (NPWP) and Land Availability Information within three hours. The criteria of this service are as follows:

- Investment Plan at a minimum of One Hundred Billion Indonesian Rupiah (IDR100,000,000,000.00), and/or
- Plan to use Indonesian workers over 1,000 (One thousand) people;
- Application submitted in person by prospective shareholders at Headquarters of PTSP BKPM.

A prospective nominee of shareholders can represent the other shareholders by attaching a power of attorney that contains the power to:

- Apply for the License
- See the Notary / Attorney
- Sign the Deed
- Agree to become of the Directors or Commissioners of the Company
- Agree to become shareholders by what percentage

BKPM is the institution that authorizes the import duty exemption on imports of machinery and/or goods and raw materials, as well as most main investment licenses.

[49]Mr. Franky Sibarani, the Head of BKPM announced on December 14, 2015 - The Investment Coordinating Board (BKPM) has continued to accelerate the realization of the investment project that has entered the construction phase. BKPM works together with the Directorate General of Customs and Excise (DJBC), to increase the acceleration of green lane status in machineries and equipment importation facilities for companies that are in construction stage to achieve the investment.

Companies in green lane can enjoy the benefits of a few minutes customs process for documentations after the issuance of Exit Goods Approval Letter (SPPB). There is no physical examination required.

This facility is not offered to a new Company since every new Company will be in red lane because is categorized as "high risk".

Before the issuance of SPPB, Customs physical investigations should be done for machineries and equipment imported by new companies. The process may takes about 3 – 5 days.

Mr. Sibarani added, the acceleration of import of machinery / equipment can be given to a Company if it meets several requirements, among others: under construction building the plant, submit latest Investment Activities Report (LKPM), with the consistency in submitting previous LKPM and a statement stating that the Company will not abuse the facility (imported goods should confirm with the import documents and to be used for the implementation of Principle License of Investment).

There were 48 companies (39FDI and 9DDI) that will be proposed by the BKPM may obtain facilities for the acceleration of import of machinery/equipment from the Directorate General of Customs. The total value of the investment plans of the 48 companies is IDR127.7 Trillion, and plan for employment of 39,219 people.

---

[49] *Press Conference of BKPM and Indonesian Customs: Jakarta, December 14, 2015. Siaran Pers BKPM dan Ditjen Bea Cukai Fasilitasi Percepatan Importasi Mesin/ Peralatan Perusahaan Yang Sedang Konstruksi*

C. Fiscal Incentives: Tax Holiday, Tax Allowance and Import Duty Facility

Based of the Law No. 25/2007 Chapter X Investment Facility Article 18, Government issued fiscal Regulations to help the growth of investment in Indonesia.

> There are three fiscal incentives:
>
> - Tax Holiday
> - Tax Allowance
> - Import Duty Facility

[50]October 6, 2015, a press conference was hold by the Indonesian Investment Coordinating Board in Jakarta, publishing new rules to accelerate Tax Holiday and Tax Allowance process.

The Government through the Investment Coordinating Board (BKPM) continues to prepare for the implementation to expedite the investment license application included in Volume II economic package. The implementation of 3-Hour Investment Services License is effective on 26 October 2015.

The agency also has issued a Regulation on the management of the mechanism of Tax Holiday and Tax Allowance, that is stipulated in Regulation of the Head of BKPM No. 18/2015 on the Amendment to Regulation of the Head of BKPM No. 8/2015 on procedures for application on Income Tax facility for investment in the certain businesses and/or in certain regions (Tax Allowance), as well as the Head of BKPM Regulation No. 19/2015 on amendments to the Regulation of the Head of

---

[50] *BKPM Press Conference: Jakarta, October 6, 2015. Siaran Pers BKPM: BKPM Terbitkan Aturan Percepatan Pengurusan Tax Holiday dan Tax Allowance*

BKPM No. 13/2015 on procedures for solicitation provision on corporate Income Tax reduction facility.

According to the Head of BKPM Mr. Franky Sibarani, the rules contain of standard completion time of filing Tax Holiday and Tax Allowance, in accordance with the economic policy package volume II, in which the processing time Tax Allowance, a maximum of 25 working days, and the processing time Tax Holiday of 45 working days.

"In the second volume of economic policy package announced last week, the arrangement of the Tax Holiday and Tax Allowance will be accelerated. Tax Allowance, which was originally 28 working days to 25 working days, while the Tax Holiday was originally 125 working days to 45 working days. We soon issue Regulations governing the mechanisms so that investors can immediately take advantage," said Mr. Sibarani.

In more detail, the Deputy Investment Services BKPM Ms. Lestari Indah explained that the acceleration time maintaining Tax Holiday and Tax Allowance is done in coordination with the Ministry of Finance. According to her, the maintenance of a Tax Allowance whole process takes 25 working days, consisting of 18 working days in the maintenance of BKPM and 7 working days at the Tax Directorate of the Ministry of Finance. Meanwhile, the process to obtain the Tax Holiday the overall process takes 45 days, consisting of 25 working days of BKPM and 20 working days at the Fiscal Policy Office, Ministry of Finance.

Income Tax facilities are granted to both for new investments and business expansion:

- Certain sectors such as attached in Annex I of this Government Regulation
- Certain sectors and certain regions as listed in Annex II of this Government Regulation

1. Laws and Regulations

The following are some of Laws and Regulations regulate the fiscal incentives:

- Government Regulation No. 94/2010
- The Regulation of Finance Minister No. 130/PMK.011/2011
- The Regulation of Finance Minister No. 159/PMK.010/2015
- The Regulation of the Head of BKPM No. 19 of 2015 on changes in the Regulation No. 13 of 2015
- The Indonesian Government Regulation No. 1 of 2007 and 52 of 2011
- The Regulation of the Head of BKPM No. 18 of 2015
- The Regulation of the Head of BKPM No. 8 of 2015
- The Regulation of the Head of BKPM No. 19 of 2015

2. Tax Holiday Incentives

9 Eligible Pioneer Industries with a minimum of IDR1Trillion (USD100 Million) investment plan:

- Basic metal industries
- Oil refinery industries and/or basic organic chemicals
- Machinery industries
- Industries of renewable resources
- Communication devices industries
- Agricultural processing
- Marine transportation
- Manufacturing industry in SEZ
- Economic infrastructures

Regulated by the Minister of Finance Regulation No. 159/PMK.010/2015 on the Facilitation of Corporate Income Tax Reduction. Signed by Indonesian Finance Minister, Bambang P.S.

Brodjonegoro on August 14, 2015. Promulgated in Jakarta on August 18, 2015 by Indonesian Minister of Laws and Human Rights, Yasonna H. Laoly. Stated Gazette of Indonesia No. 1218 of 2015.[51]

- Reduction of Corporate Income Tax given at most 100%, at least 10% of the amount of corporate payable Income Tax.
- Granted for the same percentage every year, for a maximum period of 15 years of tax, at least 5 years, commencing from the commercial production.

Taking into account the interests of maintaining the competitiveness of national industry and the strategic value of certain business activities, the Ministry of Finance may extend the facilities up to 20 years.

Who is Eligible?

- A new tax payer
- Industry pioneer
- Have a new capital investment plans that have been approved by the competent agencies, at least for IDR1,000,000,000,000.00 (One Trillion Rupiahs)
- Meet with the provisions of the ratio between debt and capital referred in the Minister of Finance Regulation on the determination of the ratio between corporate debt and capital for the purposes of calculating the Income Tax
- Submit a statement of willingness to deposit funds into the Indonesian bank totaling at least 10% of the total capital investment plans. The funds will not be withdrawn prior to the commencement of the implementation of the investment

---

[51] *Peraturan Menteri Keuangan Republik Indonesia No. 159/PMK.010/2015 tentang Pemberian Fasilitas Pengurangan Pajak Penghasilan Badan. August 14, 2015. Menteri Keuangan RI, Bambang P.S. Brodjonegoro. Lembaran Negara Republik Indonesia Tahun 2015 No. 1218.*

- Ratification of legal status determined from Indonesia or after the date of August 15, 2011

How to Apply?

Submit application to the Head Investment Coordinating Board (BKPM) with the following documents:

- NPWP (Tax ID)
- Principle License and amendments
- A statement of willingness to deposit funds into the Indonesian bank
- Certificate of Fiscal

3. Tax Allowance

Regulated by Indonesian Government Regulation No. 18 of 2015 concerning income tax facilities for investment in certain and / or in specific sector(s). Signed by the President of Indonesia, Joko Widodo on April 6, 2015. Promulgated in Jakarta by the Minister of Laws and Human Rights, Yasonna H. Laoly on April 6, 2015. Registered in the Indonesian State Gazette No. 77 of 2015.[52]

Facilities:

- Reduction of net income of 30% of the total investment in the form of tangible fixed assets including land used for main business activities, is charged for 6 years respectively at 5% per year calculated from the time of start of commercial operations

---

[52] *Peraturan Pemerintah Republik Indonesia No. 18 Tahun 2015 Tentang Fasilitas Pajak Penghasilan untuk Penanaman Modal di Bidang Bidang Usaha Tertentu dan/atau di Daerah Tertentu. 6 April 2015. Lembaran Negara Republik Indonesia Tahun 2015 Nomor 77.*

- Accelerated depreciation on tangible assets and amortization on intangible assets acquired in the framework of the new investment and/or expansion, the useful lives and depreciation rates and amortization rates are set as follows:

  ☐ **Accelerated depreciation on tangible assets:**

Tangible Assets	Life Benefit To Be	Depreciation Tariff Based Method	
		Straight Line	Declining Balance
1. Non building			
Group 1	2 years	50%	100% at once
Group 2	4 years	25%	50%
Group 3	8 years	12.5%	25%
Group 4	10 years	10%	20%
2. Buildings	10 years	10%	
Permanent	10 years	10%	–
Non Permanent	5 years	20%	–

  ☐ **Accelerated amortization on intangible assets:**

Intangible Assets	Life Benefit To Be	Amortization Tariff Based Method	
		Straight Line	Declining Balance
Group 1	2 years	50%	100% at once
Group 2	4 years	25%	50%
Group 3	8 years	12.5%	25%
Group 4	10 years	10%	20%

- Imposition of Income Tax on dividends paid to foreign taxpayers in addition to a permanent establishment in Indonesia by 10%, or a lower rate, under double taxation treaties in force.
- Compensation for losses that are more than 5 years but not lesser than 10 years, with the following conditions:
  - ☐ Additional 1 year for new investment on business fields on the list, in industrial estates and bonded zones.
  - ☐ Additional 1 year if the Company employs at least 500 Indonesian workers in 5 consecutive years.
  - ☐ Additional 1 year if the new investor needs to invest for economy and social infrastructure in the business location at least Ten Billion Rupiahs (IDR10,000,000,000.00).
  - ☐ Additional 1 year if the investor pays for research and development in the country, in order to develop products or production efficiency of at least 5% of the investment in within 5 years
  - ☐ Additional 1 year if the investor use at least 70% domestic raw materials and/or components since their 4th year of production

Income Tax facilities can be utilized after at least 80% of the capital investment plans have completed.

Minister of Finance issued a decision granting Income Tax facility after considering proposals from the Head of the Investment Coordinating Board.

Who is Eligible?

Chapter 29 the Regulation of the Head of Indonesian Investing Coordinating Board No. 19/2015 states: Taxpayer who commits in a new capital investment categorized as an industry pioneer, who did not get the facility as defined in Section 31A of the Law of Income Tax may be granted exemption or reduction of Income

Tax as referred in the Article 18 Paragraph (5) of the Law No. 25/2007.

The pioneer industry referred above is an industry that has broad relevance, value-added and high value, introduce new technology, also has a strategic value for the national economy.

Taxpayers can be granted exemption or reduction of corporate Income Tax as referred to in Article 4 of Indonesian Minister of Finance Regulation No. 159/PMK.010/2015, is a new corporate taxpayer who meets the following criteria:

- An Industry Pioneer;
- Have a new capital investment plans that have been approved by the competent agencies, at least for IDR1,000,000,000,000.00 (One Trillion Rupiahs);
- Placing funds in banks in Indonesia at least 10% (ten percent) of the total capital investment plans as referred to in point b, and should not be withdrawn before the commencement of the implementation of the realization of the investment; and
- Meet with the provisions of the ratio between debt and capital referred in the Minister of Finance Regulation on the determination of the ratio between corporate debt and capital for the purposes of calculating the Income Tax;
- Have status as a legal entity whose ratifications Indonesia set a maximum of 12 months before this Regulation comes into force or endorsement set since or after the entry into force of this Regulation.

The exemption or reduction of Income Tax referred above may be used with following requirements:

- Has done the realization of investments; and
- Has done commercial production.

Taking into account the interests of maintaining the competitiveness of national industry and the strategic value of certain business activities, the Minister of Finance may grant Industry Pioneers exemption or reduction of corporate Income Tax, in addition to Industry Pioneers coverage.

> The Industry Pioneers included:
> - Basic metal industry
> - Petroleum refining industry and/or organic basic chemicals derived from petroleum and natural gas
> - Machinery industry
> - The latest in the field of industry resources
> - Communication equipment industry

The commencement of commercial production shall be determined by the Director General of Taxation, which of procedures regulated by the Director General of Taxation.

How to Apply?

The application to be submitted in person at the Front Office, Central PTSP BKPM with the required documents as listed on Appendix I of the Regulation, and:

- The application letter signed by the board on stamp duty in accordance with the format set forth in Appendix II of the Regulation, which is an integral part of this Chief Regulation;
- Principle License / Investment Permit and its amendments issued by BKPM or Principle Permit and amendments issued by the Investment Board and One Stop Services Province;
- Deed recording of entity and its amendments equipped with endorsement / approval from the Ministry of Justice or the District Court;
- Recording of an entity Taxpayer Identification Number (TIN / NPWP);

- Assessment of the fulfillment of the criteria as a pioneer industry
- The original affidavit stating the ability to put funds in in the Indonesian bank
- Taxpayer fiscal certificate
- Explanation of sources of financing of Company's investment and supporting documents
- Explanation of fulfillment of the provisions of the amount of the ratio between debt and capital referred to the Regulation of the Minister of Finance that regulates the determination of the ratio of debt and capital companies for the purposes of calculation of Income Tax
- Stamped power of attorney if the application is not handled directly by the taxpayer's board in accordance with the format contained in Annex III, which is an integral part of this Chief Regulation. This provision does not apply if the entity:
  - ☐ Directly owned by the Central Government or Local Government;
  - ☐ Ownership consists of stocks listed in the stock exchanges in Indonesia.

Process & Procedure

Upon the submittal of documents at the Front Officer of PTSP BKPM Center (One Stop Integrated Service of Investment Coordinating Board), the documents have to follow through some clarification and eligibility with provisions:

- In the case of Principle License / Investment Permit issued Investment by BKPM, the Taxpayer to be present to do the clarification;
- In the case of Principle Permit issued by the Province Investment Agency and One Stop Integrated Service, clarifications to be done by presenting the taxpayer and

the representative of the Board of Investment and One Stop Integrated Services Province.

Receipt as formed in Appendix IV of the Regulation to be issued when it is decided and clarified that the application meets the requirements.

A Clarification Technical Meeting will follow the clarification of eligibility referred above, to be done by representatives from technical ministries, the Ministry of Finance, experts, academics and associations on their respective businesses petitioned the facilities.

The Meeting Decision to be done based on the Technical Clarification Meeting.

Results of eligibility clarification, Technical Clarification Meeting, and Decision Meeting respectively set forth in Minutes signed by all meeting participants using the format as contained in Appendix V of the Regulation.

In case the application is accepted, the Head of BKPM issues a Proposed Reduction Facility Corporate Income Tax / Tax Holiday by using the format as listed in Annex VI of the Regulation.

In case the application is rejected, the Head of BKPM make Rejection Letters by using the format as contained in Annex VII of the Regulation.

The Period of time of clarification process until the publication of acceptance / rejection the proposal is 25 (twenty five) working days after the issuance of a receipt.

In the event of a technical clarification process or when a taxpayer fails to complete documents by the deadline as stated in the Minutes of the Technical Clarification, the application is returned to the taxpayer.

Documents Required

- Application Letter
- Letter of Authorization / Power of Attorney from the Board of Director
- Principle Licenses and the amendments
- NPWP (Tax ID)
- Deeds and any amendments as well as the ratification / approval / notification from the Ministry of Justice and Human Rights – in a Company folder:
  - ☐ Deed of Incorporation;
  - ☐ Deed of Adjustment Act PT (if any);
  - ☐ Deed of Change of Name (if any);
  - ☐ Deed of Change of Domicile (if any);
  - ☐ Deed in connection with changes in Purpose and Objectives of Company (if any);
  - ☐ Deed of Amendment of Capital and/or Last Shares (if any);
  - ☐ Deed of Latest Directors (if any).

- A fully stamped explanatory letter on the fulfillment of the criteria of the study as industry pioneer, along with studies.
- The original affidavit on ability to deposit funds in the Indonesian bank
- A fiscal statement issued by the Directorate General of Taxes
- A fully stamped statement on the source of financing of investment, with supporting documents
- A letter of explanation on fulfillment of the provisions of the amount of the ratio between debts and capital

4. Import Duty Facility

> 2 years import duty exemption of machines, goods, materials for productions, or 4 years for companies using minimum of 30% locally produced machines.

Import duty facility granted as long as machinery, goods and materials have:

- not been produced domestically
- been produced domestically, but have not meet the required specifications
- been produced in the country, but the amount are not sufficient for industry

Given to industries that produces goods and/or services, including:

- Tourism and culture
- Public transportation
- Public health services
- Mining
- Construction
- Telecommunication
- Ports

Regulated by the Minister of Finance Regulation No. 176/PMK.011/2009 regarding duty exemption on imports of machinery and goods and materials for construction or industrial development within the framework of investment. Signed by Indonesian Minister of Finance, Ms. Sri Mulyaniindrawati on November 16, 2009. Promulgated in Jakarta by Indonesian Minister of Laws and Human Rights, Mr. Patrialis Akbar on November 16, 2009. State Gazette No. 432 of 2009.[53]

---

[53] *Peraturan Menteri Keuangan No. 176/PMK.011/2009 Tentang Pembebasan Bea Masuk Atas Impor Mesin Serta Barang Dan Bahan Untuk Pembangunan Atau Pengembangan Industri Dalam Rangka Penanaman Modal. 16 November 2009. Berita Negara Republik Indonesia Tahun 2009 No. 432.*

Import duty facility granted as long as machinery, goods and materials have:

- not been produced domestically
- been produced domestically, but have not meet the required specifications
- been produced in the country, but the amount are not sufficient for industry

If the Company has not completed the importation within 2 years, the facility can be extended for another year.

Companies that perform construction or development, except for the industry that produces services, using at least 30% domestically produced machineries, the import duty exemption can be granted for the purposes of production / additional production for 4 years, with the import period of 4 years, valid from time when the import duty exemption granted. This facility does not apply to motor vehicle assembly industry, except motor vehicle component industry.

How to Apply?

Submit application to the Head of Investment Coordinating Board (BKPM), together with the following documents:

- Deed of Incorporation
- Investment approval
- NPWP / Tax Identification Number and receipt of Taxable Entrepreneur application
- Customs Identity Number (NIK)
- Import Identification Number (API / APIT / API-P)
- List of machines, quantity, type, detailed technical specifications

- Brief description of production processes for industries that produce goods, or a brief description of business activities for the service industry
- A statement from the relevant authorities regarding the composition of the engine, in case the Company is using domestically produced machineries
- List of goods and materials including the amount, type, and detailed technical specifications
- Import customs declaration, or invoice for machines purchased domestically

Further details can be found in the Regulation of the Minister of Finance of the Republic of Indonesia No. 176/PMK.011/2009 regarding the exemption of import duty of machinery as well as goods and materials for construction or industrial development within the framework of investment, dated 16 November 2009.

14 | Exchange Control and Landing

Note from Author: There are translations of Laws and/or Regulations in this Chapter. I emphasized readability rather than word-for-word. When there are contradictions and discrepancies as to interpretation of any provision of the Law, the original version of the Law written in Bahasa Indonesia shall prevail.

A. Medium of Exchange

Regulated by the Law No. 7 of 2011 dated 28 June 2011[54], on Currency (the Currency Law), and the Regulation of Bank Indonesia No. 17/3/PBI/2015[55] regarding the Obligation to Use Rupiah in the Territory of the Republic of Indonesia:

As the currency of the Republic of Indonesia, Rupiah is required to be used for cash or non-cash bill or coin transactions the territory of the Republic of Indonesia. Except for foreign transactions, such as:

- Transactions related to the state budget;
- Grants given by or to a foreign state;
- International trade transactions;
- Bank deposits denominated in foreign currencies; and

---

[54] *Undang Undang Republik Indonesia No. 7 Tahun 2011 Tentang Mata Uang. 28 Juni 2011. Presiden Republik Indonesia Dr. H. Susilo Bambang Yudhoyono. Promulgated in Jakarta by Indonesian Minister of Laws and Human Rights, Mr. Patrialis Akbar on June 28, 2011. State Gazette No. 64 of 2011.*

[55] *Peraturan Bank Indonesia No. 17/3/PBI/2015 tentang Kewajiban Penggunaan Rupiah di Wilayah Negara Kesatuan Republik Indonesia. Signed by Mr. Agus DW Martowardojo, the Governor of Bank Indonesia on March 31, 2015. Promulgated in Jakarta by Indonesian Minister of Laws and Human Rights, Mr. Yasonna H. Laoly on March 31, 2015. State Gazette No. 70 of 2015.*

- International finance transactions.
- Business activities in foreign currencies
- Securities transactions

B. Book Keeping / Records

Regulated by the Regulation of Indonesian Ministry of Finance No. 609/KMK.04/1994[56] Regarding Book Keeping In Foreign Languages and Currencies in addition of Rupiah in the Framework of Foreign Investment, Contract of Work, Production Sharing Contracts, and Other Business Activities or Agency:

> Taxpayers can keep bookkeeping in foreign languages and currencies other than Rupiah. Foreign languages and currencies allowed by this decision are English language and US Dollar. However it must first approved by the Minister of Finance.

The application may be submitted no later than thirty days before the fiscal year begins. Finance Minister shall make a decision on the application no later than thirty days from receipt of the application. In the event there is no decision received from the Ministry of Finance within thirty days, the taxpayer's request is considered accepted.

The taxpayer should submit Surat Pemberitahuan Masa dan Tahunan (Annual Notice Period) and its annexes in Indonesian language, and shall make tax payments in Indonesian Rupiah.

---

[56] *Keputusan Menteri Keuangan Republik Indonesia No. 609/KMK.04/1994 Tentang Penyelenggaraan Pembukuan Dalam Bahasa Asing Dan Mata Uang Selain Rupiah Bagi Wajib Pajak Dalam Rangka Penanaman Modal Asing, Kontrak Karya, Kontrak Bagi Hasil, Dan Kegiatan Usaha Atau Badan Lain.* December 21, 1994. Mr. Mar'ie Muhammad, Indonesian Finance Minister.

Tax to be paid in Indonesian Rupiah using the prevailing exchange rate according to the Decree of the Minister of Finance at the time payment is made.

Financial Statements in the form of Balance Sheet and Profit and Loss Calculation are presented in English and denominated in US Dollar and Rupiah.

Director General of Taxation is authorized for and on behalf of the Minister of Finance to receive the request and provide a decision on the licensing operation for the English bookkeeping and US Dollar currency. (December 21, 1994).

C. Foreign Exchange Control

Regulated by the Law No.24 of 1999 concerning Foreign Exchange Flow and Exchange Rate System[57]:

- Bank Indonesia has the authority to request information and data concerning the activities of the Foreign Exchange performed by residents.
- Each resident is obliged to provide information and data of the Foreign Exchange activities, directly or through other parties designated by Bank Indonesia.
- Bank Indonesia establishes provisions on various types of foreign exchange transactions conducted by the bank.
- Bank Indonesia proposes Exchange Rate System to be set by the Government.
- Bank Indonesia implements exchange rate policy based on Exchange Rate System above

---

[57] *Undang Undang Republik Indonesia No. 24 Tahun 1999 Tentang Lalu Lintas Devisa dan Sistem Nilai Tukar. Signed by the President of Indonesia Mr. Bacharuddin Jusuf Habibie on May 17, 1999. Promulgated in Jakarta by Indonesian Secretary Minister of the State Mr. Muladi on May 17, 1999. State Gazette No. 67 of 1999.*

D. Offshore Borrowing

> Indonesian companies are, in general, permitted to borrow money from offshore lenders whether denominated in foreign currency or Indonesian Rupiah.

In accordance with Article 3 Paragraph 2 of Law No. 24/1999 on Foreign Exchange Traffic and Exchange Rate System, the PMA obliged to provide information and data on the activities of the Foreign Exchange Traffic directly or through other parties as regulated by Bank Indonesia.

The definition of Foreign Exchange Traffic in accordance with Article 1 Paragraph 1 of Law 24/1999 is the transfer of assets and financial obligations between residents and nonresidents, including transfers of assets and financial obligation between residents abroad.

The definition of Residents according to Article 1 Paragraph 3 of Law 24/1999 is a person, legal entity or other entities reside or plan to reside in Indonesia at least for one year, including representative and diplomatic staff of the Republic of Indonesia abroad.

As an offshore Debtor, PT PMA shall comply with the provisions in Bank Indonesia Circular Letter No. 15/17/DINT/2013 concerning Foreign Exchange Activity Reporting Form on Foreign Debt Plan, the Amendment of Foreign Debt Plan, and Financial Information, where PMA required to report the plan of the foreign debts through online https://www.bi.go.id/lkpbuv2 no later than March 15 of the current year at 24:00. The reporting applies to short-term and long-term debts.

E. Onshore Borrowing

Most major Indonesian banks (which includes the branch offices of foreign banks operating in Indonesia) may provide credit facilities in Indonesian Rupiah or in foreign currency. Indonesian banks are, however, prohibited from granting credit facilities to non-residents, unless the lending is for personal use of the non-resident (e.g. personal credit cards and loans).

15 Tax Basics

Note from Author: There are translations of Laws and/or Regulations in this Chapter. I emphasized readability rather than word-for-word. When there are contradictions and discrepancies as to interpretation of any provision of the Law, the original version of the Law written in Bahasa Indonesia shall prevail.

The taxes regulated in the Indonesian Government Regulation No. 94 of 2010 Regarding Calculation Of Taxable Income And Payment Of Income Tax In The Current Year.[58]

Tax advice in Indonesia is generally obtained from accredited tax consultants at Indonesian accounting firms.

Most Indonesian taxes are similar to those that investors would expect to find in other jurisdictions. These include:

- Income Tax, which includes Corporate Income Tax, Capital Gains Tax, Individual Income Tax, Withholding Tax on employee's remuneration and Withholding Tax on various payments to third parties; and
- Value Added Tax (VAT) and Luxury Goods Sales Tax (LGST), levied on goods and services used for manufacturing, business and consumption in Indonesia (subject to certain criteria).

Taxation in Indonesia is determined on the basis of residency. A Company is treated as being an Indonesian tax resident for

---

[58] *Peraturan Pemerintah Republik Indonesia No. 94 Tahun 2010 Tentang Penghitungan Penghasilan Kena Pajak Dan Pelunasan Pajak Penghasilan Dalam Tahun Berjalan. Signed by Dr. H. Susilo Bambang Yudhoyono, the President of Indonesia on December 30, 2010. Promulgated in Jakarta by Mr. Patrialis Akbar, Indonesian Minister of Laws and Human Rights on December 30, 2010. State Gazette No. 161 of 2010.*

taxation purposes if it has been incorporated or is domiciled in Indonesia. A foreign business engaging in business activities in Indonesia via a permanent establishment (PE) will typically assume the same tax obligations as a resident taxpayer.

The Indonesian tax regime incorporates both a self-assessment system and a withholding tax system.

The fundamental of tax legislation in Indonesia include:

- ☐ The General Provisions and Taxation Procedures, Law No. 28 of 2007;
- ☐ The Income Tax Law No 36 of 2008; and
- ☐ The Value Added Tax, 'Goods and Services and Sales Tax on Luxury Goods', Law No 42 of 2009.

Foreign companies intending to invest in Indonesia should obtain detailed tax advice from an accredited Indonesian tax consultant.

Indonesian Government Regulation No. 94 of 2010

A. Taxation Object

Taxable income in the form of dividends of the Income Tax Law do not include the provision of bonus shares carried out without depositing derived from:

- ■ Capitalization of share premium to shareholders who have deposited capital or have bought shares above the nominal price, as long as the total nominal value of shares owned after the distribution of bonus shares do not exceed the amount of contributed capital; and
- ■ Capitalization excess of fixed assets revaluation as referred in Article 19 Paragraph (1) of the Income Tax Law.

In the event of a transfer of property from the Company to its employee(s), the profits in results of the difference between market prices of such assets and the residual book value accrued to the Company.

Share premium arising from the excess of the market value of stock and par value shares, excluding tax object.

Share discount arising from the excess of the nominal value of stock and stock market value, not a deduction from gross income.

Share of profits received or accrued by the unit holders of Collective Investment Contract included gains on repayment of participation unit are not included as taxation object.

The provisions of the share of profits included gains on repayment of participation unit also apply to foreign tax subject unit holders.

Direct and/or indirect distribution of profits derived from retained earnings include retained earnings based on the projected income for the year is subject to tax, except for share of profits referred in Article 4 Paragraph (3) f of the Income Tax Law.

B. Calculation on Taxable Income

Gain or loss on differences of foreign currency exchange are recognized as income or expense based on the accounting system adopted and applied consistently in accordance with Financial Accounting Standards applicable in Indonesia.

Gains or losses on differences of foreign exchange that are directly related to the Taxpayers' business:

- Subject to Income Tax that are final; or
- Excluding tax object,

are not recognized as income or expense.

Gains or losses on differences of foreign exchange as referred above that are not directly related to the business of Taxpayers:

- Subject to Income Tax that are final; or
- Excluding tax object,

are recognized as income or expense as long as these costs used to obtain, collect and maintain income.

Input tax that cannot be credited as referred in Article 9 Paragraph (8) of the Law of Value Added Tax on Goods and Services and Sales Tax on Luxury Goods can be deducted from gross income as long as it can be proven the Input Tax:

- Has been paid; and
- With regard to the expenses associated with activities to obtain, collect and maintain income.

Input Tax deductible from gross income above with respect to the expenditure to acquire tangible assets and/or intangible assets and other costs that have useful life of more than 1 year as referred to in Article 11 and Article 11A Income Tax Act, must be capitalized by spending or charges and imposed through depreciation or amortization.

The cost of the development of industrial plants older than 1 year with only 1 time production, are capitalized during the period of development and as part of the cost of goods sold when the industrial plant products are sold.

The cost of maintenance of cattle aged more than 1 year and only 1 time production, are capitalized during the breeding period and as part of the cost of goods sold at the time the cattle are sold.

The loan without interest from shareholders received by the taxpayer in the form of a Limited Liability Company allowed if:

- The loan is originated from shareholders' private funds, it does not come from a third party;
- The shareholder(s) lender have already paid-up its capital;
- The shareholders lenders are not in a state of loss;
- The Limited Liability Company borrower is experiencing financial difficulties.

If the loan received by the taxpayer in the form of limited liability of shareholders does not comply with the provisions referred above, the interest rate to be paid by the borrower at a reasonable rate.

Expenses and costs that are not deductible in the taxable income determination for domestic taxpayers and permanent establishments, include:

- The cost to acquire, collect and maintain income, that:
  - ☐ Is not subject to tax;
  - ☐ The imposition of tax is final; and/or
  - ☐ Taxed based on deemed profit as referred in Article 14 of the Income Tax Act and the Special Deemed Profit as referred in Article 15 of the Law on Income Tax.
- Income Taxes are borne by the party that create earnings.

C. Repayment of Income Tax by Taxpayer

Indonesian individuals who derive income on the Income Exempted From Tax (PTKP) in connection with the projects from agencies that are not obliged to withhold tax as provided in Article 21 Paragraph (2) of the Income Tax Act, shall:

- Have a Taxpayer Identification Number (NPWP);
- Perform its own calculation and payment of payable Income Tax in the current year; and

- Report the calculation and payment of payable Income Tax payable in the current year in Annual Notice.

D. Repayment of Income Tax through Other Party

- Depending on the events that occurred beforehand, Income Tax Withholding by the parties referred in Article 21 Paragraph (1) of the Income Tax Act at the end of the month:
  ☐ When the payment occur; or
  ☐ Payable concerned income,
- Collection of Income Tax by the parties referred to in Article 22 Paragraph (1) of the Income Tax Act, made at the time of payment or other specific regulated by the Ministry of Finance.
- Depending on the events that occurred beforehand, Income Tax Withholding by the parties referred in Article 23 Paragraph (1) and Paragraph (3) of Income Tax Act, at the end of the month:
  ☐ Pays income;
  ☐ Provided for repayment of income;
  ☐ Maturity payment of concerned income,
- Depending on the events that occurred beforehand, Income Tax Withholding by the parties referred to in Article 26 Paragraph (1) of the Income Tax Act, at the end of the month:
  ☐ Pays income;
  ☐ Provided for repayment of the amount of income;
  ☐ Maturity payment of income is concerned,

In the case of tax withholding article 23 Income Tax Act or Article 26 of the Income Tax Act under the provisions referred to in Article 15 carried out in different tax years with the recognition of Income Tax, the Income Tax that has been withheld can be credited in the year of tax cuts.

With the Regulations of Director General of Taxation, may be set the recognition of income and expenses in certain respects in accordance with Government policy.

Income Tax on royalty payments as referred in Article 23 Paragraph (1.a.3) of the Income Tax Act to be done by profit sharing cut by the party obligated to pay.

In terms of income not subject to final Income Tax with separate Government Regulation, that income subject to Income Tax rates as referred in Article 17 of the Income Tax Act.

Income Tax deducted or withheld based on tariff withhold or collection referred in Article 21 (5a), Article 22 Paragraph (3), and Article 23 Paragraph (1a) of the Income Tax Act, may be credited against Income Tax payable for the same tax year after the taxpayer possess a Taxpayer Identification Number.

Taxpayers can apply for exemption of Income Tax withholding and collection by other party to Director General of Taxation, if the Taxpayers can prove there is no Income Tax debts in the current tax year due to:

- Fiscal losses;
- Entitled to carry out fiscal loss compensation; or
- Income Taxes paid is greater than the Income Tax payable,

Taxpayers can apply for exemption on Income Tax cuts and/or collection that can be credited to Director General of Taxation, if the Income Taxed final.

In calculating the Income Tax referred in Article 26 (4) of the Income Tax Act, to the permanent establishment Income Tax payable in a tax year, the tax losses cannot be offset against taxable income after deducting Income Tax.

The Income Tax payable on the taxable income after deducting taxes from a permanent establishment in Indonesia as referred in Article 26 (4) of the Income Tax Act to be paid in full before Notice of Annual Income Tax submitted.

Where a permanent establishment extends the period of filing the Notice of Annual Income Tax referred in Paragraph (1), the Income Tax payable based on based on preliminary calculations must be paid in full prior to delivery of the notice of extension of time of the Notice of Annual Income Tax.

E. Application of Treaty on Double Tax Agreement & Exchange of Information

Double Taxation Treaty applies to an individual or entity, by a Certificate of Domicile as the evidence, with:

- In the country of Indonesia; and/or
- From agreed partner countries in Double Taxation Treaty,

The Director General of Taxation may execute agreements with partner countries in order to exchange information, the mutual agreement procedure, and billing assistance.

In the case of differences in tax provisions found in international treaties and the Income Tax Act, the tax treatment to be based on the provisions of the agreement until the termination of the agreement, provided that such agreement is made in accordance with the Law on International Agreements.

The implementation of tax treatment shall be done after obtaining the approval from the Minister of Finance.

F. Separate Accounting and Changes in Fiscal Year

The taxpayer must keep books separately in terms of:

- Business income subject to Income Tax that is final and not final;

- Receive tax object income and non tax object income; or
- Receive and do not receive tax facilities as provided in Article 31A of the Income Tax Act.

Cost together for Taxpayer which cannot be separated in order to calculate the amount of taxable income, shall be allocated proportionately.

Taxpayers who change the fiscal year and has received approval from the Director General of Taxation referred in Article 28 Paragraph (6) of Law General Provisions and Tax Procedures, must report income received or accrued in the fiscal year that are not included in the new fiscal year in the Notice of Annual Income Tax separately for taxable year concerned.

The compensable residual tax losses derived from previous tax years can be compensated by the income for Parts of Fiscal Year and subsequent Fiscal Tax.

G. Exemption or Reduction Corporate Income Tax in Connection with Investment

A taxpayer who invests in a new investment categorized as an Industry Pioneer, who did not receive the facility as defined in Section 31A of the Income Tax Act, can be granted exemption or reduction of corporate Income Tax as referred to in Article 18 Paragraph 5 Law No. 25/2007 on Investment.

An Industry Pioneer is an industry that has broad relevance, value-added and high externalities, introduces new technology, and has a strategic value for the national economy.

16 Land

Note from Author: There are translations of Laws and/or Regulations in this Chapter. I emphasized readability rather than word-for-word. When there are contradictions and discrepancies as to interpretation of any provision of the Law, the original version of the Law written in Bahasa Indonesia shall prevail.

A. Main Laws

- Law No. 5/1960 on Basic Regulations on Agrarian;
- Law No. 25 of 2007 on Investment;
- Government Regulation No. 40 of 1996 on Right to Cultivate (HGU), Right to Build (HGB) and Right to Use the Land (HP);
- Government Regulation No. 24 of 1997 on Land Registration;
- Regulation of Agrarian Minister No. 2 of 1993 on Procedures of Location Permit and Land Titles
- Decree of Agrarian Minister No. 21 of 1994 on Procedure of Land Procurement
- Regulation of Agrarian Minster No. 2 of 1997 on Land Acquisition and Right to Build Land
- Regulation of Agrarian Minister No. 2 of 1999 on Location Permit;
- Regulation of Agrarian Minister No. 5 of 2015 on Location Permit

According to the Regulation of the Minister of Agrarian and Spatial Planning / Head of National Land Agency No. 5 of

2015[59], Location Permit granted to companies that have received investment approval in accordance with the provisions of the legislation to obtain land with an area that has been determined, so that when the Company succeeded in land acquisition in the designated area, the Company or its group may control over the land with:

- No more than 400Ha if it is used for industrial purposed, and if the land is located in 1 Province,
- No more than 4,000Ha statewide
- The area is doubled in Papua and West Papua.
- There is list of different sizes of land for different kind of purposes.

The Location Permit is granted for 3 years. The land should be possessed within the time of the permit. If the land acquisition has not completed in 3 years, the permit may be extended for one year if the land has been completed for more than 50%. If the land acquisition less than 50%, the permit cannot be extended.

If the land acquisition cannot be completed within the time line, the land that has been acquired may be used to implement the investment plan with the adjustment of the construction area as an integral field. Land acquisition can be performed again by the permit holder on the location of the land that lies on the land that already acquired to integrate the plot.

In the case of acquisition of land less than 50% of the land area designated in the permit, the land that has been acquired is released to the Company or any other party who qualify.

---

[59] *Peraturan Menteri Agraria dan Tata Ruang / Kepala Badan Pertanahan Nasional No. 5 Tahun 2015 Tentang Izin Lokasi. Signed by Mr. Ferry Mursyidan Baldan, Indonesian Minister of Agrarian and Spatial Planning / Head of Land Office on April 28, 2015. Promulgated in Jakarta by Mr. Yasonna H. Laoly, the Minister of Laws and Human Rights on April 28, 2015. State Gazette No. 647 of 2015.*

B. Agrarian, Spatial and Land Regulations in Investment Activities

The Regulation of the Minister of Agrarian and Spatial Planning / Head of National Land Agency No. 2/2015 on Service Standards and Agrarian Settings, Spatial and Land in Investment Activity[60], an implementing Regulation of the Indonesian President Regulation No. 97/2014 on Implementation of One Stop Integrated Services[61].

This Regulation regulates the type of service, requirements, costs, timing and procedures, for conducting service in agrarian settings, spatial planning, and land in the investment activities.

The service implementer of this Regulation is the Ministry of Agricultural and Spatial Planning / National Land Agency, Regional Office, and the Regency/City Office.

Types of One Stop Integrated Service (PTSP):

- Information about the availability of land;
- Technical considerations of land;
- Measurements of the ground plane;
- Determination of the land rights;
- The registration of the decision of land rights; and
- Complaints management.

---

[60] *Peraturan Menteri Agraria dan Tata Ruang / Kepala Badan Pertanahan Nasional No. 2 Tahun 2015 Tentang Standar Pelayanan dan Pengaturan Agraria, Tata Ruang dan Pertanahan Dalam Kegiatan Penanaman Modal.* Signed by Mr. Ferry Mursyidan Baldan on January 23, 2015. Promulgated in Jakarta by Mr. Yasonna H. Laoly on February 4, 2015. Gazette No. 184 of 2015.

[61] *Peraturan Presiden Republik Indonesia No. 97 Tahun 2014 Tentang Penyelenggaraan Pelayanan Terpadu Satu Pintu.* Signed by Dr. H. Susilo Bambang Yodhoyono, the President of Republic of Indonesia, on September 15, 2014. Promulgated in Jakarta by Mr. Amir Syamsudin on September 18, 2014. State Gazette No. 221 of 2014.

C. PTSP Procedures

- The applicant filed the application, furnished with the land and other related documents.
- In the case the file is not complete, the authority is entitled to return the proposal to the applicant to be completed.
- The file processed by PTSP after complete documents received by the authorities and the applicant has paid the fees.
- The file is to be returned to the applicant when there is found a dispute, conflict, case or other legal issues.

D. PTSP Implementation Results Reporting

Officials of the Ministry of Agricultural and Spatial Planning / National Land Agency or the Head of the Regional Office and Head of District / Municipal Ministry of Agricultural and Spatial Planning / National Land Agency as the authority in the implementation of PTSP, are required to provide a report on the results of the implementation of the OSS to the Minister of Agrarian and Spatial / National Land Agency, as follows:

1. Reporting by officials of the Ministry of Agricultural and Spatial Planning / National Land Agency, are conducted regularly every 6 months; and
2. Reporting to the Head of the Regional Office and Head of District / Municipal Ministry of Agricultural and Spatial Planning / National Land Agency is conducted, regularly every month.

E. Land Acquisition Procedures in Investment Framework

Acquisition of land for investment by a Company specifically regulated in the Regulation of the Minister of Agrarian / BPN No. 21 of 1994 on Land Acquisition Procedures For Company in Connection with Investment ("Kepmenag No. 21/1994")[62].

Acquisition of land is any activity to gain the land through the transfer of the rights over land or by delivery or release of the land's rights by granting compensation to those entitled. The Company may only exercise the acquisition of land in the area specified in the licensed location. Acquisition of the land in order to permit the implementation of the location can be done by:

- The transfer of land rights, or
- Through the delivery, or
- Release of land rights followed by entitlements.

Acquisition of land in the framework of the investment based on the Ownership Rights (HM) can be carried out as follows:

Upon the request of the rights holder or their proxies on the HM, land can be converted to Building Rights (HGB). Application for change of such rights shall be submitted to the Head of Land Office by attaching a form and HM certificate, or if the land does not have a HM certificate, include evidence of HM to register the conversion.

---

[62] *Keputusan Menteri Negara Agraria / Kepala Badan Pertanahan Nasional No. 21 Tahun 1994 Tentang Tata Cara Perolehan Tanah Bagi Perusahaan Dalam Rangka Penanaman Modal. Signed by Ir. Soni Harsono, Indonesian State Minister of Agrarian / Head of National Land Board, December 7, 1994*

For the HM that has already certificate

- The Head of the Land Office will issue a warrant for fees deposited within 3 days after the receipt of the application of HM;
- Within 7 days after the receipt deposit charges, changes in the status of the land rights recorded in the land book HM and certificate, as well as a other common list;
- The new certificate of HGB and new land book are issued.

For the HM that has not have certified:

- The Head of the Land Office completes the inventory of land and makes an announcement within 10 business days after receipt of the request;
- The Head of the Land Office issues an order to deposit money within 3 working days after the time of announcement, if there is no objection;
- Changes of rights implemented by issuing a new land book and HGB certificate within 7 days after submitting proof of deposit.

The transfer of HGB executed by PPAT deed, and recorded in the land book and certificate as well as other general list. In this case, the location permit valid as a transfer license of rights and where necessary applies as license expenditure of land reform object and other permits or fatwa according to the applicable provisions required under HGB removal on state land.

1. Leasehold

- A Leasehold (HGU) may be granted by the State for a maximum period of 95 years
- Renewed in advance for 60 years with an option to be further renewed for 35 years.

- May only be used for cultivation purposes.
- It may be transferred or mortgaged.

2. Building Rights

- Building Rights (HGB) may be granted by the State for 30 years
- May be extended for another 20 years.
- For the purposes of Foreign Investment, the foreign investor may apply for HGB and its extension simultaneously, making the total term 50 years.
- After the expiry of the term of HGB and its extension, the holder may re-apply for HGB in the same plot of land, provided that city planning still permits it.
- This is a right to erect and possess construction on land.
- The right may also be transferred or mortgaged.

A Foreign Investment Company that requires land for a factory or storage would, in most cases, apply for this type of permit, as it is the closest thing to land ownership available in Indonesia. If the land is not HGB land, it is necessary for the landowner to first convert a HM / HGU / HP land title to a HGB title. This is usually done through a binding agreement with the landowner to convert the existing land right to the HGB with approval of the Land Office before entry into a sale and purchase agreement for the land.

3. Right Of Use

- A right to use and/or collect produce from land.
- Right of Use (HP) may be granted by the State for 70 years
- Renewed in advance for 45 years with an option to be further renewed for 25 years.

- Despite the right of its holder to use the land and/or collect produce from the land, the holder has the obligation to preserve the land, the buildings on it and its environment.
- This land right can be transferred if the land is directly controlled by the State with approval from the State, but otherwise it cannot be transferred unless explicitly stated in the relevant agreement.

17 Infrastructure

To implement the provisions of Article 61, 62, 63, 71, 108, 111 Paragraph 3 of Law No. 3 of 2014 on Industry, Indonesian Government feels the need to establish a Government Regulation on the Development of Industrial Facilities & Infrastructures. In August 2014, the Indonesian President issued a Draft of Regulation on the Development of Industrial Facilities and Infrastructures.

Keys on facilities and infrastructures according to The Indonesian Law No. 3 of 2014[63]:

- Industrial standardization (Article 61);
- Industrial infrastructures (Article (62);
- Industrial estate (Article 63);
- National System of Industrial Information (Article 71);
- Industrial Business License, Business Expansion License, Industrial Estate License, Requirements to do Business in the Industrial Estate (Article 108);
- Fiscal and Non-Fiscal Facilities (Article 111).

Industrial infrastructure may be provided within and/or outside the area designated for industry. The industrial infrastructure at least include:

- Industrial land in the form of industrial areas and/or areas designated for industry;

---

[63] *Undang Undang Republik Indonesia No. 3 Tahun 2014 Tentang Perindustrian. Signed by Dr. H. Susilo Bambang Yudhoyono, the President of Indonesia on January 15, 2014. Promulgated in Jakarta by Mr. Amir Syamsudin, the Minister of Laws and Human Rights. State Gazette No. 4 of 2014*

- Energy and electricity network facilities;
- Telecommunications network facilities;
- Water resources facilities;
- Sanitation facilities;
- Transport network facilities.

The provisions of industrial infrastructure is done through:

- Procurement by the Government or Local Government which costs sourced from the Central Government budget revenues and expenditures or Local Government budget revenue and expenditure;
- Cooperation between the Government and/or the Local Government and the private sector, state-owned enterprises or regionally owned enterprises and private; or
- Entirely financed by the private sector.

The Draft of Regulation on the Development of Industrial Facilities and Infrastructures included provisions on:

- Industrial standardization;
- Industrial Estate;
- National System of Industrial Information;
- Non-Fiscal Facilities;
- Administrative Sanctions.

The Regulation of Government of Republic of Indonesia No. 36/2005 on the Implementation Regulations of Law No. 28/2002 on Building[64]: The scope of this Government Regulation includes provisions for the function of the building, the requirements

---

[64] *Peraturan Pemerintah Republik Indonesia No. 36 Tahun 2005 Tentang Peraturan Pelaksanaan Undang Undang No. 28 Tahun 2002 Tentang Bangunan Gedung. Signed by Dr. H. SB Yudhoyono, the President, September 10, 2005. Promulgated by Mr. Hamid Awaludin, the Minister of Laws and Human Rights on September 10, 2005. State Gazette No. 83 of 2005.*

of the building, the organization of the building, the role of the community, and guidance in building management.

Building permits are permits issued by the District/City Government to the owners of new buildings to build, modify, extend, reduce, and/or caring for the building in accordance with the administrative and technical requirements that apply.

The application for building construction permit submitted by the owner of the building to local Governments to obtain building permits.

Type of functions of building defined by statute:

- The function of the building must fulfill technical requirements, both in terms of layout of the building and its surroundings, as well as the reliability of building construction.
- Purpose, such as residential function, religious functions, business functions, social and cultural functions, and special functions.
- One building can have more than one function.
- The owner may apply to change of function and classification of a building through a new building permit application; it has to meet technical and administrative requirements.
- The change of function and classification of the building is regulated by Local Government through Building Permit, except if the building has a special function designated by Government.

Below are some of building requirements:

- Technical and administrative requirements in accordance with the function of the building
- Administrative requirements are:
  - ☐ Land rights status, and/or land use permit of the land rights owner
  - ☐ Building right status

- ☐ Building construction permit
- ■ Technical requirements of the building include structure, design and reliability of the building
- ■ Administrative and technical requirements for cultural buildings, semi-permanent buildings, emergency buildings, and buildings built in disaster areas to be adapted with the local culture and social condition.

Building Management and Environmental Plan (RTBL) is prepared by the local Government or by a partnership of local Government, private and/or public in accordance with the level of problems in the environment/regions concerned.

RTBL prepared based on the pattern arrangement of buildings and environments that include repair, redevelopment, new construction, and/or preservation for developed region, protected and conserved region, potentially developed new areas, mixture areas.

RTBL prepared by technical consideration of building experts team and public opinions.

Some of reliability requirements are as follows:

- ■ Safety, such as:
    - ☐ Construction, structure, fire hydrants;
    - ☐ Passive protections functions, such as: risks of fire, building materials;
    - ☐ Active protection functions: volume, area, height, number and condition of occupants.
- ■ Health, such as: ventilation, natural and/or artificial lights, sanitation, clean water, sewer, etc.
- ■ Comfort, such as: accessibility, circulation, safety and health requirements, temperature, sound, etc.
- ■ Convenience, such as: facilities, accessibilities, parking, corridors, rooms, elevators, stairs, signs, public telephones, toilets, etc.

18 Industrial Zones

Demand for industrial land is around 1,000 ha per year, about 600 ha (60%) land demand is in Bekasi and Karawang, West Java, and the rest is scattered in other areas.

Based on HKI (Industrial Park Association) data as of June 2012, the total industrial land in Indonesia reached 27,320.6 ha. According to the Regulations, developers can build the industrial area up to 70% of the total available land. The 30% is for the development of infrastructure, and green open spaces. Total of the land that can be built is 19,124.4 hectares, and 58.6% or 11,212.48 ha have been occupied. Therefore, total land ready to offer is 7,911.98 Ha. HKI consists of 61 industrial parks with 7,211 companies as the tenants[65].

According to Indonesian Law No. 3 of 2014[66], Industrial estates are built in the area designated for industry in accordance with the area spatial plan, to support industrial activities efficiently and effectively in the center of industrial growth areas, as industrial infrastructure

An industrial estate may be developed by private enterprises, a state-owned entity, region-owned enterprises, or a cooperative. In certain cases, the Government initiates the construction of an industrial estate.

---

[65] *Source: BKPM*

[66] *Undang Undang Republik Indonesia No. 3 Tahun 2014 Tentang Perindustrian. Signed by Dr. H. Susilo Bambang Yudhoyono, the President of Indonesia on January 15, 2014. Promulgated in Jakarta by Mr. Amir Syamsudin, the Minister of Laws and Human Rights. State Gazette No. 4 of 2014*

19 Trading

Note from Author: There are translations of Laws and/or Regulations in this Chapter. I emphasized readability rather than word-for-word. When there are contradictions and discrepancies as to interpretation of any provision of the Law, the original version of the Law written in Bahasa Indonesia shall prevail.

Freight traffics into and out the Customs area is regulated by the Law No. 17 of 2006 on Customs[67]. Signed by Dr. H. Susilo Bambang Yudhoyono, the President of Republic of Indonesia on November 15, 2006. Promulgated in Jakarta by Mr. Hamid Awaludin, the Minister of Laws and Human Rights. Registered in State Gazette No. 93 of 2006. In this Law:

Customs means everything related to the monitoring of traffic of goods into and out the customs area, as well as the collection of import and export duties.

Customs area is the territory of the Republic of Indonesia covering land, waters and air space above it, as well as certain places in the Exclusive Economic Zone and continental shelf in which this Law applies.

Customs zone is an area with certain limits in seaports, airports, or other places designated for the traffic of goods that are entirely under the supervision of the Directorate General of Customs and Excise.

There are import duties and export tariffs. The determination of duties and tariffs are determined by goods classification and regulated by the Minister Regulation.

---

[67] *Undang Undang Republik Indonesia No. 17 Tahun 2006 Tentang Perubahan Atas Undang Undang No. 10 Tahun 1995 Tentang Kepabeanan. November 15, 2006. Berita Negara Republik Indonesia Tahun 2006 No. 93.*

A. Import

Goods entered into the customs territory are treated as imports, and customs duties owed. There is inspection on import goods. Certain goods may receive certain supervision in the customs area.

> Import is activities to supply goods into the Customs area.

API (Angka Pengenal Import, Import License) is regulated by the Regulation of Indonesia Ministry of Trade No. 70/M-Dag/Per/9/2015 dated September 28, 2015[68]:

> Import can performed by individuals, legal or non-legal business entities, foreign or domestic investors, the government, government institutions or entities, who have API.

There are two kinds of API:

1. API Umum (API-U, General Import License)
Is given to companies to import certain goods for trading purposes.

2. API Produsen (API-P, Import License for Producers)
- Is given to companies to import goods used as capital goods, raw materials, auxiliary materials, and/or materials to support the production process
- The imported goods are prohibited to be traded or transferred to another party

---

[68] *Peraturan Menteri Perdagangan Republik Indonesia No. 70/M-Dag/Per/9/2015 tentang Angka Pengenal Importir.* Signed by Thomas Trikasih Lembong, the Minister of Trade on September 28, 2015.

- If the imported goods are exempted from import duty and have been used by the importer for a minimum of two years from notification of the Customs import, the imported goods can be transferred to another party

Each importer is only granted one API, held by the head office of the company – it can be used by branch offices as long as it has similar business activities; valid statewide.

> Import products for the purpose of export may be relieved or exempted from import duties. The permit is given for a maximum of three years. However, the company has to pay an administration sanction of 100 percent Customs Duty owed if there is a delay in export

B. Export

Indonesian Minister of Trade Regulation No. 13/M-DAG/PER/3/2012 regarding General Regulations in Export[69]:

- Exporter is an individual, organization or business entity, whether incorporated or not a legal entity, engaged in the export.

> Export is the activity of removing items out of the area of customs.

- Goods are any tangible or intangible objects, whether movable or immovable, consumable or not consumable, which can be traded, used, utilized, or advantaged.

---

[69] *Peraturan Menteri Perdagangan No. 13/M-DAG/PER/3/2012 Tentang Ketentuan Umum di Bidang Ekspor. Signed by Ms. Gita Irawan Wirjawan, the Minister of Trade on March 19, 2012.*

- Exports are regulated by Law, with the objective of protecting national defense, public interest, health, international agreements, domestic conservation, product and raw material availability, economy, intellectual property, the environment, ecology, etc.
- Export goods are classified into:
  - ☐ Free to Export;
  - ☐ Restricted Exports Goods;
  - ☐ Prohibited to Export.
- Exporter must notice Customs for any export
- Goods may be subject to export duties, inspection.

1. Free To Export

- Can be done by individual, institutions and enterprises.
- Individuals must have:
  - ☐ Tax Identification Number (NPWP);
  - ☐ Other documents required by Laws.
- Institutions or enterprises must have:
  - ☐ Business Trade License (SIUP), or business license from the technical ministries/non-ministerial Government institutions/agencies;
  - ☐ Company Registration Certificate (TDP);
  - ☐ Tax Identification Number (NPWP);
  - ☐ Other documents required by Laws;

2. Restricted Export Goods

As an exporter, the institution or business entity should have basic exporter requirements:

- Business Trade License (SIUP), or business license from the technical ministries/non-ministerial Government institutions/agencies;
- Company Registration Certificate (TDP);

- Tax Identification Number (NPWP);
- Other documents required by Laws.

To export restricted goods, an institution or business entity should have the following requirements:

- Recognition as a Registered Exporter;
- Export Approval;
- Has Surveyor Report;
- Certificate of Origin;
- Other documents required by Laws.

The Recognition as a Registered Exported and Export Approval can be applied online to the Ministry of Trade through Trade Service Unit. The Recognition as a Registered Exporter and Export Approval to be issued 5 days after complete application received.

The Minister can restrict export with the following reasons:

- To protect national security or public interest;
- To protect the health of humans, animals, plants or the environment;
- To protect the existence of international treaties or agreements signed and ratified by the Government;
- Limited supply in the domestic market or for effective conservation;
- Limited capacity of the market in the country or region of export destinations;
- Limited availability of raw materials needed processing industry.

> The Exporter should report the export realization of Restricted Goods, online to http://inatrade.kemendag.go.id, every month, no later than the 15th of the following month.

3. Prohibited To Export

An item that is banned for exports due to considerations:

- Threaten national security or public interest, including social, cultural and moral society;
- Protecting intellectual property rights, human life, health, environment and ecology;
- Based on international treaties and agreements signed and ratified by the Government.

CLASSIFICATION OF EXPORTERS:

A. Producer Exporter

- The manufacturer exporter may submit the application and at local Trade and Industry Agency in the District/City or Province.
- Have Industry Business License and TIN/NPWP;
- Provide export realization report to the Department of Industry or agencies and appointed officials periodically every three months that approved by foreign exchange banks, attached with statements such as: no delinquency to taxes or outstanding debt, no customs violations.

B. Non-Producer Exporter

- The non-manufacturer exporter may submit the application and at local Trade and Industry Agency in the District/City or Province.
- Have a Trading License and TIN/NPWP;
- Provide export realization report to the Department of Industry or agencies and appointed officials periodically every three months that approved by foreign exchange

banks, attached with statements such as: no delinquency to taxes or outstanding debt, no customs violations.

C. General Customs Procedures

Broadly speaking customs procedures for the export of goods are as follows:

- The items to be exported shall be notified in advance to the customs office by filling out Notification of Export of Goods (PEB);
- The registration of PEB accompanied by Company Registration Number (NIPER) and include supplementary documents. PEB submitted at the earliest 7 days before the expected date of export and at the latest before the export of goods entering the customs area.

Customs Documents:

- Invoice and Packing List;
- Evidence of payment of Non-Tax State Income (Pendapatan Negara Bukan Pajak, PNBP);
- Evidence of Export Duty Payment (in the case of exported goods subject to Levy);
- Documents from related technical agencies (in the case of the exported goods affected by the provisions of prohibition and/or restrictions).

At the Customs Office that has introduced Customs Electronic Data Interchange System (PDE), exporters or Customs Clearance Services Company (PPJK) must submit PEB using PDE system to Customs.

- Export tax should be paid if the goods are subject to export tax. PEB submission can be done by the exporter or authorized to PPJK;
- Physical examination of exported goods and documents;
- Approval and loading of export goods to a carrier.

Regulation of Indonesian Minister of Trade No. 16/M-DAG/PER/2/2015 regarding the Determination of Freight and Insurance Values in Filing Notice of Export Goods (PEB) Relating the Terms of Delivery Cost, Insurance and Freight (CIF) for the Export[70]:

Freight value and insurance value are calculated based on written submissions from the Ministry / Government Institutions Non relevant Ministry represented in the membership of Freight and Insurance Value Determination Team.

Freight and insurance value to be determined in a Freight and Insurance Value Determination Team meeting, regulated by Minister.

List of export prohibited goods regulated in Indonesian Minister of Trade Regulation No. 44/M-DAG/PER/7/2012 dated 18 July 2012, minister set certain goods as goods prohibited from export reasons:

- Threat to national security or public interest, including social, cultural and moral society;
- Protecting intellectual property rights, human life, health, environment and ecosystems; and/or
- Based on international treaties or agreements signed and ratified by the Government.

---

[70] *Peraturan Menteri Perdagangan Republik Indonesia No. 16/M-DAG/PER/2/2015 Tentang Penetapan Nilai Freight dan Nilai Asuransi Dalam Pengisian Pemberitahuan Ekspor Barang Terkait Penggunaan Term of Delivery Cost, Insurance and Freight untuk Pelaksanaan Ekspor. Signed by Mr. Rachmat Gobel, the Minister of Trade on February 18, 2015.*

20 Employment

Note from Author: There are translations of Laws and/or Regulations in this Chapter. I emphasized readability rather than word-for-word. When there are contradictions and discrepancies as to interpretation of any provision of the Law, the original version of the Law written in Bahasa Indonesia shall prevail.

The Law of the Republic of Indonesia No. 13 of 2003[71]

A. Company Regulations

Every enterprise employs at least 10 (ten) worker/laborers is under an obligation to establish a set of company Regulations that shall come into force after becoming legalized by the Minister or appointed official. However, it does not apply to enterprises already having collective labor agreements.

Company Regulations shall at least contain:

- The rights and obligations of the entrepreneur;
- Working conditions;
- The rights and obligations of the worker/laborer;
- Enterprise discipline and rule of conduct; and
- The period of the validity of the company Regulations.

Any manpower shall have the same opportunity to get a job without discrimination. Every worker/laborer has the right

---

[71] *Undang Undang Republik Indonesia No. 13 Tahun 2003 tentang Ketenagakerjaan. Jakarta. 25 Maret 2003. Presiden Republik Indonesia. Megawati Soekarnoputri. Diundangkan Tanggal 25 Maret 2003, Sekretaris Negara Republik Indonesia, Bambang Kesowo. Lembaran Negara Republik Indonesia 2003 No. 39.*

to receive equal treatment without discrimination from their employer.

> Entrepreneurs are not allowed to employ children.

Any manpower shall have equal rights and opportunities to choose a job, get a job, or move to another job and earn a decent income irrespective of whether they are employed at home or abroad.

B. Work Agreement

- Work agreements can be made either orally or in writing.
- Work agreements that specify requirements in writing shall be carried out in accordance with valid legislation.

A work agreement shall be made based on:

- The agreement of the parties;
- The capability or competence to take legal actions;
- The availability/existence of the job which the parties have agreed about;
- The notion that the job which the parties have agreed about is not against public order, morality and what is prescribed in the prevailing Laws and Regulations.
- If a work agreement, which has been made by the parties, turns out to be against what is prescribed, the agreement may be abolished/cancelled, shall be declared null and void by Law.
Everything associated with, and/or the costs needed for, the making of a work agreement shall be borne by, and shall be the responsibility of, the entrepreneur.

C. Termination of Contract

A work agreement comes to an end if:

- The worker dies; or
- The work agreement expires; or
- A court decision and/or a resolution or order of the industrial relations disputes settlement institution, which has permanent legal force; or
- There is a certain situation or incident prescribed in the work agreement, the company Regulations, or the collective labor agreement that may effectively result in the termination of employment. A work agreement does not end because the entrepreneur dies or because the ownership of the company has been transferred because the company has been sold, bequeathed to an heir, or awarded as a grant.
- In the event of a transfer of ownership of an enterprise, the new entrepreneur shall bear the responsibility of fulfilling the entitlements of the worker/laborer unless otherwise stated in the transfer agreement, which must not reduce the entitlements of the worker/laborer.
- If the entrepreneur, individual, dies, his or her heir may terminate the work agreement after negotiating with the worker/laborer.
- If a worker/laborer dies, his or her heir has a rightful claim to acquire the worker's entitlements according to the prevailing Laws and Regulations or to the entitlements that has been prescribed in the work agreement, the company Regulations, or the collective labor agreement.

If either party in a work agreement for a specified time terminates the employment relations prior to the expiration of the agreement, or if their work agreement has to be ended for reasons other than what is given above, the party that terminates the relation is obliged to pay compensation to the other party in the amount of the worker's/laborer's wages until the expiration of the agreement.

D. Working Hours

The working hours are:

- 7 (seven) hours a day and 40 (forty) hours a week for 6 (six) workdays in a week; or
- 8 (eight) hours a day, 40 (forty) hours a week, for 5 (five) workdays in a week.

> The provisions concerning the working hours above do not apply to certain business sectors or certain types of work.

Female workers/laborers who feel pain during their menstruation period, and notify the entrepreneur about this, are not obliged to come to work on the first and second day of menstruation. The implementation shall be regulated in work agreements, the company Regulations or collective labor agreements.

> Entrepreneurs are under an obligation to provide workers with adequate opportunity to perform their religious obligations.

Entrepreneurs are under an obligation to provide proper opportunities to female workers/laborers, whose babies still need breastfeeding, to breast-feed their babies if that must be performed during working hours.

Every worker/laborer who uses her right to take the period of rest as specified under* item E below, shall receive her wages in full.

E. Wages and Leave Entitlements

Every worker/laborer has the right to earn a living that is decent from the viewpoint of humanity. The wages policy that protects workers/laborers shall include:

- Minimum wages;
- Overtime pay;
- Paid-wages during the absence;
- Paid-wages because of activities outside of his job that he has to carry out;
- Wages payable because he uses his right to take a rest;
- The form and method of the payment of wages;
- Fines and deductions from wages;
- Other matters that can be calculated with wages;
- Proportional wages structure and scale;
- Wages for the payment of severance pay; and
- Wages for calculating Income Tax.

The Government shall establish/set minimum wages based on the need for decent living by taking into account productivity and economic growth. The minimum wages may consist of:

- Provincial or district/city-based minimum wages;
- Provincial or district/city-based sectorial minimum wages.

The amount of wages set based on an agreement between the entrepreneurs and the worker/laborer or trade/labor union must not be lower than the amount of wages set under the prevailing Laws and Regulations.

> Entrepreneurs are prohibited from paying wages lower than the minimum wages. Entrepreneurs who are unable to pay minimum wages may be allowed to make postponement.

No wages will be paid if workers/laborers do not perform work. However, the entrepreneur shall be obliged to pay the worker/laborer's wages if the worker/laborer does not perform work because of the following reasons*:

- The workers/laborers are ill;
- The female workers/laborers are ill on the first and second day of their menstruation period;
- The workers/laborers get married, marry off their children, have their sons circumcised, have their children baptized, or because the worker/laborer's wife gives birth or suffers from a miscarriage, or because the wife or husband or children or children-in-law(s) or parent(s) or parent-in-law(s) of the worker/laborer or a member of the worker/laborer's household dies;
- The workers/laborers are carrying out or fulfilling their obligations to the State;
- The workers/laborers are performing religious obligations ordered by their religion;
- The workers/laborers come to work and are willing to work as promised but the employer does not provide the work as promised;
- The workers/laborers are exercising their right to take a rest;
- The workers/laborers are performing their trade union duties with the permission from the entrepreneur; and
- The workers/laborers are undergoing an education program required by their enterprise.

If a wages is composed of basic wage and fixed allowances, the amount of the basic wage must not be less than 75% (seventy five percent) of the total amount of the basic wages and fixed allowances.

Any claim for the payment of the worker/laborer's wages and all other claims for payments that arise from an employment relation shall expire after the lapse of 2 years since such the right is arose.

F. Trade/Labor Union

Every worker/laborer has the right to form and become member of a trade/labor union.

In performing functions, a trade/labor union shall have the right to collect and manage fund and be accountable for the union's finances, including for the provision of a strike fund.

The amount of the strike fund and procedures for collecting it as mentioned above shall be regulated under the union's constitution and/or the union's by-laws.

G. Industrial Relations

- In conducting industrial relations, the Government shall perform the function of establishing policies, providing services, taking control and taking actions against any violations of statutory manpower Laws and Regulations.
- In conducting industrial relations, workers/laborers and their organizations unions shall perform the function of performing their jobs/ work as obliged, working order to ensure production, channeling their aspirations democratically, enhancing their skills and expertise and helping promote the business of the enterprise and fight for the welfare of their members and families.
- In conducting industrial relations, entrepreneurs and their associations shall perform the function of creating partnership, developing business, diversifying employment and providing welfare to workers/laborers in a transparent and democratic way and in a way that upholds justice.

Industrial relations shall be applied through:

- Trade/ Labor Unions;
- Entrepreneurs' Organizations;

- Bipartite Cooperation Institutions;
- Tripartite Cooperation Institutions;
- Company Regulations;
- Collective Labor Agreements;
- Statutory Manpower Laws And Regulations; and
- Industrial Relations Dispute Settlement Institutes.

H. Entrepreneur's Organization

Every entrepreneur has the right to form and become a member of entrepreneurs' organization. The provisions concerning entrepreneurs' organizations shall be regulated in accordance with the prevailing Laws and Regulations.

I. Bipartite Cooperation Institution

- Every enterprise employing 50 (fifty) worker/laborers or more is under an obligation to establish a bipartite cooperation institution.
- The bipartite cooperation institution shall function as a forum for communication and consultation on labor issues at an enterprise.
- The membership composition of the bipartite cooperation institution shall include the entrepreneur's representatives and the worker / laborer's representatives who are democratically appointed by workers/laborers to represent the interests of the worker/laborer in the relevant enterprise.
- The provisions concerning the procedures for establishing the membership of the bipartite cooperation institution shall be regulated with a Ministerial Decision.

J. Tripartite Cooperation Institution

- Tripartite cooperation institution shall provide considerations, recommendations and opinions to the Government and other parties involved in policy making and problem solving concerning labor issues/ problems.
- The tripartite cooperation institution shall consist of:
  - ☐ The National Tripartite Cooperation Institution and the Provincial, District/City Tripartite Cooperation Institutions; and
  - ☐ Sector-based National Tripartite Cooperation Institution and sector-based Provincial, District/ City Tripartite Cooperation Institutions.
- The membership of tripartite cooperation institutions shall consist of representatives from the Government, entrepreneurs' organizations and trade/labor unions.
- Procedures and organizational structures of tripartite cooperation institutions shall be regulated with a Government Regulation.

K. Employing Foreigners

Every employer that employs a foreign worker is under an obligation to obtain written permission from the Minister.

> An individual person is prohibited from employing a foreign worker.

Employers of a foreign worker must have a plan concerning the utilization of a foreign worker that are legalized by the Minister or appointed official.

The plans for the utilization of a foreign worker shall at least contain the following information:

- The reasons why the service of a foreign worker is needed or required;
- The position and/or occupation of the foreign worker within the organizational structure of the enterprise;
- The timeframe set for the use of the foreign worker; and
- The appointment of an Indonesian worker as associate for the foreign worker.

The Regulation of the Minister of Labor of the Republic of Indonesia No. 16 of 2015[72] amended by No. 35 of 2015 on Procedure on Foreign Manpower[73], and the Regulation of the Minister of Labor No. 13 of 2015 on the Positions that can be occupied by foreign workers in the category rental services, employment, travel agents, and other business supports, screening services group and domestic employment in the country[74], described as follows:

---

[72] *Peraturan Menteri Ketenagakerjaan Republik Indonesia No. 16 Tahun 2015 Tentang Tata Cara Penggunaan Tenaga Kerja Asing. Jakarta. 29 Juni 2015. Menteri Ketenagakerjaan Republik Indonesia, M. Hanif Dhakiri. Diundangkan tanggal 29 Juni 2015, Menteri Hukum dan HAM Republik Indonesia, Yasonna H. Laoly. Berita Negara Republik Indonesia 2015 No. 964.*

[73] *Peraturan Menteri Ketenagakerjaan Republik Indonesia No. 35 Tahun 2015 Tentang Perubahan Atas Peraturan Menteri Ketenagakerjaan No. 16 Tahun 2015 Tentang Tata Cara Penggunaan Tenaga Kerja Asing. Jakarta. 23 Oktober 2015. Menteri Ketenagakerjaan Republik Indonesia, M. Hanif Dhakiri. Promulgated on 23 October 2015 by Director General Legislation Indonesian Ministry of Laws and Human Rights, Widodo Ekatjahjana. Berita Negara Republik Indonesia 2015 No. 1599. Kepala Biro Hukum, Budiman, SH*

[74] *Keputusan Menteri Ketenagakerjaan Republik Indonesia No. 13 Tahun 2015 tentang Jabatan yang dapat diduduki oleh tenaga kerja asing pada kategori jasa persewaan, ketenagakerjaan, agen perjalanan dan penunjang usaha lainnya, kelompok jasa penyeleksian dan penempatan tenaga kerja dalam negeri. 14 Januari 2015. Menteri Ketenagakerjaan Republik Indonesia. M. Hanif Dhakiri*

> TKA (Foreign Employee) can be employed as:
>
> - Member of the Board of Directors, or Trustees members, Board members, members of the Supervisory;
> - TKA for emergency and urgent nature of work;
> - TKA for temporary work;
> - TKA for impresario service business; and
> - Marketing Director.

A TKA employer who will hire foreign workers must have RPTKA (Foreign Workers Plan, Rencana Penggunaan Tenaga Kerja Asing) authorized by the Minister or a designated official. RPTKA used as the basis for IMTA (Entry Expatriate - Entry Permit). When all the requirements are met, within three days, a decision on endorsement or RPTKA is issued by:

- Director General, to the employer who employs fifty (50) TKA or more
- Director, to the employer who employs less than fifty (50) TKA

> An IMTA is valid for one year, and may be extended in accordance with the Ministerial Decree on positions that can be occupied by TKA or RPTKA.

IMTA is the base of the application for:

- Issuance of Visa approval;
- Issuance and extension of Temporary Stay Permit (Ijin Tinggal Terbatas, ITAS);
- Change of Status ITAS to ITAP/Permanent Resident (Ijin TInggal Tetap); and
- Extension of ITAP.

IMTA should be extended every year in line with ITAP. The IMTA will be given for the maximum of two years if the TKA is the member of Board of Directors, or Trustees members, Board members, members of the Supervisory.

> RPTKA is valid in all provinces in Indonesia.

IMTA for Marketing Director valid for 5 years; can be extended.

21 Occupational Health and Safety

Note from Author: There are translations of Laws and/or Regulations in this Chapter. I emphasized readability rather than word-for-word. When there are contradictions and discrepancies as to interpretation of any provision of the Law, the original version of the Law written in Bahasa Indonesia shall prevail.

The Law No. 13 of 2003[75] states that every worker/laborer has the right to receive protection on:

- Occupational safety and health;
- Morality and decency; and
- Treatment that shows respect to human dignity and religious values.

Every enterprise is under an obligation to apply an occupational safety and health management system that shall be integrated into the enterprise's management system.

The Indonesian Law No. 1 of 1970 regarding Workplace Safety[76].

The Law regulates safety requirements in the planning, manufacturing, transportation, distribution, trade, installation, application, implementation, maintenance and storage of

---

[75] The Act of the Republic of Indonesia No. 13 of 2003 on Manpower dated 25 March 2003. Signed by Ms. Megawati Soekarnoputri, Indonesian President. Promulgated in Jakarta by State Secretary of the Republic of Indonesia, Bambang Kesowo. State Gazette No. 39 of 2003.

[76] Undang Undang No. 1 Tahun 1970 tentang Keselamatan Kerdja. Djakarta. 12 Djanuari 1970. Soeharto, Djenderal TNI. Ditetapkan di Djakarta pada tanggal 12 Djanuari 1970 Sekretaris Negara Republik Indonesia, Alamsjah, Major Djenderal T.N.I. Lembaran Negara Republik Indonesia Tahun 1970 Nomor 1.

materials, goods, products and technical production apparatus containing and can cause danger or accidents.

Conditions are contained principles of technical science collected as provisions that are arranged in order, are clear and practical, and includes the fields of construction, materials, processing and manufacturing, equipment protection tools, testing and validation, packing or wrapping, labeling, goods, technical products, and production personnel, to ensure the safety of the goods itself, the safety of workers, and public safety.

The Indonesian Minister of Labor and Transmigration Regulation No. PER-01/MEN/1980 on Safety and Health in Building Construction[77]:

- The Safety Act is enforced by MOMT (Ministry of Manpower and Transmigration);
- Regulates safety in all workplaces under the jurisdiction of the Republic of Indonesia, whether on land, in the soil, surface water, in water or in the air.
- Can be designated as work rooms or other fields which may endanger the safety or health of the workers or one in the room or field.

Through the MOMT, the Government of Indonesia has accorded increasing priority to OHS (Occupational health and safety) and the improvement of working conditions. MOMT is now actively promoting OHS, and stressing the importance of adherence to OHS principles and Regulations, in order to reduce the number of industrial accidents. Enforcement of OHS obligations remains an issue.

---

[77] *Peraturan Menteri Tenaga Kerja dan Transmigrasi No. PER-01/MEN/1980 tentang Keselamatan dan Kesehatan Kerja pada Konstruksi Bangunan. Jakarta 6 Maret 1980. Harun Zain.*

MOMT imposes obligations on employers including:

- Duties on managers;
- The requirement to establish safety and health committees in certain circumstances;
- Provide personal protective equipment (PPE);
- Obligations with respect to the application of an OHS Safety Management System;
- Obligation to provide occupation accident security;
- First aid obligations;
- Pre-employment safety obligations including health checks;
- Obligations in relation to workplace conditions; and
- Accident reporting requirements.

The Regulation of the Minister of Manpower and Transmigration of the Republic of Indonesia No. PER.02/MEN/I/2011 dated 26 January 2011 concerning Promotion and Coordination of the Labor Inspection Implementation[78], Article 6:

The improvement of performance through the optimal implementation of task and function, covers:

- Formulation of a labor inspection work plan based on the analytical result of the labor inspection object and adjusted to the development of technology and regional social economic need;
- Data development of objective labor inspection as the basis of formulation of the risk mapping of the manpower norms, and stipulation of norms, standards, procedure and criteria;

---

[78] The Regulation of the Minister of Manpower and Transmigration of the Republic of Indonesia No. PER.02/MEN/I/2011 dated 26 January 2011 on Promotion & Coordination of the Labor Inspection Implementation. Drs. H.A. Muhaimin Iskandar, M.Si. Promulgated in Jakarta on 26 January 2011 by Indonesian Minister of Law & Human Rights, Patrialis Akbar. Statute Book of the Republic of Indonesia of 2011 No. 39

- Dissemination of manpower norms to the public;
- Management of labor inspection activity in the form of examination, testing and investigation;
- Issuance of permit to use production equipment, validation of equipment/installation and protection facility, granting recommendation of Occupational Safety and Health (OSH) at the work plan;
- Determination of work accident and/or sickness due to work;
- Determination of wages calculation and/or overtime pay;
- Promotion of the establishment and improvement of the activity of the Occupational Safety and Health Committee (P2K3);
- Promotion and empowerment of Service Company of Occupational safety and Health (PJK3) and evaluation of the result of the activities.
- Promotion of establishment and improvement of activity of the work norms' candidate;
- Promotion of the Expert of Occupational Safety and Health, company's doctor and/or doctor who examines the works' health, SMK3 auditor, official, operator, and technician in the field of Occupational safety and Health (K3);
- Promotion of the establishment of the action committee of the elimination of worst forms of child labor;
- Promotion in preventing the discrimination for the application of manpower norms;
- Granting award in the manpower field;
- Coordination and cooperation with the related institution and profession association; and
- Reporting the result of labor inspection activity.

The Regulation of the Minister of Manpower and Transmigration of the Republic of Indonesia No. PER.15/MEN/XI/2011 dated 17 November 2011 on Information Network of Labor Inspection[79]:

The Information Network of Labor Inspection consist of:

- Network center; and
- Network members.

The network center is managed by the Directorate General. The network members consist of:

- The work unit of labor inspection in the institution with the scope of task and responsibility of the manpower within the Provincial Government;
- The work unit of labor inspection in the institution with the scope of task and responsibility of the manpower within the Regency/City Government; and
- Other parties.

Other parties as meant shall cover:

- Committee of Occupational Safety and Health (P2K3);
- Institution/organization/body that related to the task and function of the labor inspection pursuant to the prevailing Laws and Regulations.

To become the network member, the other party shall obtain approval from the Director General.

---

[79] *The Regulation of Indonesian Minister of Manpower & Transmigration No. PER.15/ MEN/XI/2011 dated 17 Nov 2011 on Information Network of Labor Inspection. Drs. H.A. Muhaimin Iskandar, M.Si. Enacted in Jakarta on 17 November 2011 by Indonesian Minister of Law & Human Rights Amir Syamsuddin. State Gazette No. 709 of 2011.*

The Law of Republic Indonesia No. 36 of 2009 on Health[80]:

- Everyone deserves a healthy environment for the achievement of the health status.
- Everyone has the right to obtain health information and education about a balanced and responsible.
- Everyone has the right to obtain information about her health data including measures and treatments that have been or will be received from health professionals.
- Every person is obliged to come to realize the high importance of maintaining and improving the health of communities.
- Everyone is obliged to respect the rights of others in an effort to obtain a healthy environment, whether physical, biological, and social.
- Every person is obliged to live in a healthy way to achieve, maintain, and promote a healthy lifestyle.
- Everyone is obliged to maintain and improve the health of other people for whom they are responsible.
- Every person is obliged to participate in the social health insurance program that is regulated by Law.

---

[80] *Undang Undang Republik Indonesia No. 36 Tahun 2009 tentang Kesehatan. 13 Oktober 2009. Dr. H. Susilo Bambang Sudhoyono. Diundangkan tanggal 13 Oktober 2009. Menteri Hukum dan HAM Republik Indonesia. Andi Mattalatta. Lembaran Negara Republik Indonesia Tahun 2009 No. 144.*

22 Intellectual Property[81]

Note from Author: There are translations of Laws and/or Regulations in this Chapter. I emphasized readability rather than word-for-word. When there are contradictions and discrepancies as to interpretation of any provision of the Law, the original version of the Law written in Bahasa Indonesia shall prevail.

Indonesia is a signatory to the Trade Related Aspects of Intellectual Property Rights Agreement (TRIPS), a schedule to the General Agreement on Tariffs and Trade Agreement (GATT) of the WTO. Indonesia has also ratified the Paris Convention for Protection of Intellectual Property and the Convention Establishing the World Intellectual Property Organization (the WIPO Convention). Following ratification of these conventions, Indonesia passed several legislative instruments to improve its compliance with TRIPS, the Paris Convention and the WIPO Convention.

IP rights registrable in Indonesia include patents, trademarks, designs and copyright. Registration is the basis upon which intellectual property rights in Indonesia are typically claimed. Foreign businesses that do not have a place of business in Indonesia must lodge IP applications through an Indonesian IP attorney or agent.

The Government body responsible for the administration, registration and enforcement of IP rights is the Directorate General of Intellectual Property Rights (DJHKI/DGIP). The DGIP website (www.dgip.go.id) provides a searchable database for patents, trademarks, designs and copyright registrations.

---

[81] *Direktorat Jenderal Kekayaan Intelektual, Kementerian Hukum dan Hak Asasi Manusia, Indonesia. http://www.dgip.go.id*

A. Patent

1. Term of Patent Protection

- According to Article 8, Paragraph 1 of Law No. 14 of 2001, Patent is granted for a period of 20 years from the date of receipt and the period cannot be extended.
- According to Article 9 of Law No. 14 of 2001, Patent is granted for a period of 10 years from the date of receipt and the period cannot be extended.

2. Violations and Penalties

Imprisonment of 4 years and/or a maximum fine of IDR500,000,000.00 (Five hundred million Rupiah) to any person who deliberately and without rights infringes any patent holder to perform any of the actions that make, use, sell, import, lease, assign, or available for sale or rental or delivery of the patented product and to use the patented production process to make products and other actions.

Imprisonment of 4 years and/or a fine of IDR250,000,000.00 (Two hundred and fifty million Rupiah) to any person who deliberately and without rights infringes any Simple Patent holder to perform any action that make, use, sell, import, lease, assign, or available for sale or rent or delivery of patented product and to use the patented production process to make products and other actions.

3. Substantive Examination Request

Request for substantive examination filed by filling out the form provided in Indonesian language, attaching payment receipt of application fee of IDR2,000,000 (Two million Indonesian Rupiahs) for the Patent, or IDR350,000 for Simple Patent.

B. Trademark

Trademark is a brand used on goods traded by a person or persons jointly or a corporation to differentiate the product with other similar items.

Applicant, the party who filed the petition, namely:

- People/Individual;
- Association; and
- Legal entities (CV, Firm, Company).

1. Trademark License

The owner of the registered mark is entitled to grant a license to other parties with an agreement that the licensee to use the brand for some parts or whole products or services. License agreement should be recorded by DJHKI; the owner to pay for some recording fees. The registration effect relevant parties legally.

2. Basic Trademark Protection

Law No. 15 of 2001 regarding Trademark (UUM)[82].

3. Elimination of Registered Trademark

Registered marks can be eliminated because of the four possibilities, namely:

- On the initiative DJHKI;
- On the request of the owner of the Trademark;

---

[82] *Undang Undang Republik Indonesia No. 15 Tahun 2001 Tentang Merek. Signed by Ms. Megawati Soekarnoputri, the President of Indonesia on August 1, 2001. Promulgated in Jakarta by Mr. Muhammad M. Basyuni, Indonesian Minister Secretary of the State on August 1, 2001. Gazette No. 110 of 2001.*

- The court's decision based on the elimination;
- Not extended period of registration of its Trademark.

The reason for the elimination of registration of the mark, namely:

The brand is not used for 3 consecutive years in the trade of goods and/or services from the date of registration or use of the latter, unless there is a reason that can be accepted by DJHKI, such as:

- The import ban;
- The prohibition relating to permits for circulation of goods that use brand concerned or a decision of the authorities that are temporary; or other similar prohibitions stipulated by Government Regulation;
- Brand used for the type of goods/or services that are not in accordance with the type of goods and/or services applied for registration, including the use of a brand that does not comply with the registration.
- Registered marks can be canceled by a commercial court decision that desultory Law remains on the lawsuit stakeholders pursuant to Article 4, Article 5 and Article 6 UUM.

4. Authority

The authority to hear the elimination or registered trademark lawsuit is the commercial court.

5. Period of Legal Protection of The Registered Mark

Trademark receives legal protection period of 10 years, and is valid from the date of receipt of the letter of application. Upon the request of the owner of the Trademark, the protection period may be extended each time for the same period of time.

6. Extension of the Term of Protection of the Trademark

May be submitted in writing by brand owners or their proxies within a period of 12 months prior to the expiration of the term of protection.

7. Sanctions for Perpetrators of Criminal Acts in the Field of Brand

- Imprisonment of 5 years and/or a fine of IDR1,000,000,000 (One Billion Rupiah) to any person who intentionally and without right to use the Trademark of another party for goods and/or services produced and/or traded (Article 90 UUM).

> The nature of the offense of Trademark criminal seizure is complaint-based offense.

- Imprisonment of 4 years and/or a fine of IDR800,000,000 (Eight hundred million Rupiah) to any person who intentionally and without right to use the same brand in principle with the trademark of another party for goods and/or services produced and/or traded (Article 91 UUM).
- Sanctions for the person/party who empowers the infringing goods or services referred to above

Article 94 Paragraph (1) UUM states: "He who empowers the goods and/or services that are known or should be known that the goods and/or services are the result of the offenses referred to in Article 90, Article 91, Article 93, shall be punished a maximum confinement of 1 year or a fine of not more IDR200,000,000 (Two hundred million Rupiah)."

C. Copyright

Copyright council is appointed and dismissed by the President on the proposal of the Ministry of Justice and Human Rights, that have the tasks to assist the Government in providing counseling, guidance and coaching copyright. The council members consist of representatives of the Government, representatives of professional organizations and community members who have competence in the field of copyright.

Intellectual Property Rights (IPR) Consultant is intellectual property consultant who is officially registered in the Directorate General of Intellectual Property.

Copyright Law (UUHC) was first regulated in Laws No. 6 of 1982 on Copyright. Subsequently amended by Law No.7 of 1987. In 1997 has amended again with the Law No. 12 of 1997. In 2002, the UUHC has amended in Law No.19 of 2002. Some of the implementing Regulations in the field of copyright are as follows:

- Indonesian Government Regulation No. 14 of 1986 Jo Indonesian Government Regulation No.7 of 1989 on Copyrights Council;
- Indonesian Government Regulation No.1/1989 on the Translation and/or Multiple Copyrights for the Benefit of Education, Science, Research and Development;
- Indonesian Government Regulation No. 17/1988 on the Agreement on Mutual Legal Protection Against Copyright on Phonogram between the Republic of Indonesia to the European Communities;
- Indonesian Presidential Decree No. 25/1989 on the Ratification of Agreement on Mutual Legal Protection Against Copyright between Indonesia and USA;
- Indonesian Presidential Decree No. 38/1993 on the Ratification of Agreement on Mutual Legal Protection Against Copyright between Indonesia and Australia;

- Indonesian Presidential Decree No. 56/1994 on the Ratification of Agreement on Mutual Legal Protection Against Copyright between Indonesia and UK;
- Indonesian Presidential Decree No. 18/1997 on Ratification Berne Convention for the Protection of Literary and Artistic Works;
- Indonesian Presidential Decree No. 19/1997 on Ratification WIPO Copyrights Treaty;
- Indonesian Presidential Decree No. 74/2004 on Ratification of WIPO Performances and Phonogram Treaty (WPPT);
- Indonesian Minister of Justice Regulation No. M.01-HC.03.01 of 1987 regarding Registration of Invention;
- Indonesian Minister of Justice Regulation No. M.04.PW.07.03 of 1988 on Copyright Investigation;
- Indonesian Ministry of Justice Circular No. M.01.PW.07.03 of 1990 regarding the Authority of investigating criminal acts on copyrights;
- Indonesian Ministry of Justice Circular No. M.02.HC.03.01 of 1991 on the obligation to attach Tax Identification Number in the Invention Registration and Recording of Transfer of Reserved Rights.

Term of Protection One Creation

- The copyright in the invention (in accordance with the provisions of Article 29 of Law HC):
  - ☐ Books, pamphlets, and all other written works;
  - ☐ Drama or musical drama, dance, choreography;
  - ☐ All forms of art, such as painting, sculpture and art Sculpture;
  - ☐ Batik art;
  - ☐ Song or music with or without lyrics;
  - ☐ Architecture;
  - ☐ Lectures, lectures, speeches and other similar creatures;
  - ☐ Props;

- ☐ Map; and
- ☐ Translation, interpretation, adaptation and potpourri.
- The copyright is valid for the life of the author and continues until 50 years after the author dies. If owned by 2 or more persons, the copyright is valid for life of the author who died most recently and lasts up to 50 years thereafter.
- The copyright in the creation (in accordance with the provisions of Article 30 of Law HC)
  - ☐ Computer programs, cinematography, database, photography, works resulting from adaptations shall be valid for 50 years since it was first announced;
  - ☐ Changeable a published work shall be valid for 50 years since first published;
- If a creation is owned or held by a legal entity, the copyright is valid for 50 years since it was first announced.
- Copyright owned/held by the state is based on:
  - ☐ Article 10 Paragraph (2) UUHC valid indefinitely;
  - ☐ Article 11 (1) and (3) UUHC valid for 50 years since it was first published.

D. Industrial Designs

1. Priority Rights

Priority Right is the right of an applicant to file an application originated from countries that are members of the Paris Convention for the Protection of Industrial Property or the Agreement Establishing the World Trade Organization to obtain acknowledgment that the Filing Date filed to the destination country, which is also a member of the Paris Convention or the Establishment Agreement of the World Trade Organization, having the same date of the Receipt Date in the country of origin during the period of time specified in the Paris Convention.

Application for priority rights should be filed at the latest of 6 months from the date of receipt of the application was first received by other countries that are members of the Paris Convention for the Protection of Industrial Property or the Agreement Establishing the World Trade Organization.

2. Industrial Design Rights

Industrial Design Rights is an exclusive right granted by the Republic of Indonesia to a Designer for his/her creation for a given period of time, or to give permission to another party to use the right.

3. Exclusive Right

Exclusive rights is the right to carry out industrial design and to prohibit others without the owner's consent to make, use, sell, import, export and/or distribute goods given industrial design.

4. Basic Protection of Industrial Design

- Law of the Republic of Indonesia Number 31 of 2000 regarding Industrial Design, which became effective December 20, 2000
- Indonesian Government Regulation No. 1 of 2005 on the Implementation of the Law of the Republic of Indonesia Number 31 of 2000 regarding Industrial Design.
- Right Holder of Industrial Design entitled to grant a license to other parties under licensing agreement to conduct acts as referred to in Article 9, unless otherwise agreed.
- License agreements shall be recorded in the General Register of Industrial Designs at the Directorate General with the payment of fee as regulated in this Law.

- License Agreement that is not recorded in the General Register of Industrial Designs shall not apply to any third party.
- License agreement referred to in Paragraph (1) shall be announced in the Official Gazette of Industrial Designs.

5. License

- Industrial Design Right Holder may grant a license to other parties under licensing agreement to conduct acts as referred to in Article 9, unless otherwise agreed.
- License agreements shall be recorded in the General Register of Industrial Designs at the Directorate General, some fees apply as regulated in this Law.
- License Agreement that is not recorded in the General Register of Industrial Designs shall not apply to any third party.
- License agreement as referred in Paragraph (1) shall be announced in the Official Gazette of Industrial Designs.

6. The Form and Content of the License Agreement

- License agreements shall not contain provisions that may cause adverse effects on the Indonesian economy or contain provisions which result in unfair competition as stipulated in the legislation in force.
- The Directorate General shall refuse registration of a licensing agreement that contains the provisions referred to in Paragraph (1).
- The provisions concerning the recording of a licensing agreement regulated by Presidential Decree.

7. Protected Industrial Design

Industrial Design

Industrial design is considered new if, on the Filing Date, such industrial design is not the same as previous disclosures, although there may be some similarities.

Previous disclosure, referred to is the disclosure of which before:

- Receipt date; or
- Priority date, if the application is filed with priority right;
- Has been announced or used in Indonesia or outside Indonesia.

An industrial design has not been published if within a period of 6 months prior to the Filing Date, the industrial design:

- Has been displayed in a national or international exhibition in Indonesia or overseas that is official or officially recognized; or has been used in Indonesia by the designer in an experiment with the purpose of education, research or development.
- Does not conflict with the legislation in force, public order, religion and morality.

8. Cancellation of Industrial Design

Registered Industrial Design has been can be canceled by:

a. Rights Holders on Request

Registered industrial design may be canceled by DJHKI upon written request submitted by the right holder. If the industrial design has been licensed, there must be a written consent of the licensee recorded in the public register of industrial design, which is attached to the registration cancellation request. If there is no agreement, the cancellation cannot be done.

b. A Lawsuit (Court Decision)

The lawsuit cancellation of registration of industrial designs may be submitted by interested parties on the grounds referred to in Article 2 or Article 4 UUDI to the Commercial Court. The decision of the Commercial Court submitted to DJHKI 14 (fourteen) days after the date of the judgment.

9. Term of Protection of Industrial Designs

Protection of the Rights of Industrial Design granted for a period of 10 years from the filing date. The start date of the protection period referred recorded in the General Register of Industrial Designs and published in the Official Gazette of Industrial Designs.

10. Request Objections to Industrial Design

Since the announcement of the commencement date of application for industrial design, each party may file a substantive objection to DJHKI by paying a fee for each filing objections to any petition filed objections. The appeal must be received by the Directorate General, at the latest, 3 months from the date of commencement of the announcement. The applicant can submit a rebuttal to objections submitted to DJHKI later than 3 months from the date of notification by DJHKI.

23 Environmental Regulations

Note from Author: There are translations of Laws and/or Regulations in this Chapter. I emphasized readability rather than word-for-word. When there are contradictions and discrepancies as to interpretation of any provision of the Law, the original version of the Law written in Bahasa Indonesia shall prevail.

The relevant Law in relation to environmental Regulation is contained in the Law No.32 of 2009 on Environmental Protection and Management and its supplementary Regulations. Government controls the prevention, countermeasures, and recovery management of environment[83].

One of the instruments used by Governments in the prevention of environmental pollution is the AMDAL. AMDAL (Analisis Mengenai Dampak Lingkungan Hidup), Environmental Impact Analysis, is a study on important impact of a business and/or planned activities on the environment that is necessary for the process of making decision in business and/or activities.

Every business and/or activity that may raise significant Indonesian environmental impacts must prepare an AMDAL. The AMDAL document is reviewed by an AMDAL appraisal commission and, based on the commission's recommendation, the Minister, Governors or Regents/Mayors decides on the environmental feasibility or infeasibility of the business and/or activity.

---

[83] *Undang Undang Republik Indonesia Nomor 32 Tahun 2009 Tentang Perlindungan dan Pengelolaan Lingkungan Hidup. Presiden Republik Indonesia. Jakarta, 3 October 2009. Dr. H. Susilo Bambang Yudhoyono. Diundangkan di Jakarta pada tanggal 3 Oktober 2009. Menteri Hukum dan Hak Asasi Manusia Republik Indonesia, Andi Mattalatta. Lembaran Negara Republik Indonesia Tahun 2009 Nomor 140.*

Every business and/or activity that is not required to prepare an AMDAL must have an environmental management and monitoring program (UKL-UPL). Governors or Regents/Mayors are required to stipulate the kinds of businesses and/or activities that must have a UKL-UPL. Businesses and/activities not required to have either an AMDAL or a UKL-UPL are obliged to prepare a statement of readiness to manage and monitor the environment.

Every business or activity that is required to obtain an AMDAL or UKL-UPL is required to hold an environmental license. Significant impacts are determined based on the following criteria:

- Number of residents affected by business plan and/or activities;
- Area affected;
- Intensity and duration of the impact;
- Environmental components that will be affected;
- Cumulative nature of the effects;
- Turning or irreversibility of the impact; and/or
- Other criteria in accordance with the development of science and technology.

Business criteria and/or activities that have an important impacts that must be equipped with EIA consists of:

- Changing the form of land and the landscape;
- Exploitation of natural resources, both renewable and non-renewable;
- Processes and activities that potentially can cause pollution and/or damage to the environment and waste of natural resources and a decline in utilization
- Processes and activities which may affect the natural environment, artificial environment, as well as the social and cultural environment;

- Processes and activities which will affect the preservation of natural resource conservation and/or protection of cultural heritage;
- Introduction of species of plants, animals, and microorganisms;
- The manufacture and use of biological and non-biological materials;
- Activities that have a high risk and/or affect national defense; and/or
- The application of the technology is expected to have great potential to affect the environment.

An environmental license will only be issued by the Minister of Environment/Governor/Regent/Mayor after receiving or reviewing an AMDAL or UKL – UPL recommendation. In this respect, a decision on the environmental feasibility of a business and/or activity is the basis of the issuance of an environmental license.

Environmental licenses are a pre-condition to the acquisition of activity or business licenses from different Ministries. The elucidation of this provision states that a business and/or activity license includes a license with another name, such as an operating permit and construction permit. If an environmental license is revoked, all licenses subsequently obtained as a result of the environmental license, such as any activity or business licenses, will also be revoked.

The determination of the occurrence of environmental pollution is measured through environmental quality standards:

- Water quality standards;
- Waste water quality standard;
- Sea water quality standard;
- Air quality standard;
- Emissions quality standard;
- Disturbances quality standard; and

- Other quality standards in accordance with the development of science and technology

AMDAL document contains:

- Assessment of the impact of the business and/or activities plan;
- Activities evaluation of the area location of the business and/or activities;
- Public feedback and responses to the business plan and/or activities;
- Forecasts of the magnitude and nature of the important impact that occurs when a business plan and/or the activity implemented;
- Holistic evaluation of the impact that occurred to determine the eligibility or ineligibility of the environment; and
- Management plans and environmental monitoring.

Every business and/or activity that is required to have an AMDAL or environmental impact analysis or UKL-UPL is required to have an environmental permit. Environmental permits issued by the Minister, governor or regent/mayor, in accordance with their authority.

In order to preserve the environment, Government and Local Governments are required to develop and implement environmental economic instruments.

The environmental economic instruments shall include:

- Economic development activities planning;
- Environment funding; and
- Incentives and/or disincentives.

Instruments of economic development activities planning include:

- The balance of natural resources and the environment;
- Preparation of gross domestic product and gross regional domestic product which includes the depletion of natural resources and environmental damage;
- Compensation mechanism/environmental services rewards among regions; and
- Environmental costs internalization.

Environmental funding instruments include:

- Environmental restoration guarantee fund;
- Pollution and/or damage prevention and restoration of the environment fund; and
- Trust fund/support for conservation.

Incentives and/or disincentives, among others applied in the form:

- Procurement of goods and services that are environmentally friendly;
- The application of taxes, levies, and environmental subsidies;
- Financial institutions development system and environmentally friendly stock market;
- Development of waste disposal permit trading system and/or emissions;
- The development of environmental services payment system;
- Environmental insurance development;
- The development of environmentally-friendly labeling system; and
- The performance reward system in the field of environmental protection and management.

24 Other Costs Of Doing Business

A. Man Power Costs

1. Minimum wage per month by province[84]

No.	Province	2014 IDR/Month	2015 per Month	
			IDR	USD
1	N. Aceh D.	1,750,000	1,900,000	152.00
2	N. Sumatera	1,505,850	1,625,000	130.00
3	W. Sumatera	1,490,000	1,615,000	129.20
4	Riau	1,700,000	1,878,000	150.24
5	Riau Island	1,665,000	1,954,000	156.32
6	Jambi	1,502,230	1,710,000	136.80
7	S. Sumatera	1,825,600	1,974,346	157.95
8	B. Belitung	1,640,000	2,100,000	168.00
9	Bengkulu	1,200,000	1,500,000	120.00
10	Lampung	1,399,037	1,581,000	126.48
11	W. Java	Varies by region		
12	C. Java	Varies by region		
13	E. Java	Varies by region		
14	DKI Jakarta	2,441,000	2,700,000	216.00
15	Banten	1,325,000	1,900,000	152.00

[84] *Indonesia Ministry of Manpower and Transmigration*
 Exchange Rate: USD1 = IDR12,500

No.	Province	2014 IDR/Month	2015 per Month IDR	2015 per Month USD
		Continued from previous page...		
16	DI Yogyakarta	Varies by region		
17	Bali	1,542,600	1,621,712	129.74
18	W.Kalimantan	1,380,000	1,560,000	124.80
19	C. Kalimantan	1,723,970	1,896,367	151.71
20	E. Kalimantan	1,886,315	2,026,126	162.09
21	S. Kalimantan	1,620,000	1,870,000	149.60
22	EN Tenggara	1,150,000	1,250,000	100.00
23	WN Tenggara	1,210,000	1,330,000	106.40
24	Maluku	1,415,000	1,650,000	132.00
25	N Maluku	1,440,746	1,577,000	126.16
26	Gorontalo	1,325,000	1,600,000	128.00
27	N Sulawesi	1,900,000	2,150,000	172.00
28	S Sulawesi	1,800,000	2,000,000	160.00
29	C Sulawesi	1,250,000	1,500,000	120.00
30	S E Sulawesi	1,400,000	1,652,000	132.16
31	W Sulawesi	1,400,000	1,655,500	132.44
32	Papua	1,900,000	2,193,000	175.44
33	W Papua	1,870,000	2,015,000	161.20

2. Average Monthly Salary based on Level and Position in Indonesia, 2014[85]

Position	Level Experience	Per Month	
		IDR	USD (approx.)
	Fresh Grad. Collage	2 – 3,KK	150 – 225
Assistant Manager	3 – 5 years	5 – 8,KK	370 – 600
Manager/Chief	7 – 10 years	10 – 15,KK	750 – 1,200
General Mgr		20 – 30,KK++	1,500 – 2250
Div. Mgr/ President/Dir/Exe.		50 – 100,KK	3,700 – 7,400
Finance Director/ CFO	12 years +	75 – 135,KK	5,500 – 10,000
Financial Ctrler	10 – 12 years	35 – 50,KK	2,600 – 3700
Finance Mgr	6 – 7 years	22 – 28,KK	1,600 – 2,000
Engineering Dir.	10+ years	55 – 80,KK	4,000 – 6,000
Engineering Mgr	10+ years	30 – 45,KK	2,250 – 3,350
Production Eng.	3 – 5 years	3.5 – 6,KK	260 – 450
HR Senior Exe./ Officer	3 – 6 years	5 – 12,KK	370 – 900
Learn&Dev. Mgr	5 – 8 years	17 – 28,KK	1,260 – 2,100
HR Manager	5 – 10 years	15 – 25,KK	1,200 – 1,900
IT Country Mgr	10+ years	75 – 150,KK	5,600 – 11,200

---

[85] Source: Dunia Lowongan Kerja (Indonesian's World Job Vacancies) 2014 http://infolokersatu.blogspot.com/2014/11/daftar-standar-gaji-di-indonesia-untuk-berbagai-posisi.html

Position	Level Experience	Per Month	Position
Continued from previous page...			
Sales Regional Dir	7+ years	50 – 75,KK	3,700 – 5,560
Acc/Sales Mgr	5+ years	20 – 35,KK	1,500 – 2,600
System/Netw. Adm.	2 – 6 years	5 – 9,KK	370 – 700
Adm./Office Mgr	4 – 6 years	10 – 15,KK	750 – 1,200
Adm. Asst./Co-coordinator	1 – 3 years	1.8 – 2.750,K	150 – 200
Executive Secretary	3 – 5 years	6.250 – 9,KK	470 – 700
Dist., Supply Chain & Logistic Mgr	6 – 7 years	20 – 25,KK	1,500 – 1,900
Shipping Supervisor	4 – 5 years	4.5 – 6,KK	350 – 450
Shipping Assistant	1 – 3 years	3.5 – 6,KK	260 – 450
Ship Op Director	10 – 15 years	45 – 90,KK	3,350 – 6,700
Ship Comm. Director	10 – 15 years	55 – 100,KK	4,100 – 7,500
Ship Cold Hub Mgr	6 – 8 years	20 – 25,KK	1,500 – 1,900
Purchasing C. Specialist	5 – 8 years	5 – 8.5,KK	375 – 650
Purchasing CS Manager	5 – 8 years	10 – 17,KK	750 – 1,300
Logistic Manager	6 – 10 years	22 – 33,KK	1,650 – 2,500
Logistic Specialist	2 – 4 years	4 – 7,KK	300 – 550
Sup Chain Manager	6 – 10 years	30 – 45,KK	2,250 – 3,350
Bus. Process Improv. Manager	6 – 10 years	25 – 35,KK	1,900 – 2,600

B. Comparative Wages in Selected Countries[86]

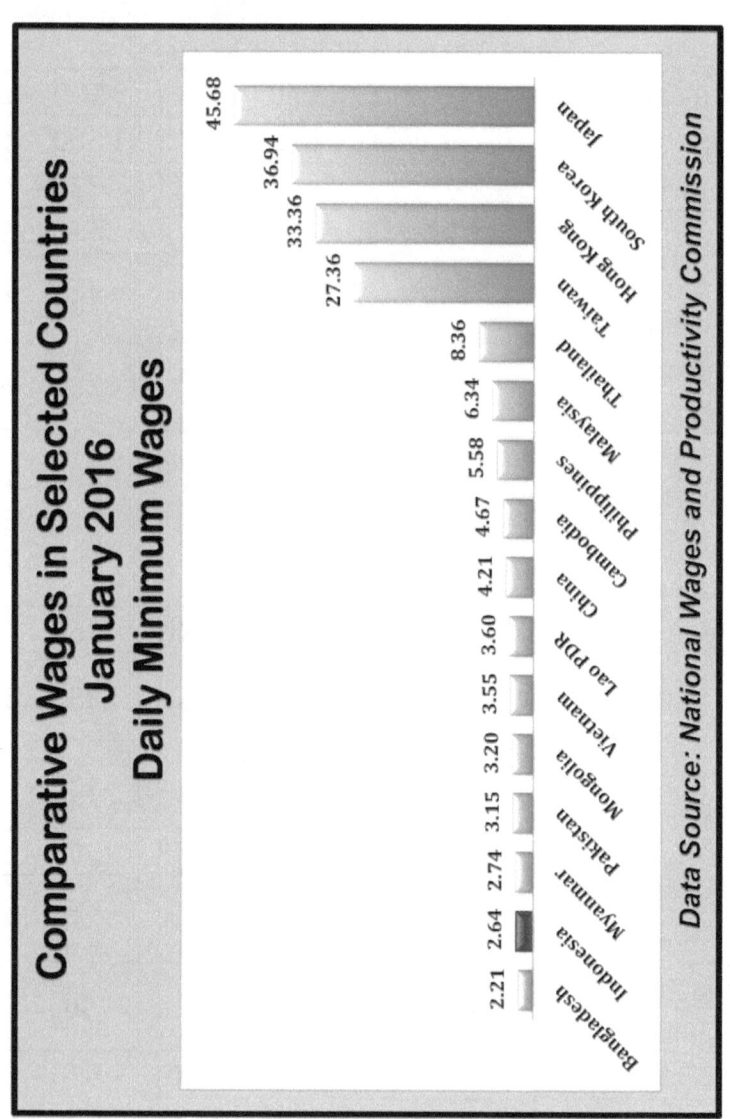

---

[86] Data Source: Department of Labor and Employment, National Wages and Productivity Commission, Philippines
http://www.nwpc.dole.gov.ph/pages/statistics/stat_comparative.html

- Bangladesh (Taka, BDT): Minimum wage for the garment industry, 2013, every 5 years.
- Indonesia (Rupiah): Minimum Wage in DKI Jakarta IDR3,100,000 (highest) and Java Tengah IDR1,100,000 (lowest) effective for the year 2016.
- Myanmar (Kyat): National Minimum wage for all sectors industries at MMK3,600/day effective, September 1, 2015
- Pakistan (Rupee): In June 2014 the Federal Government has raised the minimum wage from PKR10,000 to PKR12,000/month for unskilled workers.
- Mongolia (Tughrik): The minimum hourly wage rate was set to MNT1,142.85 effective September 1, 2013
- Viet Nam (Dong): New minimum wage, varying from VND 2,400 to 3,500 million effective January 1, 2016
- Lao (Kip): Minimum wage set at LAK900,000/month (US$111/month) effective April 1, 2015
- China (Yuan Renminbi): Lowest minimum wage is in Guangxi (at CNY830/month). Highest min. wage is in Shanghai (at CNY1,820/month)-effective 2015
- Cambodia (Riel): Effective Jan. 1, 2016 to Dec 31, 2016, minimum wage for the garment & shoe industry is KHR560,000 at US$ Cambodian riel exchange rate at KHR4000/US$
- Philippines Region IVA (Peso): Highest daily minimum wage in Non-Agri. is PHP362.50 in IV-A (Growth Corridor Area), and the lowest minimum wage is PHP267.00 (Resourced Based Area)-effective May 1, 2014.
- Thailand (Baht): As of January 1, 2013 the Minimum Wage Rates in Thailand is set at THB300 (US10.34) per day
- Taiwan (New Dollar): TWD120/hour, effective July 1, 2015
- Hong Kong (Dollar): Effective May 1 2015 the SMW is HK$32.50/hour.
- Malaysia (Ringgit): Introduction of the country's first minimum wage. The minimum wage set at MYR800/month in the states of Sabah and Sarawak and on the island of

Borneo and MYR900/month for workers on the Malaysian Peninsula
- South Korea (Won): Minimum wage level at KRW5,580/hour, Effective 2015
- Japan (Yen): The highest minimum wage is Kochi's at JPY910/hour (JPY7,280 for an 8-hr/day) while the lowest is ¥647/hr. JPY5,176 for an 8hr day in Kumamoto, updated March 23, 2014

Daily equivalent of MW computed using 30 days
Monthly equivalent of DMW computed using 30 days.

C. Some Samples of Rental Charge and Service Charge per m2/Month in South Jakarta for June 2015[87]:

Name	RC m²/month	SC m²/month	RC+SC m²/month
ANZ Tower	USD24	IDR90,000	–
Chase Plaza	IDR245,000	IDR95,000	–
IFC Tower II	IDR440,000	IDR90,000	–
Wisma BNI	USD32	USD7.5	–
Wisma Keiai Prince	USD27	USD8.5	–
Landmark Tower	–	–	USD32
Sampoerna Strategic	USD39	IDR90,000	–
Ratu Plaza	–	–	USD26
Sentral Senayan	USD57	USD7	–

[87] *Source: Multiple online advertisements sources*
http://sewakantorjakarta.org
http://www.sewakantor.org

Name	RC m²/month	SC m²/month	RC+SC m²/month
Continued from previous page...			
BEJ IDX I	USD19	USD7.85	–
Equity Tower	USD54	IDR50,000	–
Wisma Indocement	USD16	IDR100,000	–
Wisma GKBI	–	–	USD50
World Trade Centre I	USD34	IDR95,000	–
World Trade Centre II	USD44	IDR95,000	–
World Trade Centre VI	USD24	IDR95,000	–

D. Fuel Costs IDR/Liter Oct – Nov 2015[88]

No.	Province	Pertamax	Pertamax Plus	Pertamina Dex
1	Nanggroe Aceh	10,950	11,150	12,900
2	N Sumatera	10,750	11,150	12,400
3	West Sumatera	10,850	–	12,600
4	Riau	–	11,650	12,950
5	Riau Island	–	11,150	12,400
6	Batam	–	10,750	11,600
7	B Belitung	10,950	–	14,000
8	S. Sumatera	10,950	11,450	12,500
9	Jambi	10,950	–	12,950
10	Lampung	10,950	–	12,500

---

[88] *Indonesian Magazines "Daftar Harga BBM" 2015*

No.	Province	Pertamax	Pertamax Plus	Pertamina Dex
	Continued from previous page...			
11	Banten	9,300	10,200	11,900
12	Jakarta	9,300	10,300	11,900
13	West Jawa	9,300	10,300	11,900
14	DI Yogyakarta	9,300	10,300	12,300
15	Central Java	9,400	10,300	12,300
16	East Java	9,400	10,350	12,300
17	Bali	9,500	10,400	13,050
18	WN Tenggara	10,900	11,200	13,100
19	EN Tenggara	11,300	–	–
20	S Kalimantan	10,500	–	13,400
21	C Kalimantan	10,500	–	13,400
22	E Kalimantan	10,500	–	–
23	N Kalimantan	10,600	–	14,050
24	Gorontalo	11,900	–	–
25	West Sulawesi	11,750	–	14,050
26	S. Sulawesi	11,200	–	14,050
27	C. Sulawesi	11,400	–	–
28	SE Sulawesi	11,500	–	–
29	N. Sulawesi	11,500	–	–
30	Maluku	12,350	–	21,700
31	N. Maluku	13,750	–	–
32	Papua	13,150	18,300	21,700
33	West Papua	13,650	–	–

E. Water Tariff[89]

Subscriber	Block and Usage Tariff IDR per M³		
	0 – 10 M³	11 – 20 M³	> 20 M³
Type I	1,050	1,050	1,050
Type II	1,050	1,050	1,575
Type III A	3,550	4,700	5,500
Type III B	4,900	6,000	7,450
Type IV A	6,825	8,150	9,800
Type IV B	12,550	12,550	12,550
Type V/Special	14,650	14,650	14,650

F. Electricity Costs[90]

The Regulation of the Minister of Energy and Mineral Resources No. 31/2014 on tariffs of the electric power supplied by PT. Perusahaan Listrik Negara (PLN), the State Power Company[91]

---

[89] *Indonesian Investment Coordinating Board*
[90] *Source: PT. Perusahaan Listrik Negara*
[91] *Peraturan Menteri Energi dan Sumber Daya Mineral Republik Indonesia No. 31 Tahun 2014 Tentang Tarif Tenaga Listrik yang Disediakan oleh Perusahaan Perseroan (Persero) PT Perusahaan Listrik Negara. Signed by Mr. Sudirman Said, the Minister of Energy and Mineral Resources on November 5, 2014. Promulgated in Jakarta by Mr. Yasonna H. Laoly, the Minister of Laws and Human Rights on November 5, 2014. State Gazette No 1770 of 2014.*

A. Energy Cost For Business

Group	Limit	Cost Load IDR/kVA/Month	Usage Costs (IDR/kWh) and kVArh Costs (IDR/kVArh)	Prepaid IDR/kWh
B-1/TR	450 VA	23,500	Block 1: 0–30kWh : 254 Block 2: >30kWh : 420	535
B-1/TR	900 VA	26,500	Block 1: 0–108kWh : 420 Block 2: >108kWh : 465	630
B-1/TR	1,300 VA	*|	966	966
B-1/TR	2,200 VA – 5,500 VA	*|	1,100	1,100
B-2/TR	6,600 VA – 200 kVA	*|	1,352	1,352
B-3/TR	200kVA and up	**|	Block WBP = K x 1,020 Block LWBP=1,020 kVArh = 1,117 ***|	–

*| Minimum Bill (RM 1) = 40 (hour of usage) x power connected (kVA) x Cost of Usage

**| Minimum Bill (RM2) = 40 (hour of usage) x power connected (kVA) x Cost of Usage LWBP.

        Hour of usage: kWh per month divided by connected kVA

***| The cost of excess consumption of reactive power (kVArh) imposed in terms of the average power factor of each month less than 0.85

K	Comparison factors between WBP and LWBP price in accordance with the characteristics of local electrical system load (1.4 ≤ K ≤ 2), determined by the Board of Directors of PT. Perusahaan Listrik Negara
WBP	Peak Time Load
LWBP	Outside Peak Time Load

B. Energy Cost For Industrial Needs

Group	Limit	Cost Load IDR/ kVA per Month	Usage Costs (IDR/kWh) and kVArh Costs (IDR/kVArh)	Prepaid IDR/ kWh
1-1/TR	450VA	26,000	Block 1: 0–30kWh : 160 Block 2: >30kWh : 395	485
1-1/TR	900VA	31,500	Block 1: 0–108kWh : 315 Block 2: >108kWh : 405	600
1-1/TR	1,300VA	*|	930	930
1-1/TR	2,200VA	*|	960	960
1-1/TR	3,500VA – 14kVA	*|	1,112	1,112
1-2/TR	>14kVA – 200 kVA	**|	Block WBP = K x 972 Block LWBP = 972 kVArh = 1,057 ****|	–
1-2/TR	>14kVA – 200 kVA	**|	Block WBP = K x 972 Block LWBP = 972 kVArh = 1,057 ****|	–

Group	Limit	Cost Load IDR/ kVA per Month	Usage Costs (IDR/kWh) and kVArh Costs (IDR/kVArh)	Prepaid IDR/ kWh
		Continued from previous page...		
1-3/TR	> 200kVA	**|	Block WBP = K x 1,115 Block LWBP = 1,115 kVArh = 1,200 ****|	–
1-3/TR	30,000kVA and up	***|	Block WBP and LWBP = 1,191 kVArh = 1,191 ****|	–

*\| Minimum Bill (RM 1) = 40 (hour of usage) x power connected (kVA) x Cost of Usage

**\| Minimum Bill (RM2) = 40 (hour of usage) x power connected (kVA) x Cost of Usage LWBP.

***\| Minimum Bill (RM3) = 40 (hour of usage) x power connected (kVA) x Cost of Usage WBP and LWBP.

      Hour of usage: kWh per month divided by connected kVA

****\| The cost of excess consumption of reactive power (kVArh) imposed in terms of the average power factor of each month less than 0.85

K   Comparison factors between WBP and LWBP price in accordance with the characteristics of local electrical system load ($1.4 \leq K \leq 2$), determined by the Board of Directors of PT. Perusahaan Listrik Negara

WBP   Peak Time Load

LWBP Outside Peak Time Load

25 Travel and Visa

Note from Author: There are translations of Laws and/or Regulations in this Chapter. I emphasized readability rather than word-for-word. When there are contradictions and discrepancies as to interpretation of any provision of the Law, the original version of the Law written in Bahasa Indonesia shall prevail.

A. Visa On Arrival[92]

- Is given for 30 days stay;
- Can be extended in Immigration Office for one time, to have another 30 days stay;
- Issued by Indonesian Immigration at Indonesian main international airports; and
- Foreigners can apply this visa upon arrival in Indonesia, if the nationality included on Visa On Arrival countries list.

> 75 countries are exempted to enter Indonesia for Tourist Visa included the United States and Canada.

Requirements:

- Passport – validity 6 months; and
- Return/Through Ticket.
- Important: Keep the "small portion" of immigration card together with your passport for your return/out of Indonesia

---

[92] Direktorat Jenderal Imigrasi Indonesia. http://www.imigrasi.go.id

B. Visit Visa[93]

- Is given for 60 days stay;
- Issued by Indonesian Embassy or Consulates, or the guarantor could apply to the Directorate General of Immigration in Jakarta, Indonesia;
- Can be extended in Immigration Office for 5 time;
- Each extension will be given another 30 days stay; and
- Foreigners that travel frequently to Indonesia for Family, Business, and Governmental visit purposes may choose this type of visa.

Requirements:

- Passport – validity 6 months for single, 18 months for multiple;
- Application Letter & Guarantee Letter;
- Copy of Bank Accounts;
- Return/Through Ticket; and
- Re-entry Permit – for a stateless/non nationality person.

C. Multiple Visit Visa

- Valid for one year; and
- A holder of Multiple Visit Visa is given up-to 60 days stay each visit and can't be extended.

Requirements:

- Passport – validity 18 months;
- Application Letter & Guarantee Letter;
- Copy of Bank Accounts;

---

[93] *Direktorat Jenderal Imigrasi Indonesia.* http://www.imigrasi.go.id

- Return/Through Ticket; and
- Re-entry Permit – for a stateless/non nationality person.

D. Indonesian Domestic Luggage Policies

Garuda Indonesia[94]

Free Carry On Item*

Hand baggage suitable for placing in the closed overhead rack or under the passenger's seat with maximum dimensions specified by the carrier. The carry on baggage may have a maximum dimension of LxWxD = 56x36x23cm = 22x14x9", or the maximum sums of the three dimensions do not exceed 115cm = 45.27", exception for Economy class CRJ and ATR: maximum LxWxD = 41x34x17cm = 16x13.38x6.69", however the sums of the three dimensions shall not exceed 92cm = 36.22" or weight of 7Kg = 15.43Lbs.

> **Safety tips**: It is recommended to lock your luggage with TSA lock before leaving your country, and during domestic travels in Indonesia.

Checked In Luggage*

	First Class	Business Class	Economy Class
Adult	40 Kg=88 Lbs	40 Kg=88 Lbs	20 Kg=44 Lbs
Children	30 Kg=66 Lbs	30 Kg=66 Lbs	10 Kg=22 Lbs
Infant	20 Kg=44 Lbs	20 Kg=44 Lbs	10 Kg=22 Lbs

*Approximate conversion

---

[94] Garuda Indonesia. https://www.garudaindonesia.com.sg/travel-tips.shtml#Baggage-Information

Lion Air[95]

Free Carry On Item*

Passengers are allowed to carry luggage only 1 (one) piece with a maximum of weight 7Kg = 15.43Lbs, and maximum dimension of 40 x 30 x 20 cm = 15.75 x 11.81 x 7.87" and a bag of personal items for use during the trip (personal items). *

Cabin baggage is accepted subject in the cabin subject to availability of space in the overhead bin. Restricted stowage space is also available under the front seat. In the event no space being available in the aircraft to stow cabin baggage, it will be necessary to remove and load the same in the baggage hold as per safety Regulations.

Checked In Luggage*

	Business Class	Economy Class
Adult/Children	30 Kg = 66 Lbs	20 Kg = 44 Lbs

Approximate conversion

E. Major Infectious Diseases[96]

Bacterial diarrhea, hepatitis A, hepatitis E, typhoid fever, dengue fever, and malaria immunization and bring adequate medication supplies prior to departure is recommended.

Note: Highly pathogenic H5N1 avian influenza has been identified in this country; it poses a negligible risk with extremely rare cases possible among US citizens who have close contact with birds.

---

[95] *Lion Air:* https://secure2.lionair.co.id/LionResources/en/Condition_of_Carriage.pdf

[96] https://www.cia.gov/library/publications/the-world-factbook/geos/id.html

F. Customs Regulations[97]

All those who come from foreign countries are expected to fill the Indonesian Customs Declaration (usually distributed on the plane). You are expected to declare goods or money in a certain amount you bring from foreign country.

Passengers' goods are exempted from Customs Duties and Other Import Tax, if the value of goods carried less than FOB USD250 for each person or the value is less than FOB USD1,000 to each family.

If the value of the goods exceeds the amount, the passenger in the compulsory pays Customs Duties and Other Taxes Levied on the difference.

Foreign Passengers goods such as camera, video camera, radio cassette, binoculars, laptops or mobile phones to be used during their stay in Indonesia and will be taken back by the time they leave Indonesia also received exemption.

Individual is only emphasized to notify the amount of money to the Indonesian Customs officers if they bring in Indonesian Rupiah or other currency worth IDR100,000,000.00 or more.

Goods Subject To Excise Duty[98]:

- According to Law No. 39/2007, BKC is composed of:
  - ☐ Ethyl alcohol (EA) or ethanol, and
  - ☐ Beverages containing ethyl alcohol (MMEA)
- Tobacco products. Each person is allowed to bring cigarettes and alcoholic beverages to Indonesia in limited quantities

---

[97] *Direktorat Jendral Bea dan Cukai, Kementerian Keuangan Indonesia* http://www.beacukai.go.id

[98] *Undang Undang Republik Indonesia No. 39 Tahun 2007 Tentang Perubahan Atas Undang Undang No. 11 Tahun 1995 Tentang Cukai. Signed by Dr. H. Susilo Bambang Yudhoyono on August 15, 2007. Promulgated by Mr. Andi Mattalatta, Indonesian Minister of Laws and Human Rights on August 15, 2007. State Gazette No. 105 of 2007.*

as follows: Maximum 200 cigarettes or 50 cigars or 200 grams of tobacco slices; A maximum of 1 liter of alcohol and perfume in reasonable quantities or limit the amount previously mentioned are not obligated to pay Customs and Excise Duties and Other Taxes Levied.

26 Potential Investment Opportunities

Indonesia is entering an era of many and varied investment opportunities. The investor can take advantage of their natural resources to build manufacturing companies, combined with availability of work forces, strategic locations, high population, and a political climate favorable for international trade.

Samples of natural resources available in Indonesia:
- corn, cocoa, aloe Vera, coconut, rubber, cinnamon, mangosteen, soursop, vanilla, rattan, seaweed, steel, copper, manganese, and iron.

Samples of projects and industries sought after by Indonesia:
- Manufacturing, such as spare parts, auto parts and components, pharmaceutical products, computer hardware, metal / plastic / wood products, and animal feed.
- Construction, such as buildings, bridges, roads, railroads, toll roads, ports and airports, sea tolls, power plants, dams, industrial estates, and boat and ship building.

Bellow are some target projects described in the National Medium Term Development Plan (RPJM) 2015 –2019[99]:

EDUCATION

Indicator	2014 Baseline	2019
Can read and write above 15 years of age	94.1%	96.1%
Graduated university with minimum accreditation B	50.4%	68.4%
Middle School with minimum accreditation B	62.5%	81.0%
High School with minimum accreditation B	73.5%	84.6%
Trade Schools with minimum accreditation B	48.2%	65.0%

Policy Targets:

- Continued efforts to fulfill the right of people to receive quality basic education services;
- Improved access to quality secondary education;
- Strengthen the role of the private sector in providing quality secondary education service;
- Improved access to education and skills training services; and
- Improved quality of learning.

---

[99] *Ringkasan Rencana Pembangunan Jangka Menengah Nasional 2015-2019. Menteri Perencanaan Pembangunan Nasional / Kepala Bappenas. Medan 24 Januari 2015*

FOODS

Indicator	2014 Baseline	2019
Domestic Production (million Ton):		
■ Rice	70.6	82.0
■ Corn	19.13	24.1
■ Soy	0.92	2.6
■ Sugar	2.6	3.8
■ Beef	452.7	755.1
■ Seafood	12.4	18.8
Development, Improvement and Rehabilitation of Irrigation:		
■ Development and Improvement of surface irrigation lines, ground water and marsh (million Ha)	8.9	9.89
■ Rehabilitation of surface irrigation line, ground water and marsh (million Ha)	2.71	3.01
■ Development and improvement of fishpond irrigation (thousand Ha)	189.75	304.75
■ Reservoirs construction	21	49

Notes:

For the first three years, the focus is on self-supporting rice crops. Soy already is for domestic consumption, especially for tofu and tempeh. Sugar, beef and salt are for household consumptions.

Policy Targets:

1. Increase food supply through strengthening the capacity of domestic production
   Paddy: (i) Completion of sustainable land use (holding conversion of rice fields), field extension of 1 million ha, and expansion of irrigation networks; (ii) revitalization and extension of seeding systems, seed sovereign of 1000 villages, and 1000 villages using organic farming; (iii) banks for agriculture - SMEs - Cooperative; and
   Fishery products: 40 million tons (fish, etc.)
2. Increase public accessibility to foods: (i) construction of warehouses with post harvest facilities, control of imports through import mafia eradication; (ii) strengthening food reserves and the stabilization of food prices; (iii) development of a logistics system for fish.
3. Improve nutritional quality of food consumed by the community: (i) an appropriate balance of consumption of protein: eggs, fish, and meat; as well as vegetables and fruits; (ii) the use of local non-rice food.
4. Mitigate disruption to food sovereignty: (i) adapting seeds climate change, school climate and agricultural insurance.

INDONESIAN STAPLE FOOD PRODUCTION MAP

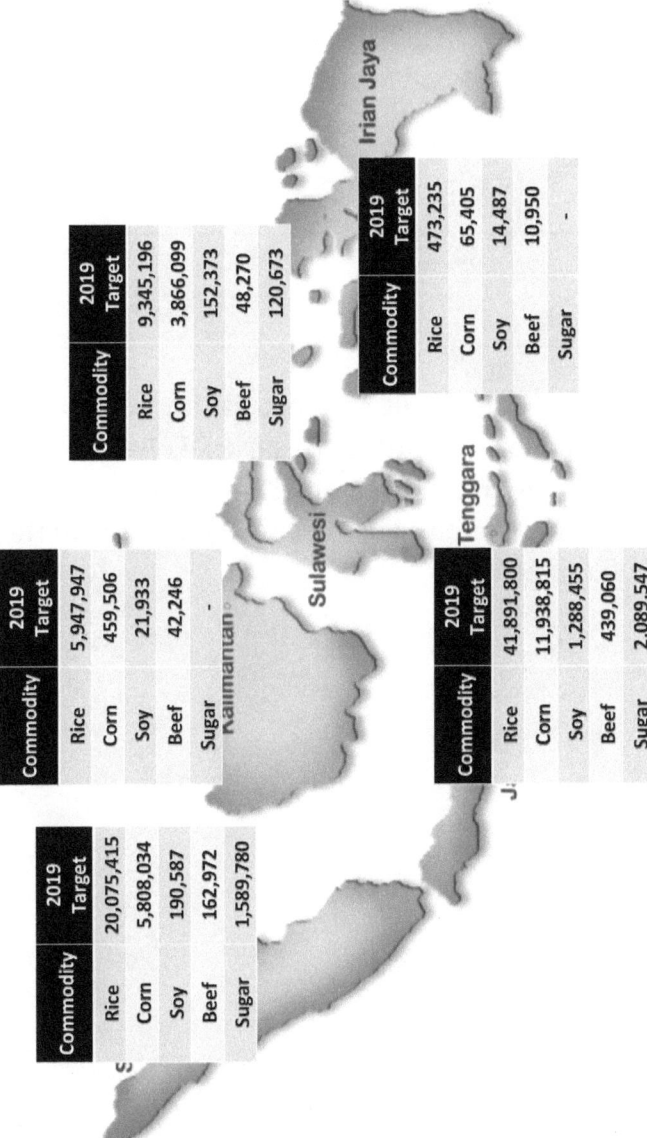

Source: Ringkasan Rencana Pembangunan Jangka Menengah Nasional (Rpjmn) 2015-2019 Kementerian Perencanaan Pembangunan Nasional/ Badan Perencanaan Pembangunan Nasional

Targets on Forest Management by Community 2015– 2019

Indicator	2015	2016	2017	2018	2019
Forest area managed by community*	2.54M	5.08M	7.62M	10.16M	12.7M
Total Watershed	5	7	10	12	15

M=million

Notes:

In the form of Community Forest (Hutan Kemasyarakatan, HKm), Village Forest (Hutan Desa, HD), People's Plantation Forest (Hutan Tanaman Rakyat, HTR), People's Forest (Hutan Rakyat, HR), Indigenous Forest and Partnership (Hutan Adat dan Kemitraan, HA).

The 49 Locations of Planned Dam Development

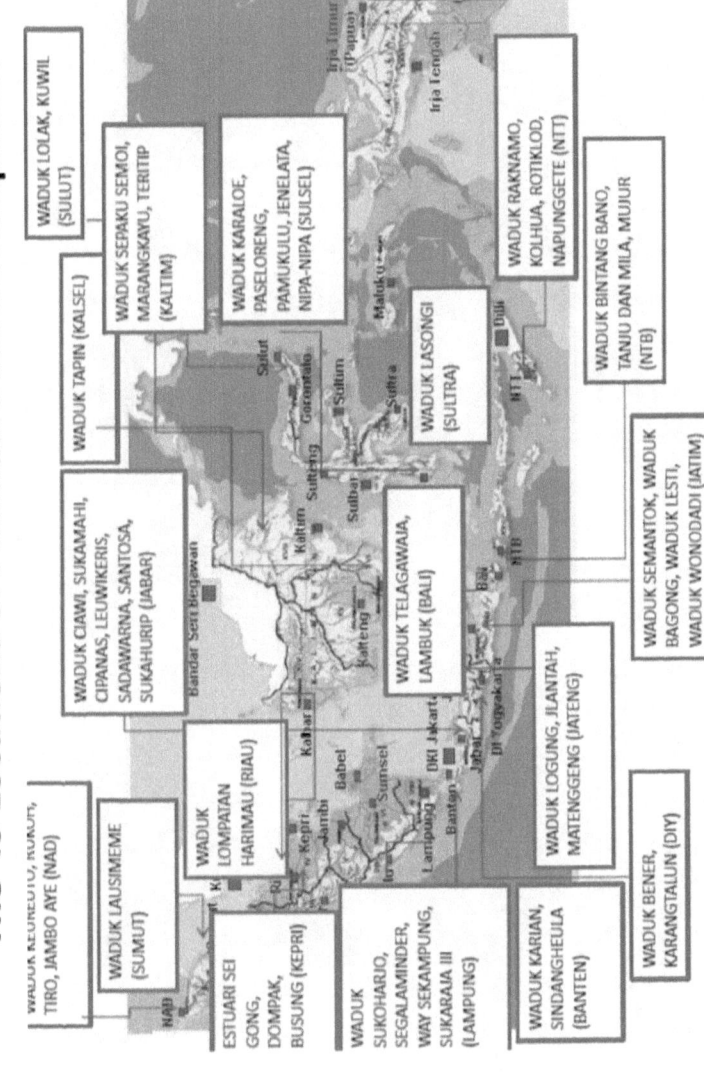

SOURCE: RINGKASAN RENCANA PEMBANGUNAN JANGKA MENENGAH NASIONAL (RPJMN) 2015-2019
KEMENTERIAN PERENCANAAN PEMBANGUNAN NASIONAL/ BADAN PERENCANAAN PEMBANGUNAN NASIONAL

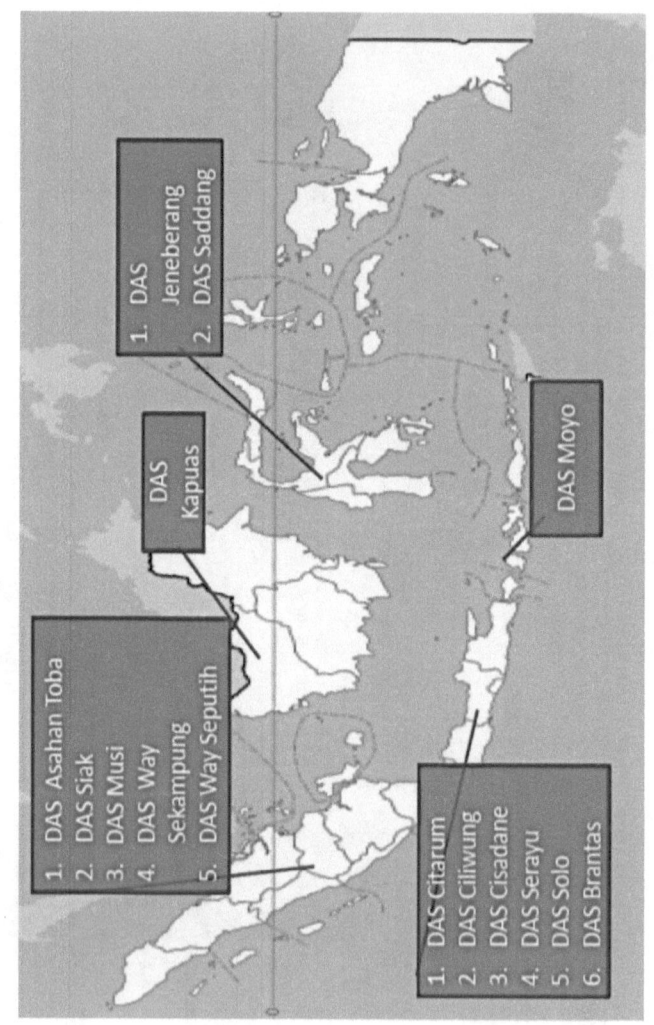

The Watersheds (DAS) to be Restored in 2015 - 2019

Source: Ringkasan Rencana Pembangunan Jangka Menengah Nasional (Rpjmn) 2015-2019 Kementerian Perencanaan Pembangunan Nasional/ Badan Perencanaan Pembangunan Nasional

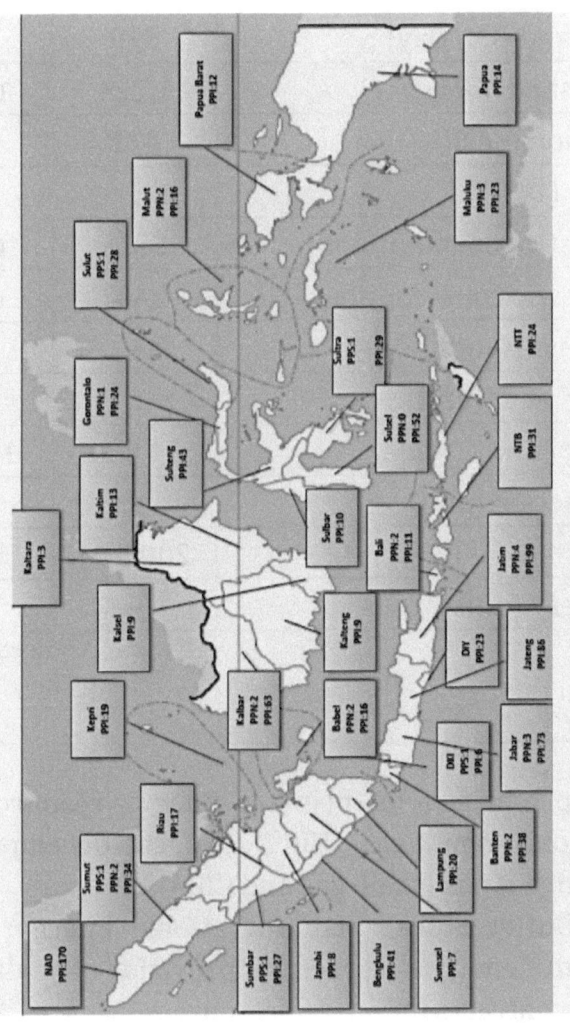

ENERGY

Indicators	2014 Baseline	2019*
Energy resources production enhancements:		
■ Oil (thousand BM/Day)	818	700
■ Gas (thousand SBM/Day)	1,224	1,295
■ Coal (million tons)	421	400
Domestic Use (DMO):		
■ Gas domestic consumptions	53%	64%
■ Coal domestic consumptions	24%	60%
Regasification onshore (unit)	–	6
FSRU Development (unit)	2	3
Gas pipe lines (Km)	11,960	17,960
SPBG Construction (unit)	40	118
City gas line	200,000	1m
New oil refinery (unit)	–	1

* with corporation

Policy Targets:

- Increase production of primary energy resources (oil, gas, and coal): new fields, IOR / EOR, the development of unconventional gas (shale gas and CBM).
- Increase Buffer Stocks and Operational Energy: (i) the government's energy reserves; (ii) provision of medium and long-term contracts for energy resources
- Increase the role of renewable energy in the energy mix: (i) incentives and the right price; (ii) use of biofuels.
- Improve accessibility: (i) encourage local use of energy resources; (ii) use of city gas; (iii) conversion of fuel oil into gas fuel.

- Increase efficiency in energy use: (i) developing incentives and funding mechanisms for saving technology / energy efficiency; (ii) energy audits; (iii) increasing the role of the energy services company (ESCO)
- Improve management, targeting and transparency of fuel subsidies.
- Harness the potential of water resources for hydroelectric power plants (electricity)

The electrification ratio and energy consumed per capita 2013

TERRITORY	Population 1000	House Hold 1000	Customers		KWh Sell		Electrification Ratio (%)	KWh Sell / Capita
			House Hold 1000	% of IDN	KWh 1000	% of IDN		
Sumatera	53,539.0	13,056.4	9,917	19.78	25,739	13.95	75.95	480.75
Java	141,985.6	38,193.2	31,655	63.13	137,029	74.28	82.88	965.09
Bali & NT	13,721.1	3,480.9	2,203	4.39	5,687	3.08	63.30	414.49
Kalimantan	14,751.4	3,674.4	2,617	5.22	6,988	3.79	71.23	473.74
Sulawesi	18,216.9	4,262.2	3,019	6.02	7,266	3.94	70.83	398.85
Maluku&Papua	6,604.1	1,537.2	733	1.46	1,773	0.96	47.72	268.48
Non Java	106,832.5	26,011.3	18,461	36.82	49,463	26.81	70.97	463.00
Indonesia	248,818.1	64,204.3	50,145	100.00	184,482	100.00	78.10	741.44

Communications

1. Universal Service Obligation serves the non-commercial communication and information service around borders and remote areas:
   - 575 base transceiver stations (BTS);
   - 100 broadcasting locations; and
   - 130 farming and fishing villages.
2. Broadband high-speed Internet use in big islands, regencies and cities:
   - Household 71% in the city; 49% in the village;
   - Mobile 100% in the city; 52% in the village; and
   - 4,000 locations: ports, schools, etc.

Internet Users
Total: 42.4 million, or 16.7% of population (2014 est.)[100]
Telephone Mobile Cellular
Total: 319 million.
Subscriptions per 100 inhabitants: 126 (2014 est.)

Maritime and Marine

Indicators	2014 Baseline	2019
■ Completion of registration of small islands in the United Nations	13,466	17,466 (completed in 2017)
■ Completion of maritime boundaries between countries	1 country	9 countries
Illegal fishing eradications:		
■ Increased adherence to fisheries	52%	87%

---

[100] CIA Library https://www.cia.gov/library/publications/resources/the-world-factbook/geos/id.html

Building national connectivity:		
■ Sea port developments to support sea tolls	–	24
■ Ferry port developments	210	270
■ Ship building	50 units	104 units
Maritime and marine economic development:		
■ Fishery product production (million tons)	22.4	40 – 50
■ Fishing port development	21 units	24 units
■ Marine conservation area enhancements	15.7M Ha	20M Ha

Policy Targets:

- Settlement boundaries and limits of the continental shelf beyond 200 nautical miles, as well as the registration and naming of islands.
- Regulation and control of the Indonesian Archipelagic Sea Lanes (Alur Laut Kepulauan Indonesia, ALKI).
- Strengthen sea surveillance agencies.
- Improve coordination in handling maritime criminal offenses.
- Promote development of a multimodal maritime transportation system.
- Achieve a balance between national, regional, and local maritime transportation.
- Accelerate development of a marine economy.
- Broaden the scope of the functions of the sea, and increase its capacity as a resource, while preserving the marine environment.
- Improve marine science and technology, develop greater insight into maritime culture, and strengthen maritime human resources.
- Enhance the dignity and standard of living of fishermen and coastal communities.

SEA TOLLS

Program	IDR Billion	
24 Ports	243,696	Including dredging, container terminals developments, land. Ships, Panjang Port, well, Bojanegara, Kendal, Pacitan, Cirebon. National ports master plans. 1,481 ports 83 ports Access roads, harbor railroad, coastal train. 12 shipyards, pioneer goods, bulk container, tug & barge, tanker and ships. Patrol boats class IA – V.
Short sea shipping	7,500	
General bulk cargo	40,615	
Non commercial ports	198,100	
Commercial Ports	41,500	
Transportation to the ports	50,000	
Shipbuilding revitalization	10,800	
Ships for 5 years	101,740	
Patrol boats	6,048	
Total	**699,999**	

Regulatory Framework of Indonesian Sea Toll

- Soft loan facility for the procurement of national ships;
- Financing through Special Allocation Funds (Dana Alokasi Khusus, DAK) for the procurement of people's boats;
- Adjustment of duty-free regulations, VAT, Income Tax for shipbuilding and supporting industries;
- More flexible rules on collateral bank guarantee; can use boat as a collateral;
- Adjustment on Regulation Permenhub 7/2013 concerning Obligation classification for Indonesian-flagged vessels on the classification board to reduce the cost of ship construction; and
- Increase domestic content level of national shipbuilding industry by 40% (new ships).

Complement concept of sea toll

Corridors	Conditions	Costs
North Belt	Pinang – Sintete is no connected. Will be done within 2017 – 2019	IDR40B
Central Belt	Wahai – Fak Fak is done in 2014. Service to be improve: ports and ships	
South Belt	Has been connected since 2013. Service to be improve: ports and ships	

Programs and Targets:

- Construction of ferry ports at 60 locations;
- Construction of 50 ferries;
- Separation of operators and regulators (establishment of port authority); and
- Construction of ships needed to overcome the bottleneck at the main traffic including the Merak – Bakauheni.

COMPLEMENT CONCEPT OF SEA TOLL

SOURCE: RINGKASAN RENCANA PEMBANGUNAN JANGKA MENENGAH NASIONAL (RPJMN) 2015-2019 KEMENTERIAN PERENCANAAN PEMBANGUNAN NASIONAL/ BADAN PERENCANAAN PEMBANGUNAN NASIONAL

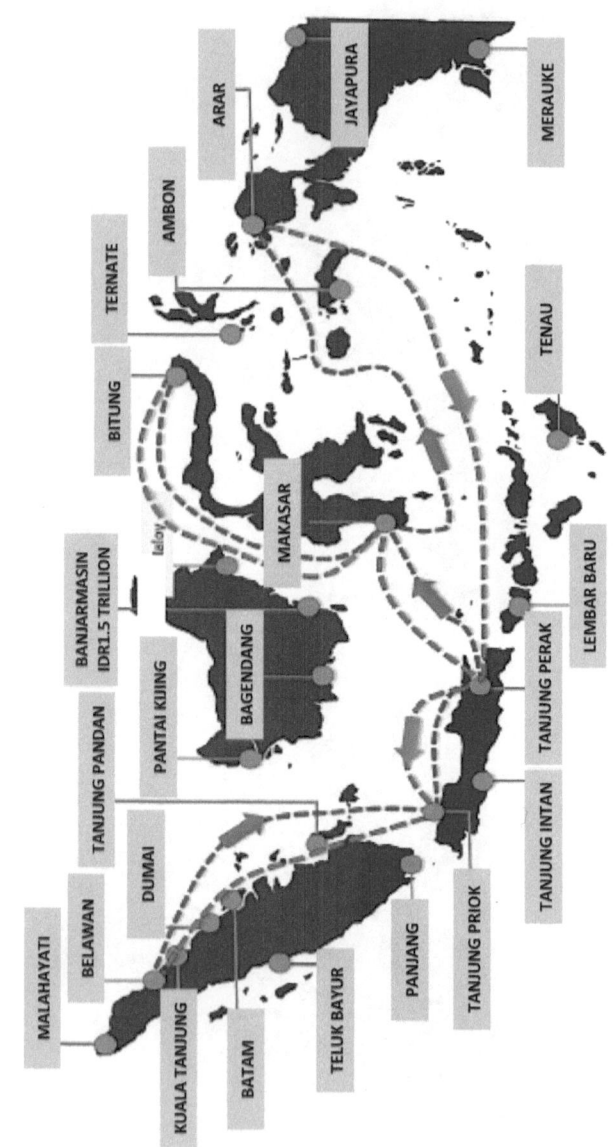

Source: Ringkasan Rencana Pembangunan Jangka Menengah Nasional (Rpjmn) 2015-2019 Kementerian Perencanaan Pembangunan Nasional/ Badan Perencanaan Pembangunan Nasional

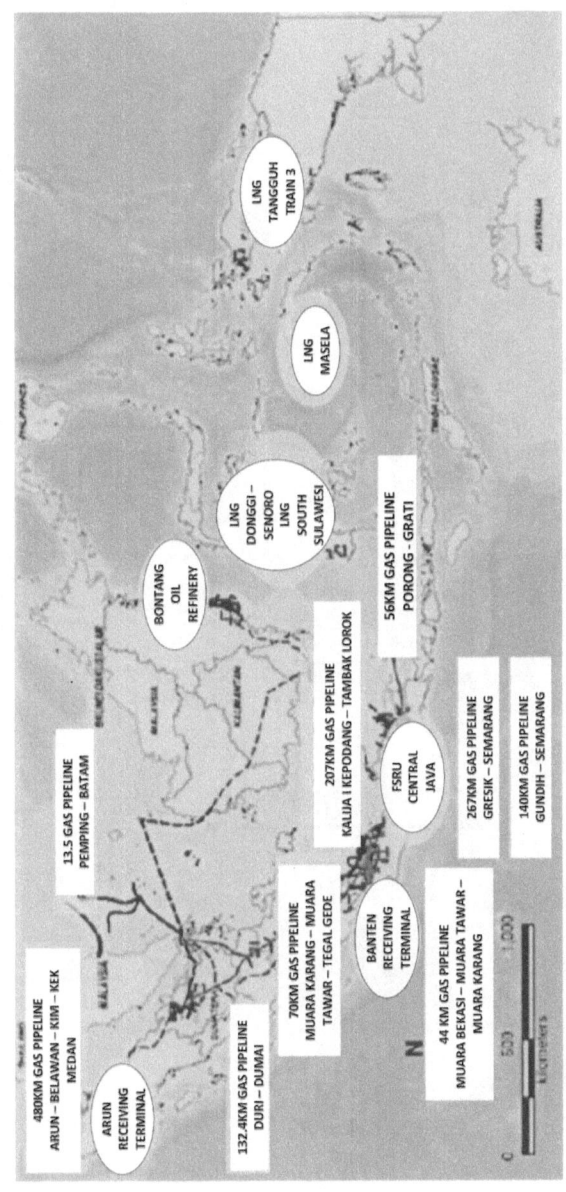

Source: Ringkasan Rencana Pembangunan Jangka Menengah Nasional (Rpjmn) 2015-2019
Kementerian Perencanaan Pembangunan Nasional/ Badan Perencanaan Pembangunan Nasional

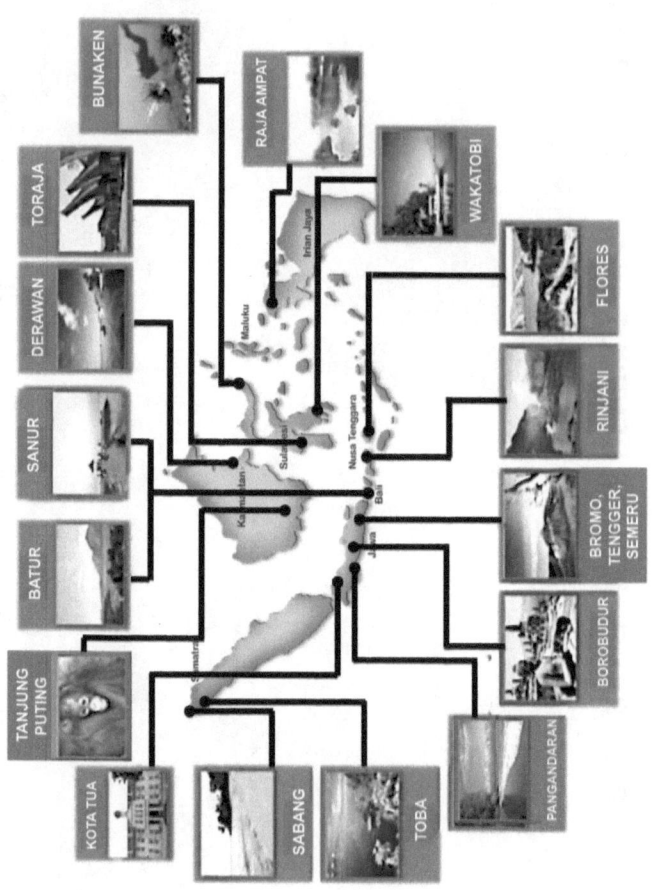

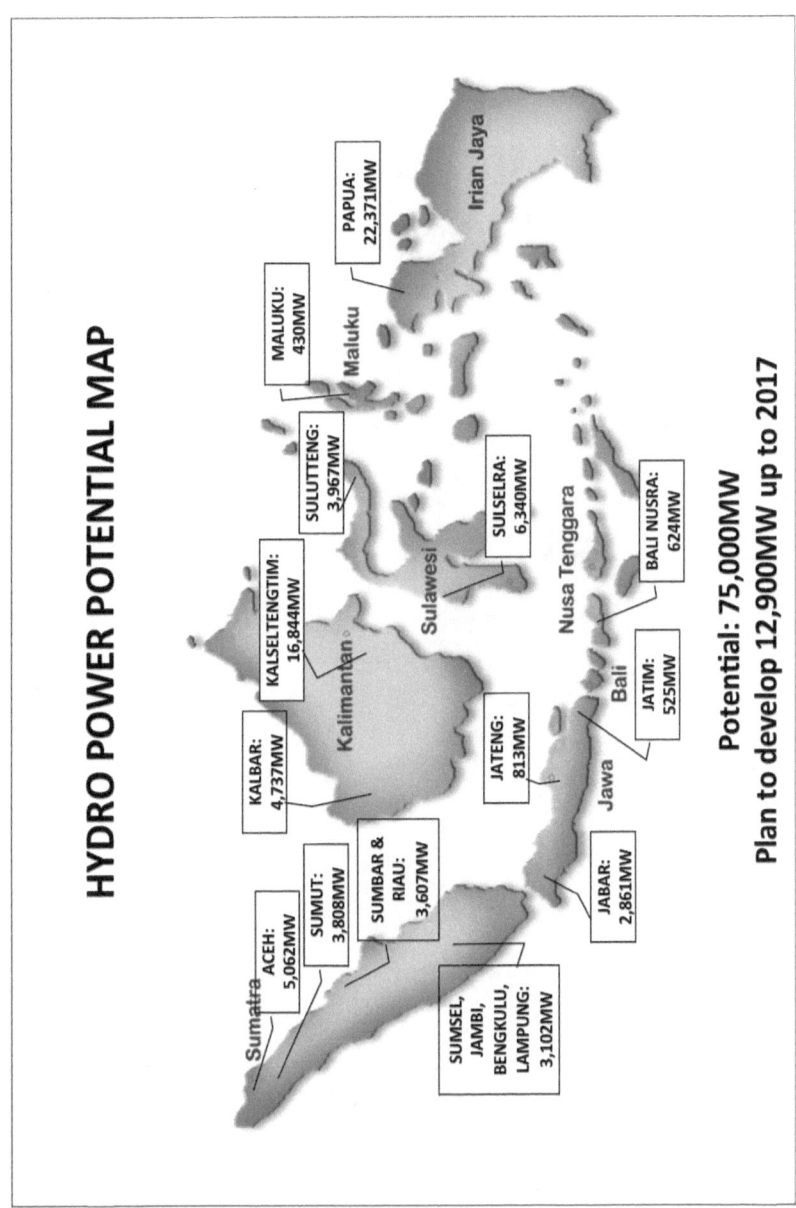

Micro Hydro and Hydroelectric Power Plants Plans

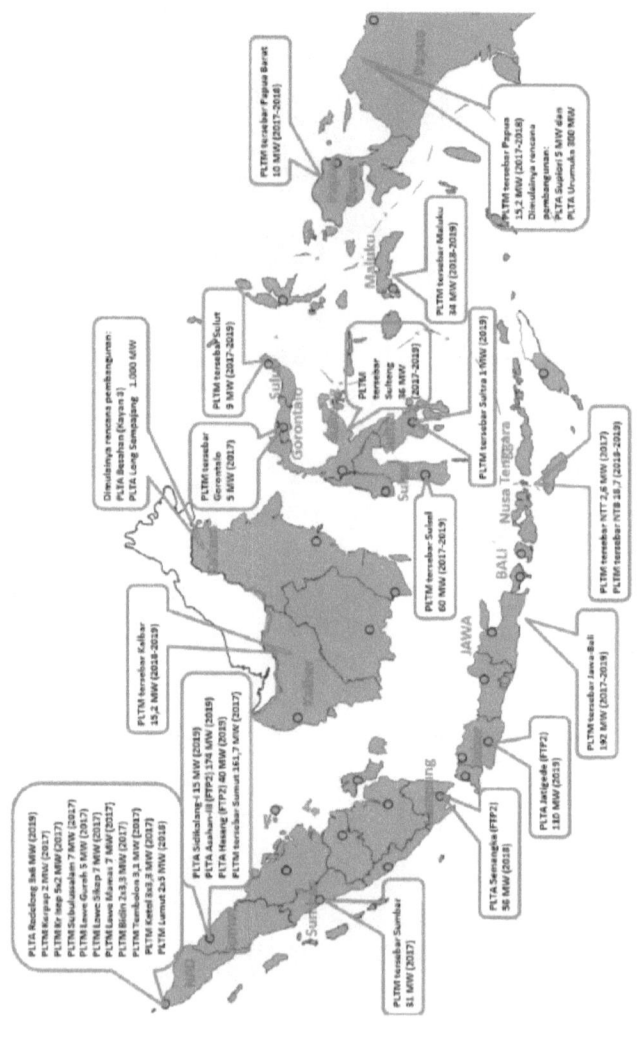

SOURCE: RINGKASAN RENCANA PEMBANGUNAN JANGKA MENENGAH NASIONAL (RPJMN) 2015-2019 KEMENTERIAN PERENCANAAN PEMBANGUNAN NASIONAL/ BADAN PERENCANAAN PEMBANGUNAN NASIONAL

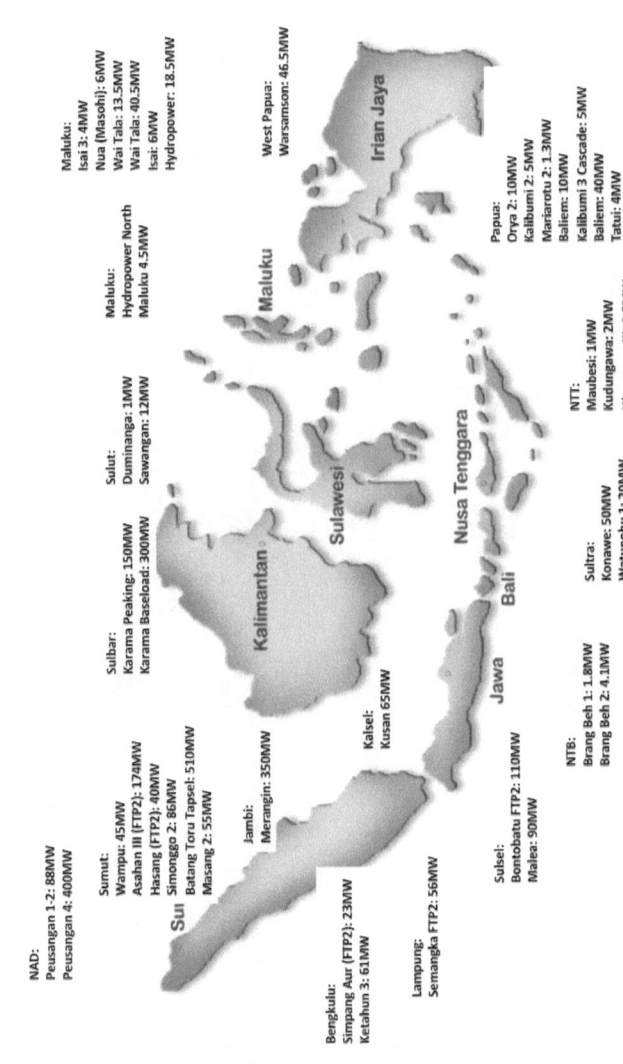

TOLL ROAD MAP

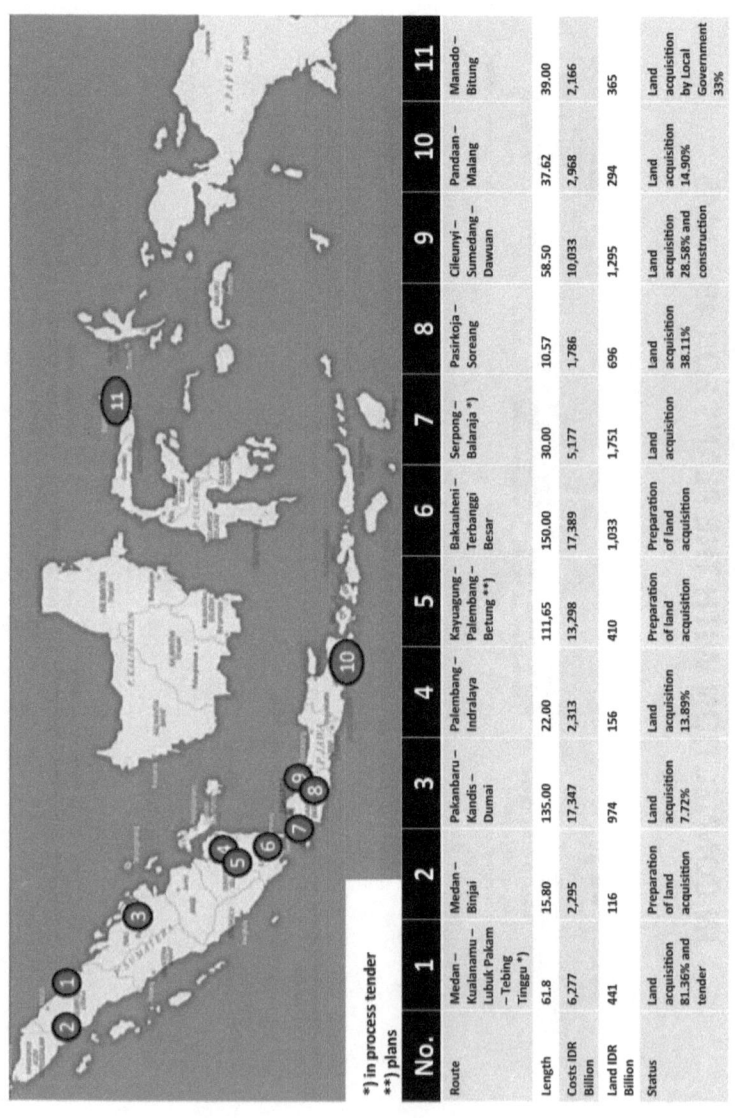

No.	1	2	3	4	5	6	7	8	9	10	11
Route	Medan – Kualanamu – Lubuk Pakam – Tebing Tinggi *)	Medan – Binjai	Pakanbaru – Kandis – Dumai	Palembang – Indralaya	Kayuagung – Palembang – Betung **)	Bakauheni – Terbanggi Besar	Serpong – Balaraja *)	Pasirkoja – Soreang	Cileunyi – Sumedang – Dawuan	Pandaan – Malang	Manado – Bitung
Length	61.8	15.80	135.00	22.00	111,65	150.00	30.00	10.57	58.50	37.62	39.00
Costs IDR Billion	6,277	2,295	17,347	2,313	13,298	17,389	5,177	1,786	10,033	2,968	2,166
Land IDR Billion	441	116	974	156	410	1,033	1,751	696	1,295	294	365
Status	Land acquisition 81.36% and tender	Preparation of land acquisition	Land acquisition 7.72%	Land acquisition 13.89%	Preparation of land acquisition	Preparation of land acquisition	Land acquisition	Land acquisition 38.11%	Land acquisition 28.58% and construction	Land acquisition 14.90%	Land acquisition by Local Government 33%

*) in process tender
**) plans

SOURCE: *RINGKASAN RENCANA PEMBANGUNAN JANGKA MENENGAH NASIONAL (RPJMN) 2015-2019 KEMENTERIAN PERENCANAAN PEMBANGUNAN NASIONAL/ BADAN PERENCANAAN PEMBANGUNAN NASIONAL*

RAILROAD PLANS 2015 - 2019

DEVELOPMENT AND CONSTRUCTION OF NEW AIRPORTS

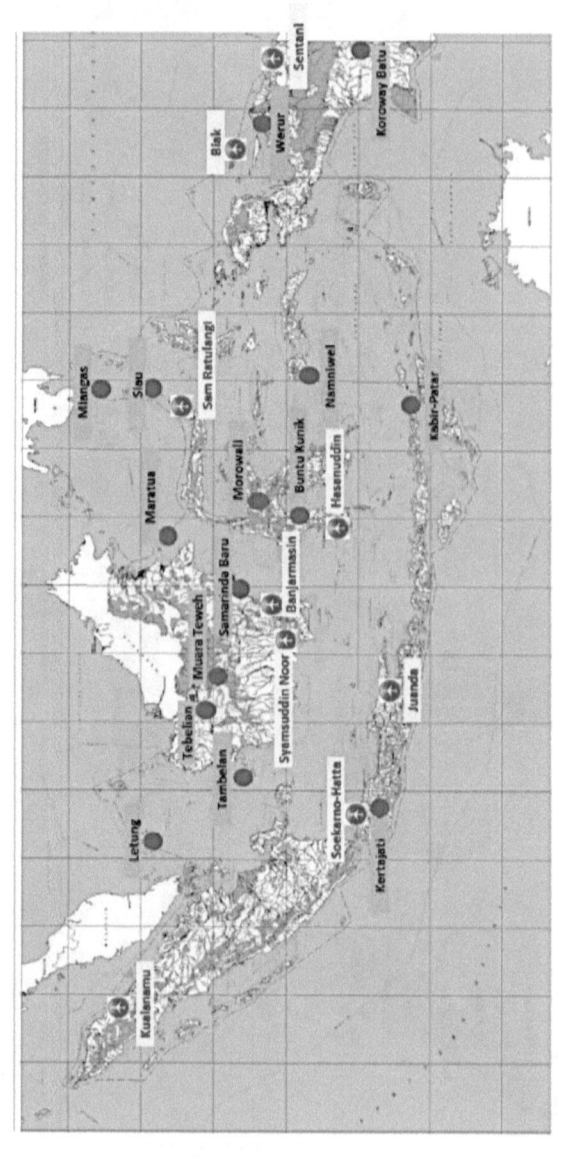

Source: *Ringkasan Rencana Pembangunan Jangka Menengah Nasional (Rpjmn) 2015-2019 Kementerian Perencanaan Pembangunan Nasional/ Badan Perencanaan Pembangunan Nasional*

SPECIAL ECONOMIC ZONES
(Kawasan Ekonomi Khusus)

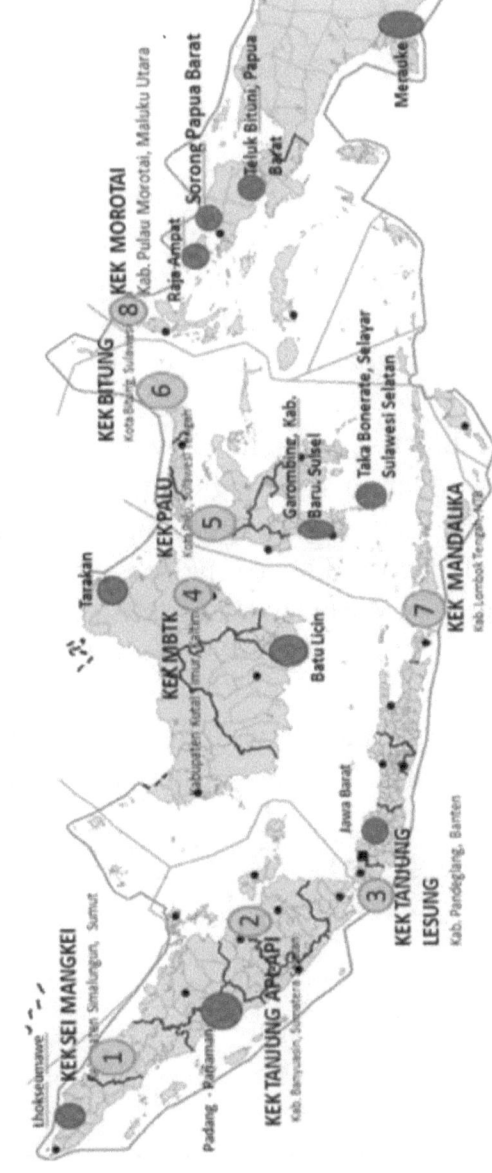

Numbered: Special Economic Zones that have already decided until 2014
Blank Circles: SEZ Indicated locations for 2014 – 2019

Source: Ringkasan Rencana Pembangunan Jangka Menengah Nasional (Rpjmn) 2015-2019 Kementerian Perencanaan Pembangunan Nasional/ Badan Perencanaan Pembangunan Nasional

The development of infrastructure to support the 14 industrial areas outside Java:

Projects:

- **Ports:** Kuala Tanjung, Tanjung Perak, Pontianak, Bitung, Makassar, Banjarmasin, Kupang, Halmahera;
- **Toll Road:** Manado – Bitung;
- **Roads:** Batulicin Ringroad, Palu – Parigi, Kupang Ringroad, Susumuk – Bintuni;
- **Railroads:** Manado – Bitung, Sei Mangke – Bandar Tinggi – Kuala Tanjung, Pasoso – Tanjung Priok, DDT and Elektrification Manggarai – Bekasi – Cikarang, Outer ring railroad;
- **Electricity:** Electric Steam Power Plants (PLTU): Kualatanjung, Asahan 3, Pangkalan Susu, Palu, NTT2, Ketapang FTP2, Bantaeng, Bengkayang, Parit Baru, Pulang Pisau; Hydroelectric and Micro Hydro Power Plants (PLTA/MH): Poso, Konawe, Morowali (PLTA/MH); Gas Power Plants: Pontianak Peaker (PLTG/MG), Morowali (PLTMN), Tangguh (PLTGU); and
- **Airports:** Mutiara Palu, Eltari Kupang, Halu Oleo Kendari, Sam Ratulangi Manado, Syamsuddin Noor Banjarmasin.

PROJECTS	INVESTMENT IDR Billion
■ Airports	8,200
■ Roads	8,079.74
■ Railroads	10,085.00
■ Electricity	10,477.06
■ Ports	17,664.00
■ Water	939.00
TOTAL	**55,444.80**

27 Challenges

A. Indonesia "Doing Business" Reports

According to 2015 World Bank Doing Business Report:

"Doing Business" indicators are frequently used by more than 50 countries' Government Reform Committees, including Indonesia. It is used as one input to inform their programs for improving the business environment, also to ensure coordination of efforts across agencies at the inter-ministerial level or for reporting directly to the president or the prime minister.

The focus of the Doing Business indicators remains to be the regulatory regime faced by domestic firms engaging in economic activity in the largest business city of an economy.

Although Doing Business was not originally designed to inform opinions by foreign investors, in application, investors may find the data helpful as an intermediary for the quality of the national investment climate.

Studies done in the World Bank Group's Global Indicators Group demonstrated that countries that have sensible rules for domestic economic activity also tend to have good rules for the activities of foreign subsidiaries engaged in the local economy.

Interestingly, the Doing Business data does not suggest that reforming business regulations is easier in small economies just because their Government structures tend to be less complex. Eight of the 11 economies with a population of more than 100 million reformed in at least one of the areas measured by Doing Business in 2013/14, while only 18 of the 34 economies with a population of less than 1 million did so. Among the 11 large economies, China, Mexico and Russian Federation each implemented 2 reforms making it easier to do business, while India and Indonesia each implemented 3. Reforms make it easier to do business in the 11 large economies in 2013/2014[101].

Economy	Reforms Reducing Regulatory Complexity & Cost	Reform Strengthening Legal Institutions
Bangladesh	1	0
Brazil	0	0
China	2	0
India	2	1
Indonesia	3	0
Japan	0	0
Mexico	0	2
Nigeria	0	0
Pakistan	1	0
Russian Federation	2	0
United States	1	0

The three reforms implemented in Jakarta and Surabaya, Indonesia are:

- Paying taxes less costly for companies by reducing employers' health insurance contribution rate.
- Getting electricity easier by eliminating the need for multiple certificates guaranteeing the safety of internal installations, and eliminating the need for electrical contractors to obtain

---

[101] *World Bank. 2014. Doing Business 2015: Going Beyond Efficiency. Washington, DC: World Bank. DOI: 10.1596/978-1-4648-0351-2. License: Creative Commons Attribution CC BY 3.0 IGO*

multiple certificates guaranteeing the safety of internal installations. Although it increased the cost by introducing a security deposit for new connections, it lowered labor taxes.
- The Ministry of Law and Human Rights started to electronically issue the approval letter for the deed of establishment to make starting a business in Indonesia easier.

Doing Business highlights how easy or difficult it is for a local entrepreneur to open and run a small to medium-size business when complying with relevant Regulations. Measuring and tracking the changes in Regulations affecting 11 areas in the life cycle of a business: starting a business, dealing with construction permits, getting electricity, registering property, getting credit, protecting minority investors, paying taxes, trading across borders, enforcing contracts, resolving insolvency and labor market Regulation.

The 10 topics included in the ranking in Doing Business 2016: starting a business, dealing with construction permits, getting electricity, registering property, getting credit, protecting minority investors, paying taxes, trading across borders, enforcing contracts and resolving insolvency. The labor market regulation indicators are not included in this year's aggregate ease of doing business ranking, but the data are presented in this year's economy profile.

How has Indonesia made starting a business easier—or not? By Doing Business report year from DB2011 to DB2016[102]

DB Year	Reform
DB2011	Indonesia eased business start-up by reducing the cost for company name clearance and reservation and the time required to reserve the name and approve the deed of incorporation.
BD2012	Indonesia made starting a business easier by introducing a simplified application process allowing an applicant to simultaneously obtain both a general trading license and a business registration certificate.
DB2015	Indonesia made starting a business easier by allowing the Ministry of Law and Human Rights to electronically issue the approval letter for the deed of establishment. This reform applies to both Jakarta and Surabaya.
DB2016	Indonesia made starting a business in Jakarta easier by reducing the time needed to register with the Ministry of Manpower.

Indonesia ranked 109 in Doing Business 2016; and ranked 120 in Doing Business 2015. Doing Business 2015 ranking shown is not last year's published ranking but a comparable ranking for Doing Business 2015 that captures the effects of such factors as data revisions and the changes in methodology.[103]

---

[102] *World Bank. 2016. Doing Business 2016: Measuring Regulatory Quality and Efficiency. Washington, DC: World Bank Group, DC: World Bank Group. DOI; 10.1596/978-1-4648-0667-4. License: Creative Commons Attribution CC BY 3.0 IGO*

[103] *World Bank. 2016. Doing Business 2016: Measuring Regulatory Quality and Efficiency. Washington, DC: World Bank Group, DC: World Bank Group. DOI; 10.1596/978-1-4648-0667-4. License: Creative Commons Attribution CC BY 3.0 IGO*

The rankings are measured to June 2015 and based on the average of each economy's distance to frontier (DTF) scores for the 10 topics included in this year's aggregate ranking. The distance to frontier score benchmarks economies with respect to regulatory practice, showing the absolute distance to the best performance in each Doing Business indicator. An economy's distance to frontier score is indicated on a scale from 0 to 100, where 0 represents the worst performance and 100 the frontier. For the economies for which the data cover 2 cities, scores are a population-weighted average for the 2 cities. *Source: Doing Business Database*

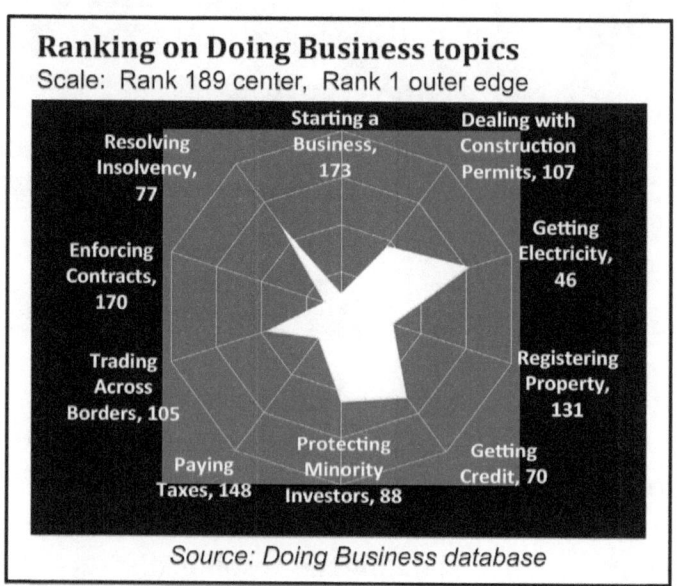

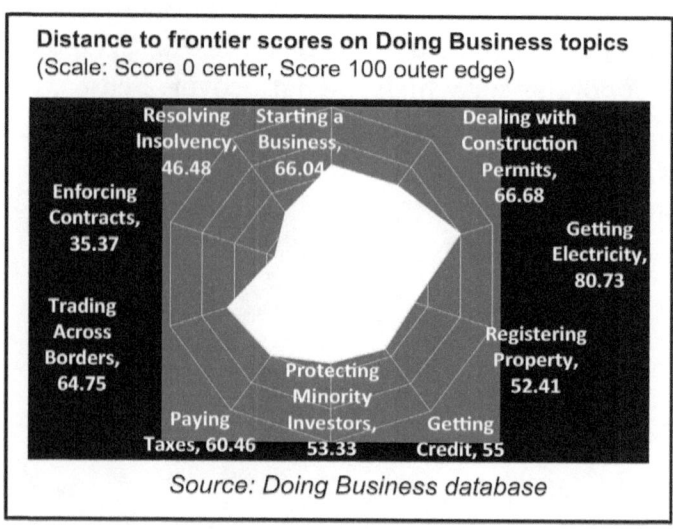

Indonesia compare to the best in the world, 2016:

	IDN	COMPARISON	
Corruption[104] (rank of 174)	107	1	Denmark
Doing Business – rank	109	1	Singapore
Doing Business – DTF score	58.12	87.34	Singapore
Starting a Business – rank	173	1	New Zealand
Starting a Business – score	66.04	99.96	New Zealand
Cost (% of income/capita)	19.9	0	Slovenia
Time – days	47.8	0.50	New Zealand
Dealing with construction permits – rank	66.68	92.97	Singapore
Procedures – number	17	7	5 Economies
Reliability of supply & transparency of tariff index (0-8)	7	8	18 Economies

According to data collected by Doing Business, starting a business there requires 13.00 procedures, takes 47.80 days, costs 19.90% of income per capita and requires paid-in minimum capital of 31.00% of income per capita.

---

[104] *Transparency International: Corruption Perceptions Index 2014: Results. Table and Rankings.* https://www.transparency.org/cpi2014/results

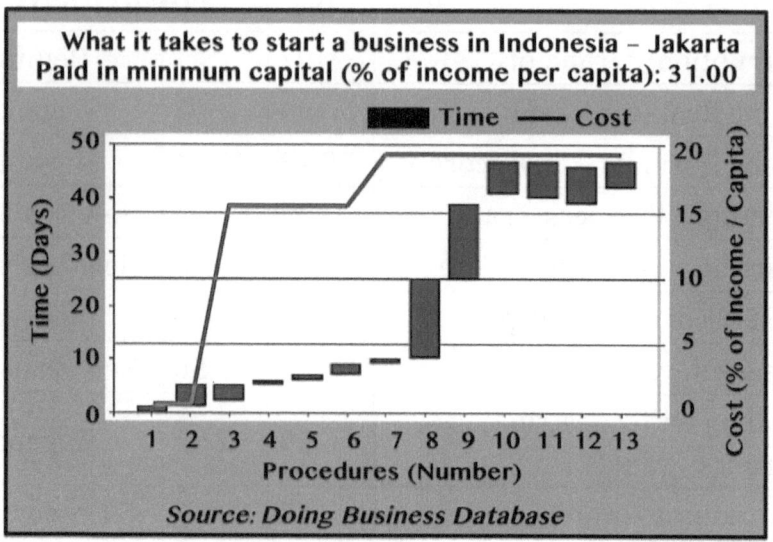

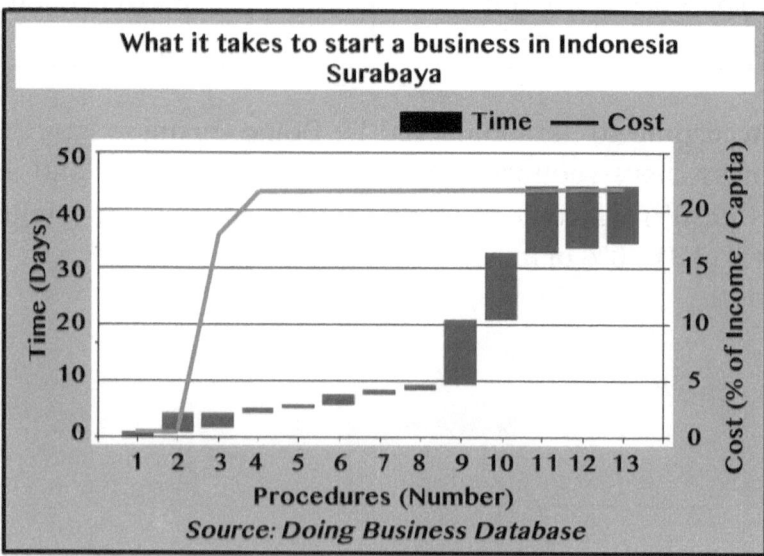

Note: Time shown in the figure above may not reflect simultaneity of procedures. Online procedures account for 0.5 days in the total time calculation.

B. Challenges

The Government of Indonesia has published the new National Medium Term Development Plan (RPJMN) 2015-2019 that target overall reforms in areas such as education, infrastructure, governance, investment, environmental policies, taxation, and creating supportive welfare system for its most vulnerable citizens.

Over the last 15 years, Indonesia's economic has rose relatively steady between 5.0 - 6.6 percent, however it is not directly proportional to the environmental conditions. Indonesia's economic development still relies on donations of natural resources, which amounted to approximately 25% of Gross Domestic Product (GDP), especially oil, mineral resources, and forests. This causes the depletion of natural resources and environmental degradation. Environmental quality that is reflected on the quality of water, air and land is still low - the index of environmental quality in 2012 was 64.21.

Strategic issues expected as obstacles on investments for the period 2015-2019, among others[105]:

- The distribution of investments. Java Island is still a center of investment in Indonesia. Contributing factor is the availability of adequate infrastructure facilities, such as: roads, ports, communications, and labor. The country outside of Java, especially in the Eastern part of Indonesia is relatively under-developed although laden with natural resources.
- The ratio of contributions of domestic investment in Java to total domestic investment amounted to 58.0 percent in 2010 and 62.3 percent in the period from January to September

---

[105] *Rancangan Awal Rencana Pembangunan Jangka Menengah Nasional, RPJMN 2015 – 2019 Buku II Agenda Pembangunan Bidang, Kementerian Perencanaan Pembangunan Nasional/Badan Perencanaan Pembangunan Nasional, Republik Indonesia. 2014 http://www.bpkp.go.id/*

2014. While the contribution of FDI in Java against the total FDI amounted to 70.9 percent in 2010 and 53.4 percent in January-September 2014

Investment in the manufacturing sector rose, but mostly for the fulfillment of the domestic market. World Bank reported that Japan and China are the largest trading partners and source of FDI for Indonesia. However, FDI inflows are more for the to produce sufficient goods for the domestic market.

Complicated bureaucracy and inefficient licensing processes are due to licensing authorities coming from separate Ministries/Institutions. Some licensing procedures have not been able to be transferred to PTSP (One Stop Integrated Service) by Local Governments because Local Governments receive authorities from related ministries based on its Regulation. This causes diversities in the issuance of licenses, including from the Governor/Regent, the Head of Department, and PTSP. Meanwhile, institutionally, PTSP still is diverse, which is the body, departments, offices and units.

In total, of the 491 areas that already form PTSP, 187 PTSP (28 percent) have SOP, and 239 PTSP have reduced costs. Thus, the numbers of PTSP that have had the SOP and have reduced the cost have not reached 50 percent. Up to June 2014, total licensing in Indonesia is 19,747 licenses. PTSP signed 15,342 licenses, or 78 percent of total licenses, that are: Governor/Regent (6 percent or 1,212 licenses), Local Secretaries (2 percent or 383 licenses), related SKPD (14 percent or 2,810 licenses).

The length of time to obtain a license needs to be addressed, especially for some sectors. For example, a plantation has a process time of licensing that reaches 939 (nine hundred and thirty-nine) days, the industrial sector 793 (seven hundred and ninety three) days, and the transport sector 743 (seven hundred and forty-three) days. The time to obtain the permits for three sectors above need to be shortened and simplified, to make easy to do business.

Corporations have not been able to take advantage of fiscal incentives optimally, partly because the capital requirement proposed for fiscal incentives (tax holiday) is considered too large (IDR1 Trillion), so filing for tax holiday is difficult to reach. Secondary sectors such as food industries are the most frequent to take advantage of import duty facilities, while the other sectors have not utilized the facility optimally.

Availability of Infrastructure and Energy. In addition to the problem of inefficient bureaucracy and corruption, the lack of availability of infrastructure is one of the factors inhibiting investment into Indonesia. World Bank reported infrastructure ranking for Indonesia in 2014 is 2.92, compare to Germany (the best) 4.32 and Somalia (the worse) is 1.50.[106] Cooperation between Government and private sectors in developing infrastructure is still hampered because there are unsynchronized Government Regulations at the central level, within central level and local. In addition, local Government has not taken an optimum role in the construction of infrastructure.

Land Procurement and Licensing. One factor inhibiting investors to invest in Indonesia are still many obstacles in the land provision and permit process.

Regulations: Investor has to pay higher costs due to disharmonized and distorting Regulations that caused by unclear, out of date Regulations – some provide negative economic impacts.

Workforce: Less conduciveness of labor market, include the high cost of redundancy, rigidity of employment, acceptance and

---

[106] *World Bank. Logistics Performance Index. Global Ranking 2014* http://lpi.worldbank.org/international/global?sort=asc&order=Infrastructure

termination of employment, flexibility of wages determination and the relationships between employees and employer.

Anti-competitive behavior: Persistently high anti-competitive behavior that could hamper incentives to invest and inhibit the growth of manufacturing industry and new businesses.

BKPM report on the Investment Coordinating Board Strategic Plan[107] established the main challenges associated with the development of capital investment, grouped into 4 challenges as follows:

- The governance development to create an effective and efficient bureaucracy;
- Economic growth;
- Accelerating equitable developments among regions; and
- Global economic pressures.

1. The Governance Development to Create an Effective and Efficient Bureaucracy

In order to reach the effectiveness and efficiency of governance, Government needs to improve the integrity, accountability, effectiveness, and efficiency of bureaucracy in organizing governance, development and public services related to investment is the implementation of One Stop Integrated Service (PTSP) in their entirety at the central, provincial and district/city. PTSP was formed to provide ease of licensing and non-licensing services to investors. However, to this day, there are not all Ministries and Institutions that have the authority to delegate or assign the licensing process to PTSP Center (BKPM).

---

[107] *Rencana Strategis Badan Koordinasi Penanaman Modal Tahun 2015-2019 (Investment Coordinating Board Strategic Plans 2015 – 1029).*

Not all Provincial and District/Municipal PTSP receive the delegation or the delegation of authority to process permits and non-permits from the Governor and Regent/Mayor. Additionally still occurring unevenness nomenclature.

2. Economic Growth

One of contributing factors is the low economic efficiency or economic productivity demonstrated by the low contribution of Total Factor Productivity (TFP) in economic growth.

IMF, Global Economic Prospects 2016 said general Government debt has increased in many developing countries. Commodity exporter fiscal deficits have astronomically deteriorated more than expected, while remaining mostly steady in other developing countries. As a result, the number of countries where debt has soared from pre-crisis levels, potentially vulnerable to global shifts in investor sentiment.[108]

World Bank said that growth in Indonesia decreases by around 0.4 percentage point due to spillovers from growth slowdown in China.

The IMF (2011) estimates that a 1-percentage-point growth decline in Japan would reduce growth in China by 0.18 percentage point, and by less than this in Indonesia and Korea. Japan financial sector is largely domestically orientated; financial spillovers from Japan are smaller than those from other systemically important economies[109].

---

[108] *World Bank Group. 2016. Global Economic Prospects, January 2016: Spillovers amid Weak Growth. Washington, DC. World Bank, Washington, DC. World Bank. doi: 10.1596/978-1-4648-0675-9. License" Creative Commons Attribution CC BY 3.0 IGO*

[109] *World Bank Group. 2016. Global Economic Prospects, January 2016: Regional Integration and Spillovers. East Asia and Pacific. World Bank Group. 2016. Global Economic Prospects, January 2016: Spillovers amid Weak Growth. Washington, DC. World Bank, Washington, DC. World Bank. doi: 10.1596/978-1-4648-0675-9. License" Creative Commons Attribution CC BY 3.0 IGO*

3. Accelerating Equitable Developments Among Regions

The Government continues to encourage equity investment mainly outside Java, especially Papua and West Papua. Infrastructure limitations become one of the challenges to achieve the target of investment equalization. Investments based on natural resources processing driven outside Java. Therefore, the challenge is to ensure availability of infrastructure, especially energy (electricity and gas) as well as logistics.

The availability of infrastructure is still very limited. The average of national electrification ratio in 2014 is about 81.5%. The electrification ratio in Eastern Indonesia is much lower than the average national electrification ratio. In addition to the low ratio of electrification, power quality (service level) is still low. Meanwhile, the development of processing industries based on natural resources, particularly smelters require very large and stable electricity[110].

4. Global Economic Pressures

There are four risks of global economic pressures that may influence investment in Indonesia, namely:

A. The Deceleration of World Economy

The pessimistic scenario continues. In October 2015, the IMF said in the World Economic Outlook (WEO), the sources of slower growth in an economy is diverse, ranging from commodity price declines, to overhangs from past rapid credit growth, to political turmoil; Countries with multiple diagnoses are faring worst,

---

[110] *Rencana Strategis Badan Koordinasi Penanaman Modal Tahun 2015-2019 (Investment Coordinating Board Strategic Plans 2015 – 1029)*

in some cases also facing higher inflation. According to IMF, another factor that discourages investment is low aggregate demand. Slow expected potential growth, dampens aggregate demand, further limiting investment. In its more extreme forms, political conflict has created a large global stock of displaced persons, both within and across borders. The economic and social costs are immense[111].

Financial condition for emerging markets have tightened since the spring, especially in recent weeks: With the first increase in U.S. policy rates approaching and a worsening of the global outlook, financial conditions Dollar bond spreads and long-term local-currency bond yields have increased by 50 to 60 basis points on average, and stock prices are weaker, while exchange rates have depreciated or come under pressure.

B. The Low World Commodity Prices

Changes in prices affect both the output gap and potential output itself. For many commodity exporters with flexible exchange rate regimes, weakening commodity prices have triggered sizable currency depreciation. Declining commodity prices, reduced capital flows to emerging markets and pressure on currencies, and increasing financial market volatility,

---

[111] *International Monetary Fund. 2015. World Economic Outlook: Adjusting to Lower Commodity Prices. Washington (October)*

downside risks to the outlook have risen, particularly for emerging market and developing economies.

The IMF said in World Economic Outlook: Adjusting to Lower Commodity Prices – October 2015, renewed declines in commodity prices will put downward pressure on headline inflation in advanced economies in the coming months and could delay the expected pickup in core inflation as the recovery progresses[112].

World Bank Global Economic Prospects January 2016 said weaker commodity prices would exacerbate the impact on commodity exporters (Indonesia, Malaysia, Mongolia)[113].

C. World Liquidity Shortage

Liquidity—the degree to which assets can be bought or sold without affecting the price, generally taken to mean the ease with which an investor can quickly buy or sell a security without moving its price.

Non-resident investors remain key players in the local currency bond markets of Indonesia and Malaysia, holding around 40 percent of domestic Government bonds.

Global debt issuance has exploded since the financial crisis, with borrowers taking advantage of low interest rates. Easy money continues to increase global financial stability risks.

Prolonged monetary ease may also encourage excessive financial risk taking, in the form of increased portfolio allocations to riskier assets and increased willingness to leverage balance sheets.

---

[112] *International Monetary Fund. 2015. World Economic Outlook: Adjusting to Lower Commodity Prices. Washington (October)*

[113] *World Bank Group. 2016. Global Economic Prospects, January 2016: Regional Integration and Spillovers. East Asia and Pacific. World Bank Group. 2016. Global Economic Prospects, January 2016: Spillovers amid Weak Growth. Washington, DC. World Bank, Washington, DC. World Bank. doi: 10.1596/978-1-4648-0675-9. License" Creative Commons Attribution CC BY 3.0 IGO*

Accommodative policies aimed at supporting the recovery and promoting economic risk taking have facilitated greater financial risk taking.

These structural changes in credit markets, together with the expected normalization of monetary policy in the United States, have raised market and liquidity risks in ways that could compromise financial stability if left unaddressed.

As Regulation of banks tightens, the liquidity, particularly of European and US credit markets, has evaporated. The interest rates rise.

As has expressed by BKPM, the Bank of England, as well as a slew of major bond-market investors and analysts from other countries, Mr. Robert Stheeman, the head of the UK Debt Management Office said that it is not just company bond markets that have been affected. Sovereign debt may also be hit. He warned that the gilt market is potentially threatened by falling liquidity[114].

Many asset prices drop significantly during liquidity crises. Hence, asset prices are subject to liquidity risk and risk-averse investors naturally require higher expected return as compensation for this risk.

Unexpected behavior of such new financial assets can lead to market participants disengaging from risks they don't understand and investing in more liquid or familiar assets.

Some economists argued that financial liberalization and increased inflows of foreign capital, especially if short term, can aggravate illiquidity of banks and increase their vulnerability. The onset of capital outflows can have particularly destabilizing consequences for emerging markets.

Given the limited access of emerging markets to world capital markets, illiquidity resulting from contemporaneous loss of

---

[114] *The Telegraph, UK, 21 Mar 2015. Liquidity crisis could spark the next financial crash http://www.telegraph.co.uk/finance/markets/11487546/Liquidity-crisis-could-spark-the-next-financial-crash.html*

domestic and foreign investor confidence is nearly sufficient to cause a financial and currency crises, the 1997 Asian financial crisis being one example.

D. Increasing Competition with Neighboring Countries

After enactment of the MEA, competition is increased with Malaysia, Thailand, and Vietnam. Currently, the competitive position of Indonesian workers is relatively low compared to other ASEAN countries, meaning that Indonesia can no longer rely on cheap labor. Other factors are less competitive in the field of infrastructure, techno readiness and financial market development.

Indonesian Rupiah Depreciation

Indonesian Rupiah has depreciated since the beginning of 2012, driven by:

- External factors: US Dollar appreciation against almost all currencies as a result of a Federal Fund Rates increase plan and Quantitative Easing Policies of the ECB (European Central Bank) and the BOJ (Bank of Japan) followed by a number of countries.
- Internal factors: the current deficit transactions (current account). There are mismatch risks of private foreign debts that only 13.6% to hedge cash (foreign exchange hedging).

Decline in the Rupiah is relatively better than other countries, however there remain structural problems, namely a current deficit account amounting to USD26 Billion (2.95% of GDP) in 2014.

C. Efforts and Plans to Tackle Challenges

1. National Medium Term Development Plan[115]

Some strategic issues emphasized in mainstreaming governance policies, and plans:

- Increase transparency on information and public communication;
- Increase public participation in policy formulation;
- Increase the bureaucracy capacity through national and regional bureaucratic reform implementation; and
- Improve the quality of public services.

The implementations:

- Establishment of Documentation and Information Services Center (PPID) in the framework of public disclosure;
- The creation of spaces of participation and public consultation;
- Preparation of grand design and road map bureaucratic reform;
- Institutional arrangements that include Government agencies functions structuring and organizational structure;
- Structuring management of Government agencies;
- Management development apparatuses;
- CPNS selection system through the CAT system;
- Development and application of 2-Government;

---

[115] *Rancangan Awal Rencana Pembangunan Jangka Menengah Nasional, RPJMN 2015 – 2019 Buku II Agenda Pembangunan Bidang, Kementerian Perencanaan Pembangunan Nasional/Badan Perencanaan Pembangunan Nasional, Republik Indonesia. 2014*
http://www.bpkp.go.id/public/upload/unit/sesma/files/Buku%20II%20 RPJMN%202015-2019.pdf

- Application of 2-Archive;
- Implementation of apparatus performance accountability system;
- The expansion of e-Service for public services;
- The implementation of standards of public service in the Public Service Unit;
- Implementation of One Stop Integrated Services for the main service, licensing and investment;
- Complaints unit formation information technology based society; and
- Build management system and public information services are reliable and professional.

2. Corruption

A pilot bureaucracy reform program was started in 2004 in the Ministry of Finance, and in 2008 the program was rolled out to many other ministries and agencies before extension to the regional level in 2013. Its principle objectives are to:

- Tackle corruption, collusion and nepotism;
- Improve service delivery;
- Improve civil servants' capacity and accountability;
- Upgrade human resource management policies and practices; and
- Address overlapping, inconsistent and vague laws and Regulations.

The reform program has been a success, and rolling it out to the regions should continue. The Government has committed to publish a "Grand Design and Roadmap for Bureaucratic Reform" by 2019.

A. Corruption Eradication Commission (KPK)

The KPK was established in 2002 as an ad hoc corruption-fighting agency, independent from the Executive, Legislature and Judiciary. It works alongside incumbent agencies such as the Attorney General's Office and national police and is authorized to conduct pre-investigation, investigations and prosecutions against corruption cases that:

- Involve law enforcement, state officials and other individuals;
- Have generated significant public concern; and/or
- Have lost the state at least IDR 1 Billion (USD70, 000).

Based on Article 6 Law No. 30/2002[116], KPK has mandates to conduct investigation and prosecution of corruption cases, to prevent corrupt practices, to coordinate with Government agencies, supervise corruption case handled by other law enforcement authorities (the national police force and Attorney General's Office) and also to monitor the implementation of good governance throughout the country.

The KPK is led by five commissioners and has a staff of around 1,200, including some 250 investigators and prosecutors. The commissioners operate as a panel and all investigations need to be vetted by it. The investigators and prosecutors of the KPK are typically experienced agents recruited mainly from the Indonesian National Police and the Attorney General's Office.

Experts from other Government agencies are also taken on, particularly financial experts. While not ideal from the point of view of independence and avoiding possible contagion of

---

[116] *Undang Undang Republik Indonesia No. 30 Tahun 2002 Tentang Komisi Pemberantasan Tindak Pidana Korupsi. Signed by Ms. Megawati Soekarnoputri, the President of Indonesia, on December 27, 2002. Promulgated in Jakarta by Indonesian Minister Secretary of State, Mr. Bambang Kesowo on December 27, 2002. State Gazette No. 137 of 2002*

corruption from one agency to the next, thorough testing and vetting has been largely successful in avoiding this problem.

The KPK's focus has been on high profile cases, and the public perception of its effectiveness is high. The Corruption Eradication Commission (KPK) has handled as many as 439 cases from 2004 to July 2015, consists of 205 cases of bribery, procurement of 133 cases, 44 cases of misuse of funds, extortion 20 cases, permitting 18 cases, 14 cases of Money Theft Criminal Acts (TPPU), and five cases of hindering the process of the Commission. The convictions it has obtained include Government ministers, top management and officials from private companies, provincial governors, police, judges and prosecutors.

As stipulated in the 1999 Governance Law, all state officials are obliged to submit a wealth report to the Commission within two months of starting or finishing their tenures. This includes the President and Government ministers. President Joko Widodo was the first president to require all ministerial candidates to be vetted by the KPK, as well as by the Financial Transaction Reports and Analysis Centre (PPATK) which tracks international money transfers with a view to uncovering corruption, fraud and tax avoidance.

B. Public Watch

Indonesia citizens become more and more critical toward their Government, especially regarding corruption. There are some private non-profit organizations such as Indonesia Corruption Watch,[117] Transparency International[118], Masyarakat Pemantau Aset-aset Negara (MAPAN), Forum Indonesia untuk Transparansi Anggaran (Fitra), Indonesia Procurement Watch (IPW). Since Joko Widodo became president, it is not as easy as previous years for Government officials to practice corruption.

---

[117] *http://www.antikorupsi.org*
[118] *http://www.ti.or.id*

3. Bureaucracy

As described in Rancangan Awal RPJMN 2015 – 2019, Indonesian Government is aware that the quality of governance is a prerequisite to achieve national development goals, both short term, medium and long term.

The Government needs to share power with private sectors and civil societies. Interactions require space equality between relevant actors so transparency, accountability, participation, and others etc. can be realized.

Several attempts have been made by the Government in order to encourage the expansion of public participation as actors of development. In 2011 the Government of the Republic of Indonesia agreed on the Declaration of Principles on Open Government which gave birth to the Open Government Partnership (OGP), which encourages the Government to open up and open spaces of citizen participation through a variety of collaborative schemes for the creation of Government transparency[119].

The involvement of Indonesia cannot be separated from the issuance of Law No. 14 of 2008 on Public Information (KIP). UU KIP is the basis for establishing the application of the principles of governance in governance. In addition, to institutionalize public disclosure, they created an Organizations Documentation and Information Management Officer (PPID) for 34 ministries, 36 State/Organization Ministerial/LNS/LPP, 23 provinces, 98 districts and 36 cities.

The low quantity of PPID is caused due to the low commitment of the leadership of the public body about the importance of the role of PPID, the limited capacity of the human resources information management, communications infrastructure, and

---

[119] *World Bank. 2014. Doing Business 2015: Going Beyond Efficiency. Washington, DC: World Bank. DOI: 10.1596/978-1-4648-0351-2. License: Creative Commons Attribution CC BY 3.0 IGO*

the lack of encouragement and optimally efforts to carry out a public service function.

4. Licensing Reformation

> A slowdown in China's real GDP growth has a significant impact on neighboring countries, especially commodity exporters such as Indonesia.

As spillover economic slowdown from China continues, when China reforms focus on lowering leverage in the economy, while shifting growth away from credit-fueled investment in housing and industry towards consumption and services, Indonesia BKPM as a front line investment institution is aware of the need for comprehensive regulatory reformation in providing better licensing systems to receive better outcome for Indonesia investment.

The reformation can be done by:

- Minimizing economic institutions through the creation of productive business climate and legal certainty for businesses;
- Improvement of governance by doing, among other things, the right Government policies; and
- The use of globalization to improved domestic interests.

Duplications or repetitions of Government Regulations with Government Agencies and Local Government/Regional Centers have caused:

- Ineffectiveness;
- Unharmonious and distorted information;
- Unclear procedures, time and costs; and
- High transaction costs for corporation.

> Efforts need to be done, such as:
>
> - Harmonization of policies;
> - Simplification of licensing and non-licensing requirements; and
> - Repair disharmonized legislation and the end the bottlenecking of Regional Centers.

The following are improvements Indonesia reported by Doing Business 2016[120]:

- **Starting a Business**
  Indonesia made starting a business in Jakarta easier by reducing the time needed to register with the Ministry of Manpower.
- **Getting Credit**
  Indonesia improved access to credit by enabling searches of the collateral registry by the debtor's name. This reform applies to both Jakarta and Surabaya.
- **Paying Taxes**
  Indonesia made paying taxes easier and less costly for companies by introducing an online system for paying social security contributions and by reducing both the rate and the ceiling for the contributions paid by employers. This reform applies to both Jakarta and Surabaya.

Doing Business 2016 as well as World Bank reported that Indonesia reduced regulatory complexity and cost, and

---

[120] *World Bank. 2016. Doing Business 2016: Measuring Regulatory Quality and Efficiency. Washington, DC: World Bank Group, DC: World Bank Group. DOI; 10.1596/978-1-4648-0667-4. License: Creative Commons Attribution CC BY 3.0 IGO*

strengthened legal institutions, in 2014/15 to make easier to start a business[121]:

- Indonesia introduced an online system for filing and paying social security contributions.
- Introduced or improved online procedures.
- Made it easier to pay taxes.
- Introduced or enhanced electronic systems.
- Cut or simplified post-registration procedures (tax registration, social security registration, licensing).
- Reduced labor taxes and mandatory contributions.
- Strengthened legal rights of borrowers and lenders.
- Created a unified or modern collateral registry for movable property.

Doing Business also reported that Indonesia eased the burden of third-party involvement in incorporation by launching online services related to business start-up that enabled notaries to complete company name searches and reservations more quickly, in 2007. The following year it introduced standard business incorporation forms. And in 2009 Indonesia reduced notary fees—including the fees for notarizing company deeds—by amending the official fee schedule. These changes have led to time and cost savings for entrepreneurs.

If Indonesia keeps up the pace in adopting international good practices in the business start-up process, entrepreneurs starting a simple business, like the one in the Doing Business case study, soon will no longer need to involve third parties. The online system (Sisminbakum, Sistem Administrasi Badan Hukum) was introduced on January 31, 2001, by a decree of the Minister of Justice and Human Rights (decree M-01.HT.01.01 of October 4, 2000).

---

[121] *World Bank. 2016. Doing Business 2016: Measuring Regulatory Quality and Efficiency. Washington, DC: World Bank Group, DC: World Bank Group. DOI; 10.1596/978-1-4648-0667-4. License: Creative Commons Attribution CC BY 3.0 IGO*

GDP growth is expected to accelerate to 5.4 percent on average in 2016-18 in assumption by implementation of a reform package announced by the Government in September – October 2015 to unlock investment and boost productivity growth[122].

5. Infrastructure Reformations

To encourage investment more evenly, in 2015-2019, the Government has committed to build power infrastructure of 35.9 GW. The committed to build 172 new ports, 65 new dock crossings, 15 new airports, 3,258 Km of railway lines, 2,650 Km of new roads, and 1,000 Km of highways. In addition, they will develop 14 Industrial Zones (KI) and 7 Special Economic Zones (SEZ) outside of Java.

To achieve these targets, in the next five years, Indonesia needs a IDR5,519.4 Trillion investment for infrastructure. Of these amount, Government funding will provide around 40.14%, or around IDR2,215.6 Trillion for 5 years into the future. That leaves a difference in funding of about IDR3,303.8 Trillion (Bappenas, 2014). The Government will conduct a review of the structure of the state budget by, among other things, reducing fuel subsidies and allocate the savings to infrastructure development.

A decrease in the exchange rate is relatively better than in other countries, but there still are structural problems and the current account deficit of USD 26 Billion (2.95% of GDP) in 2014. To maintain the resilience of the balance of payments, Bank Indonesia targets a balance of payments deficit in 2015 at the range of 2.5-3.0% of GDP.

---

[122] *World Bank Group. 2016. Global Economic Prospects, January 2016: Spillovers amid Weak Growth. Washington, DC: World Bank. Washington, DC: World Bank. doi:10.1596/978-1-4648-0675-9. License: Creative Commons Attribution CC BY 3.0 IGO*

The sources of the current account deficit (current account) is primarily:

- The trade deficit due to declining commodity prices;
- The service account deficit which is very large due to higher dependence to foreign transport services (freight) so it is necessary to encourage the export trade transactions of the free on board (FOB) into a cost, insurance and freight (CIF) by developing shipping services, logistics and insurance.
- The amount of capital repatriation. Almost all ASEAN countries to provide incentives for reinvestment.

To improve the performance of balance of sheets through increasing exports and reducing imports, it takes strong policies to encourage structural reforms. In the field of investment, the policy is geared to maintain the trust, encouraging reinvestment (reducing remittances), and encouraging investment priority sectors. Also, strengthen the balance of trade by substituting import of raw materials for industrial sectors, focus more on exports and tourism.

This policy is intended to increase the efficiency of the licensing process, increase the certainty of investing and doing business in Indonesia, as well as encourage more healthy and fair competition. The strategy adopted is: To become a high-income country in 2030, the Indonesian economy needs to grow between 6-8 percent per year. To achieve such high, sustainable, economic growth, Indonesia must be inclusive and remain supported by policies that protect the stability of the economy. High economic growth, that is sustainable and inclusive, will be achieved through a comprehensive reform. It can be achieved by policies, that:

- Streamline economic institutions through the creation of a productive business climate and legal certainty for businesses;

- Improve governance, by doing right Government policies, among other things; and
- Harness globalization for the benefit of domestic interests.

The Government will conduct a review of the structure of the state budget by reducing fuel subsidies and allocate the funds to infrastructure development, among other things.

The next challenge is to encourage private participation in infrastructure development, either through a Public Private Partnership scheme (PPP) and non-KPS (Business to Business).

In addition, the Indonesian Government has committed to join the Asian Infrastructure Investment Bank (AIIB) that was initiated by the Chinese Government. Thus the next challenge is the utilization of the G-20 agreement or AIIB to support infrastructure development in Indonesia.

28 Abbreviation/Acronyms

AANZFTA	ASEAN-Australia-New Zealand Free Trade Area
ACIA	ASEAN Comprehensive Investment Agreement
ACIF	ASEAN Community in Figures
ACFTA	ASEAN China Free Trade Area
AD	Anno Domini Nostri Iesu, In The Year of Our Lord Jesus Christ
AEC	ASEAN Economic Community
AIA	Framework Agreement on ASEAN Investment Area
AIFTA	ASEAN India Free Trade Area
AIIB	Asian Infrastructure Investment Bank
AIR	ASEAN Investment Report
AJCEP	ASEAN Japan Comprehensive Economic Partnership
AMDAL	Analisis Mengenai Dampak Lingkungan Hidup, Environmental Impact Assessment
API	Angka Pengenal Importir, Import License
API-P	Angka Pengenal Importir – Produsen, Producer's Import License
APIT	Angka Pengenal Importir Tetap, Permanent Import License
API-U	Angka Pengenal Importir – Umum, General Import License
ASEAN	Association of Southeast Asian Nations

ASEAN – 6	Brunei Darussalam, Indonesia, Malaysia, the Philippines, Singapore and Thailand
ASEAN IGA	ASEAN Investment Guarantee Agreement
ATIGA	ASEAN Trade in Goods Agreement
ATR	ASEAN Trade Repository
Bappenas	Badan Perencanaan Pembangunan Nasional, National Development Planning Agency
BC	Before Christ
BIT	Bilateral Investment Treaties
BKPM	Badan Koordinasi Penanaman Modal, Investment Coordinating Board
BKPMD	Badan Koordinasi Penanaman Modal Daerah, Regional Investment Coordinating Board
BOJ	Bank of Japan
BPJS	Badan Penyelenggara Jaminan Sosial, Social Security Administrator
BPK	Badan Pengawas Keuangan, Financial Supervisory Agency
BPMPTSP	Badan Penanaman Modal dan Pelayanan Terpadu Satu Pintu, Board of Investment and One Stop Integrated Services
BPN	Badan Pertanahan Nasional, National Land Agency
BPUPKI	Badan Penyelidik Usaha Persiapan Kemerdekaan Indonesia, Preparatory Work for Indonesian Independence Committee
C	Celsius
CAT	Computer Assisted Tests
CIA	Central Intelligence Agency
CIF	Cost, Insurance and Freight
CLMV	Cambodia, Lao PDR, Myanmar, Viet Nam

CPNS	Calon Pegawai Negeri Sipil, Candidates for Civil Servants
CV	Commanditaire Vennootschap, is a limited partnership, an alliance founded by an individual or individuals who entrusted money or goods to an individual or individuals who run the company and act as a leader.
DDI	Domestic Direct Investment
DGIP	Directorate General of Intellectual Property Rights (DJHKI)
DJHKI	Direktorat Jenderal Hak Atas Kekayaan Intelektual
DPA	Dewan Pertimbangan Agung, Supreme Advisory Council
DPD	Dewan Perwakilan Daerah, Regional Representative Council
DPR	Dewan Perwakilan Rakyat, House of Representatives
DTF	Distance to Frontier
DJBC	Direktorat Jenderal Bea dan Cukai, The Directorate General of Customs and Excise
EAP	East Asia and Pacific
ECB	European Central Bank
EODB	Ease of Doing Business
EU	European Union
F	Fahrenheit
FDI	Foreign Direct Investment
FET	Fair and Equitable Treatment
FOB	Free on Board
GDP	Gross Domestic Product
Golkar	Partai Golongan Karya
GNI	Gross National Income

GW	1 Giga Watt = 1,000 Mega Watts
HAM	Hak Azazi Manusia, Human Rights
HGB	Hak Guna Bangunan, Building Rights
HGU	Hak Guna Usaha, Business Use Rights
HKI	Himpunan Kawasan Industri Indonesia, Indonesian Industrial Estate Association
HM	Hak Milik, Ownership Rights
HP	Hak Pakai, Right to Use
Humas	Hubungan Masa, Public Relations
ICSID	International Centre for Settlement of Investment Disputes
ICT	Information and Communication Technology
ICW	Indonesia Corruption Watch
IDR	Indonesian Rupiah (Rp)
IIA	International Investment Agreement
IMB	Ijin Mendirikan Bangunan, Building Construction Permit
IMF	International Monetary Fund
IMTA	Ijin Masuk Tenaga Kerja Asing, Foreign Workers Entry Permit
IP	Intellectual Property
IS	Islamic State
ISBN	International Standard Book Number
ISO	International Standardization of Organization
ISIC	Indonesian Standard Industrial Classification
ISIS	Islamic State of Iraq and Syria
ITAS	Ijin Tinggal Sementara, Temporary Stay Permit
ITAP	Ijin Tinggal Tetap, Permanent Stay Permit
Jokowi	Joko Widodo, Indonesian President
KBLI	Klasifikasi Baku Lapangan Usaha Indonesia, ISIC
KEK	Kawasan Ekonomi Khusus, SEZ

K3	Keamanan dan Keselamatan Kerja, Work Safety & Security
KI	Kawasan Industri, Industrial Zone
KIP	Keterbukaan Informasi Publik, Public Disclosure
KPPA	Kantor Perwakilan Perusahaan Asing, Representative Office of Foreign Company
KP3A	Kantor Perwakilan Perusahaan Perdagangan Asing, Representative Office of Foreign Trade
KPBPB	Kawasan Perdagangan Bebas dan Pelabuhan Bebas, Free Trade Zone and Free Port
KPS	Kerjasama Pemerintah dan Swasta, Government and Private Business Cooperation
KTP	Kartu Tanda Penduduk, ID Card
KUHP	Kitab Undang Undang Hukum Pidana, Criminal Codes
KY	Komisi Yudisial, Judicial Commission
LGST	Luxury Good Sales Tax
LKPM	Laporan Kegiatan Penanaman Modal, Investment Activities Report
LLC	Limited Liability Company
LNS	Lembaga Non Struktural, Non Structural Institution
LWBP	Luar Waktu Beban Puncak, Outside peak load time
OECD	Organization for Economic Co-operation and Development
OGP	Open Government Partnership
OHS	Occupational Health and Safety
OJK	Otoritas Jasa Keuangan, the Financial Service Authority
PAN	Partai Amanat Nasional

PBNU	Pengurus Besar Nahdlatul Ulama, Executive Board of NU
PD	Partai Demokrat
PDE	Pertukaran Data Elektronik, Electronic Data Exchange
PDI-P	Partai Demokrasi Indonesia – Perjuangan
PDRM	Polisi Diraja Malaysia, Malaysian Police
PE	Permanent Establishment
PEB	Pemberitahuan Ekspor Barang, Export Goods Notice
Pertamina	Persatuan Perusahaan Pertambangan Minyak dan Gas Bumi Nasional, Association of National Mining and Oil and Gas
PJK3	Perusahaan Jasa Keselamatan dan Keselamatan Kerja, Work Safety and Security Service Company
PKS	Partai Kebangkitan Bangsa
PLN	PT. Perusahaan Listrik Negara
POA	Pelaporan Orang Asing, Foreigner Report
Polri	Kepolisian Republik Indonesia, Indonesian Police
PPAT	Pejabat Pembuat Akta Tanah, Land Titles Registrar
PPID	Pejabat Pengelola Informasi dan Dokumentasi, Information and Documentation Management Officer
PPJK	Pengusaha Pengurus Jasa Kepabeanan, Customs Service
PPE	Personal Protective Equipment
PPP	Purchasing Power Parity
PPP	Public Private Partnership
PMA	Penanaman Modal Asing, Foreign Investment
PMDN	Penanaman Modal Dalam Negeri, Domestic Investment

PNBP	Pendapatan Negara Bukan Pajak, State Income Non Tax
PT	Perseroan Terbatas, Limited Liability Company
PTKP	Penghasilan Tidak Kena Pajak, Non-Taxable Income
PTSP	Pelayanan Terpadu Satu Pintu, One Door Integrated Service
Q3	Quarter 3
MA	Mahkamah Agung, Supreme Court
MEA	Masyarakat Ekonomi ASEAN, ASEAN Community
Mensos	Menteri Sosial, Social Minister
M&As	Mergers and Acquisitions
MK	Mahkamah Konstitusi, Constitutional Court
MNEs	Multinational Enterprises
MOLHR	Minister of Law and Human Rights
MPR	Majelis Permusyawaratan Rakyat, People's Consultative Assembly
NIK	Nomor Identitas Kepabeanan, Customs ID
NIPER	Nomor Induk Perusahaan, Company Registration Number
NPWP	Nomor Pendaftaran Wajib Pajak, TIN
NPPKP	Nomor Pengukuhan Pengusaha Kena Pajak, Taxable Taxpayer ID
NU	Nahdlatul Ulama, traditionalist Sunni Islam
RCEP	Regional Comprehensive Economic Partnership
RI	Republik Indonesia
RPJMN	Rencana Pembangunan Jangka Menengah Nasional, National Medium Term Development Plan
RPTKA	Rencana Pemakaian Tenaga Kerja Asing, Foreign Workers Adoption Plan
RTBL	Rencana Tata Bangunan dan Lingkungan, Building Management and Environmental Plan

RUPM	Rencana Umum Penanaman Modal, General Plan of Investment
RVCs	Regional Value Chains
SABH	Sistem Administrasi Badan Hukum, Legal Entity Administration System
SEZ	Special Economic Zones
Sinlapnaker	Sistem Informasi Wajib Lapor Ketenagakerjaan di Perusahaan, Report Obligatory Information Systems Company
SITU	Surat Ijin Tempat Usaha, Business Place Permit
SIUP	Surat Ijin Usaha Perdagangan, Business Trading Permit
SKK Migas	Satuan Kerja Khusus Kegiatan Usaha Hulu Minyak dan Gas Bumi, Special Unit Upstream Oil and Gas
SMEs	Small and Medium-sized Enterprises
SMK3	Sistem Manajemen Kesehatan dan Keselamatan Kerja, Occupational Health and Safety Management System
SPPB	Surat Pemberitahuan Ekspor Barang, Export Goods Notice
Tbk	Terbuka, Opened
TBNRI	Tambahan Berita Negara Republik Indonesia, Official Gazette of the Republic of Indonesia
TDP	Tanda Daftar Perusahaan, Certificate of Company Registration
TIN	Tax Identification Number
TNCs	Trade Negotiation Committees
TPP	Trans-Pacific Partnership
TTIP	Transatlantic Trade and Investment Partnership
TTPU	Tindakan Pidana Pencurian Uang, Criminal Actions on Money Theft

UK	United Kingdom
UKL	Upaya Pengelolaan Lingkungan, Environmental Management Efforts
UMKMK	Usaha Mikro, Kecil, Menengah dan Koperasi, Micro, Small, Medium Enterprises and Cooperatives
UN	United Nations
UNCITRAL	United Nations Commission of International Trade Law
UNCTAD	United Nations Conference on Trade and Development
UPTSA	Unit Pelayanan Terpadu Satu Atap, One Roof Integrated Services Unit
UPL	Upaya Pemantauan Lingkungan, Environmental Monitoring
USD	United States Dollar ($)
UTC	Universal Time Coordinated
UUG	Undang Undang Gangguan. Nuisance Law
UU	Undang Undang, Law
UUM	Undang Undang Merek, Brand Law
VAT	Value Added Tax
VOC	Vereenigde Oost-Indische Compagnie
VTIS	Vessel Traffic Information System
WBP	Waktu Beban Puncak, Peak Load Time
WEO	World Economic Outlook
WIB	Waktu Indonesia Barat, Indonesian West Time
WITA	Waktu Indonesia Tengah, Indonesian Central Time
WIT	Waktu Indonesia Timur, Indonesian East Time
WNI	Warganegara Indonesia, Indonesian Citizen
WTO	World Trade Organization

29 About the Cover

Bali Mandara Toll Road
Also known as Nusa Dua-Ngurah Rai-Benoa Toll Road.
Length: 12.7 Km (about 7.89miles)
Location: across the Gulf of Benoa, connecting the city of Denpasar and South Kuta, Badung Regency, Nusa Dua and Ngurah Rai International Airport.
Costs: IDR2.48 Trillion (about USD 220Million)
Officially opened by President Susilo Bambang Yudhoyono on 23 September 2013.
http://www.thejakartapost.com/news/2013/09/23/yudhoyono-officially-open-bali-s-first-toll-road.html

Tugu Selamat Datang (Welcome Monument)[123]

Located in the Bundaran HI, Central Jakarta, Indonesia. Completed in 1962.

During the 1960s, President Sukarno ordered several constructions and city beautification projects in preparation preparation for the Asian Games IV. This is one of them.

The design of the statue was sketched by Henk Ngantung, the Vice Governor of Jakarta at that

---

[123] *https://en.wikipedia.org/wiki/Selamat_Datang_Monument*

time. The construction of the statue was done by Indonesian sculptor Edhi Sunarso. The statue depicts two bronze statues of a man and a woman, waving in a welcoming gesture. The woman is shown holding a flower bouquet in her left hand.

The height of the figures is five meters from head to toe, or seven meters from the tip of the raised arm to toe. The two figures stand atop a pedestal. In total, the monument is about thirty meters above the ground. Selamat Datang Monument symbolizes the openness of the Indonesian nation to welcome the visitors of the Asian Games IV.

TRG 1000 Phoenix Gearbox Emas 2016 Agrindo

The newest Hand Tractor Diesel Engine Model DI900L from PT. Agrindo (Ltd.). PT. Agrindo is one of manufacturing companies in Rutan Machinery Group, pioneer in Indonesian agricultural machinery manufacturing. Rutan Group has been developing and building Indonesian agricultural systems for over 70 years.

A few years after completing her job for PT. Taiyo Electric Indonesia, a joint venture company between Taiyo Electric Co. Ltd., Japan – PT. Agrindo Ltd. – PT. Rutan Machinery Trad. Co., the Writer has worked with the Management Representative of this group of the companies to establish ISO 9001:2000 Quality Management System for the Rutan Group. She maintains friendships to this date.

Buildings in Jakarta

From various locations in Jakarta
1. APL Tower, Central Park
2. Indonesia Stock Exchange
3. Wisma BNI46
4. Bakri Tower, Rasuna Epicentrum
5. The Pakubuwono Signature
6. The Regatta Tower Jakarta
7. The Equity Tower Jakarta

In Circle:

Various kinds of Indonesian fabric, such as tenun, batik, and factory made fabrics.

Tenun is hand woven fabric, normally made of wood fiber, cotton, silk, or other materials. Produced traditionally at home in Sumatera, Java, Kalimantan, Maluku and Nusa Tenggara.

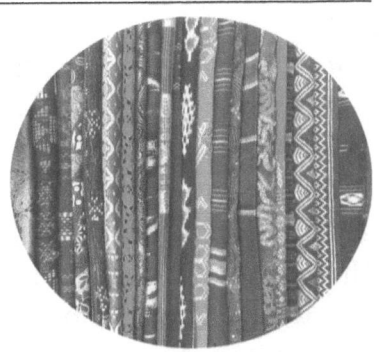

Lower Front:

A sample of various kinds of Indonesian products, made of: rubber, leather, wood, metal (steel, stainless steel, brass, etc.), plastic, fiber plants, ceramic, glass, terracotta, onyx, coconut, and paper. You also see some samples of horticultural products such as coffee, cocoa, and tea.

Back Cover:

"Kay"

Painted for, Beverly Kay Cunningham, in oil, on 16x20" canvas, by Rosye B. Salz in 2010. Beverly Kay, is Rosye's sister-in-law who passed a way from cancer in 2010. More paintings by Rosye Buray Salz can be found in http://rosye.com.

Side Cover:

Batang Garing (Tree of Life)

Symbol of Central Kalimantan Province in Borneo. Believed awarded by the Almighty God, the Heavenly Ranying Hatalla for the Ngaju Dayak tribe of Central Kalimantan, the Heart of Borneo, based on Kaharingan. A cosmology representation of the universe, at the bottom of the symbol are two receptacles, while at the very top are a hornbill and the sun. consists of three parts:

- ☐ The Heavanly Ranying Mahatalla, illustrated by spear facing upwards, the hornbill, and the sun, the source of all life on earth
- ☐ The Earth, illustrated by the tree trunks, fruits, hornbill's tail – illustrated by leaves
- ☐ The Underworld, illustrated by the Sandung (small house to place a body after they have died), which also symbolizes the

island where the children and grandchildren of King Bunu live, who later gave birth to all human beings on this earth.

Although the heavenly and earthly world are different, they are closely connected to one another and are inseparable, since they are both interdependent.

The branches where some face up and others face down means that there is an eternal balance between the earthly and the afterlife. That life on earth is temporary, and that human life is designed for the hereafter.

The Tree of Life expresses the core of the Kaharingan faith, that Human Life must be a balance and kept in harmony between man and his fellow humans, between man and his natural environment, and between man and the Ranying Hatalla.

Kaharingan comes from the Old Dayak word "Haring," which means "Life" or "Alive." Kaharingan is a religion professed by many Dayaks in Kalimantan, Indonesia. The supreme God in Kaharingan is called Ranying, or Ranying Hatalla.

Many Dayaks in Central Kalimantan that embraced the Kaharingan faith have converted to Christianity or Islam. However, most still use Kaharingan values and traditions in their daily activities, such as wedding ceremonies, some funeral traditions, family relations and traditions, agriculture, opening a field for a new construction, etc.

Moslem mosques and Christian churches stand near each other peacefully in Central Kalimantan. There are strict rules and directives on how to treat the rainforests, what may be done or taken from the forests, and what are taboo. Dayaks have certain ways of wisdom and an innate concern to preserve the forest and the natural environment. The Dayaks' local wisdom directs that trespassing these rules will destroy the balance of the forest and animals living in the forest, and so directly or indirectly will adversely damage communities living from the forest bounty.

Central Kalimantan Province area is 157,983Km² (60,997.58sq.mi.), consists of 80 percent forest. Total population in 2010 census is 2,202,599, consists of 52 percent male and 48 percent female. Natural resources and products are coal, gold, zirconia, steel, kaolin, copper, palm oil, rubber, shrimp, crab, terrapins, fish, ornamental fish, rattan, resin, Gemor bark, bird's nest, and wood waste utilization.

Investment opportunity in Central Kalimantan: infrastructure, industrial estate, railroad, construction, manufacturing, clean water development, processing plants (of iron ore, iron sand, fisheries, coconuts, palm oil, coffee, manganese, animal feed, seaweed), power plants, and agriculture such as aloe Vera, onions, corn, cocoa, rice paddy, citrus, etc.

www.ingramcontent.com/pod-product-compliance
Lightning Source LLC
Chambersburg PA
CBHW020727180526
45163CB00001B/140